GENDER, DESIGN AND MARKETING

Gender, Design and Marketing

How Gender Drives our Perception of Design and Marketing

GLORIA MOSS

GOWER

Gower Applied Business Research
Our programme provides leaders, practitioners, scholars and researchers with thought provoking, cutting edge books that combine conceptual insights, interdisciplinary rigour and practical relevance in key areas of business and management.

Published by
Gower Publishing Limited
Wey Court East
Union Road
Farnham
Surrey GU9 7PT
England

Gower Publishing Company
Suite 420
101 Cherry Street
Burlington, VT 05401-4405
USA

www.gowerpublishing.com

British Library Cataloguing in Publication Data
Gender, design and marketing : life patents, culture and development. - (Intellectual property, theory, culture)
1. Market segmentation 2. Women consumers
I. Moss, Gloria
658.8'02

ISBN: 978-0-566-08786-8

Library of Congress Cataloging-in-Publication Data
Moss, Gloria.
Gender, design, and marketing : how gender drives our perception of design and marketing/ by Gloria Moss.
p. cm.
Includes bibliographical references and index.
ISBN 978-0-566-08786-8
1. Consumer behavior. 2. Marketing--Sex differences. 3. Commercial art--Sex differences. I. Title.

HF5415.32.M675 2008
658.8'342--dc22

2008009812

Printed and bound in Great Britain by
TJ International Ltd, Padstow, Cornwall

Contents

List of Figures

List of Tables

Foreword

In setting out to write this Foreword I realize that I am a male prefacing a text by a female examining the differences between male and female designers who are servicing clients irrespective of gender ... that in turn are delivering goods and services to customers and/or consumers of either sex. Add in the permutations of culture, age and market diversity to these issues and one could be forgiven for asking the questions where do we start in trying to understand gender issues in design and does it really matter.

For the design profession it does matter. Creativity, or new ways of thinking, is exploited by innovation, which in turn is delivered by design, hence design delivers change, and gender politics, has been in the last century and is likely to continue to be a key area of change due to globalization and population dynamics.

Design being regarded as an esoteric and individual activity has escaped the need to address this issue other than in employment legislation, which considering the 'cottage industry' nature of the sector has hardly proved a burden. Equally, with design having occupied a role within 'marketing' for so long in merely adding value, it has been shielded from needing to address gender issues by advertising and marketing functions, which had to travel the same road as their audience.

Still a young profession as we now recognize it, design is having to adjust rapidly as an interface between creativity and the consumer. New models of working will require collaboration with technologists, scientists, geneticists and other professions where gender differences may well not echo those in the design sector. New technologies and rapid manufacturing will enable the designer to work directly with the consumer in providing products and indeed with access and interactivity provided by the web, the consumer is likely to become a part of the design team influencing design thinking, process and outcome.

The expansion of design activities into areas such as service and food design will affect the gender make-up of the profession and design employers will want to ensure that their design offer, which more and more will focus on emotion as a differentiating success factor, is understood and embraced by future dynamic, expanding and more easily segmented markets.

Designers tell stories, they create metaphors, they bring their own experience and influences to bear in answering needs, and in doing so we will see differences between the design outcomes of male or female designers. This book explores through research some of the differences between the two and in doing so provides the profession with information and understanding that will feed into professional practice and development.

The Chartered Society of Designers 'Genetic Matrix', which examines what a designer does in four key criteria, is used to underpin its structure for professional practice and development throughout the sector. Culture, knowledge, insight, skills and personality all play a significant role in determining the designer and the research presented in this book is extremely welcome and relevant to our own thinking and I believe to the design sector and its three key stakeholders, design providers, design users and design education.

Frank Peters FCSD FRSA MIoD
Chief Executive
Chartered Society of Designers

Introduction

This book is an introduction to the academic research on the impact of gender on design and marketing preferences. Why a book tracking the research on this topic? There is a rush of new books on gender and marketing but these are problematic in several ways. Firstly, they tend to draw their findings pretty indiscriminately from secondary sources (that is, second-hand accounts of research), and some of the research described comes from non-academic as well as academic sources. Some of what passes for truths is then presented uncritically to the reader, and this does not provide a reliable research base from which organizations can launch new marketing initiatives. By contrast, research presented in academic journals has been through the litmus test of academic peer review and can be relied upon to have greater credibility.

A second problem is that the books present a persuasive case for greater diversity in marketing without balancing this with information on the obstacles that organizations may face in implementing change. These obstacles may be structural (for example, difficulties in recruiting web designers with the right set of skills) or cultural (for example, difficulties in shifting the thinking within a particular organization) but there is not a whiff of these difficulties in the other books available on this topic.

The sort of difficulty I am talking about is illustrated by a story. A few years ago I had the good fortune to meet the person who created the design of a then-new brand of yoghurt drink. This is a grocery product for which the market is principally female shoppers. The designer showed me the original designs she had produced, which appeared on the page alongside pictures of the finished product. It was immediately apparent that the proportions she had originally used had been elongated and enlarged. This was a bit like looking at yourself in a distorting mirror in the fair, and I was intrigued as to how this had come about. She was quite clear about the process: 'My boss took my designs and improved them, to his way of thinking at least'.

If we analyse this incident it appears that her boss was using his own preferences as a barometer to gauge what the purchaser would like without questioning whether their preferences would in fact cohere. What the literature on 'diversity marketing' reveals is that ultimately there may be no universal design solutions to match all markets. The question then arises as to how a person with one set of preferences can bend these to accommodate the different preferences of another person. The problem of how people can ultimately be made to think like someone else is not covered at all in the books on gender and marketing and the problems are unlikely to end there. Imagine the intricacies of determining whose work is good enough to warrant recruitment or promotion in a world in which the notion of good design (or advertising for that matter) is not fixed. Things become very complicated indeed.

These intricacies make it timely to introduce an audience of practitioners and academics to original research from reliable and reputable sources. Who would choose to embark on a lengthy journey by car without a detailed roadmap? So it is with this topic. An outline approach can be misleading, contradictory findings can be ignored and organizations can get sucked into a way of thinking without realizing that the detail significantly alters the conclusion. For example, many of the books on gender and marketing make much of differences between men's and women's use of language without factoring in the research that has called some of the findings into question.

Much of the information gathered in this book is not available in the 'popular' books. There are two factors behind this. Firstly, this book goes straight to the original (primary) research not relying solely on secondary sources, and does this across numerous disciplines – psychology, design, marketing, Fine Art and art therapy, to name just a few. Secondly, the book focuses on an area almost wholly neglected by the other books, that of visual aesthetics. The lack of attention given to this field is one reason for the extensive coverage given to it here and although I do touch on the research regarding advertising but make no apologies for the fact that this is not a primary focus of this book. Neither are the linguistic aspects that accompany design. Readers with a primary interest in the language of advertising can find many other texts that will give them a thorough introduction to this topic.

Armed with reliable information, on the other hand, organizations can be confident of committing resources to marketing initiatives which will help build bigger market share.

Two final points. All the other books available on gender and marketing have authors who are based in the US and whose focus is largely on American business. The author of this book is based in the UK, and the vista is an expanded one that looks west to the US, at European experience too, and finds time to look east for places to refer to for research in Asia. Last but not least, it needs to be said that universities are no longer the ivory towers they used to be and those working in business schools aim to work closely with business. For much of my working life I have worked in both industry and academia, with long periods as a Human Resources expert and Fellow of the Institute of Personnel and Development, together with periods lecturing and researching in university business schools, carrying HR-type notions of diversity into the field of marketing. I am a Fellow of the UK's Institute of Personnel and Development and have carried an understanding of people, organizations and diversity into the area of marketing. Fortunately, the research I have conducted on design and marketing has been fed back to industry through consultancy, and the businesses I have helped have made huge strides forward as a result of receiving a different way of looking at the world. These companies include Marks and Spencer, Canon Cameras, BT, Bounty, Directski, Ford and local authorities.

One of the purposes of this book is to bring this information together for the first time and siphon it to a wider audience. You can now gen up on research, past and present, and become an expert, knowledgeable about the importance and significance of gender to perception. You will then be in a position to make strategic marketing decisions relating to the organization(s) you work with, and determine the basis for a reappraisal of strategy. Which company would make important strategic decisions without reliable and valid information on which to base these decisions? I can guarantee that there is much here that is new and that will afford a radically new perspective on the designed world around you.

The appearance of this information is timely since the body of knowledge on men and women as consumers, and on the way they construct designs and advertising, is growing. Since 1991, in recognition of the growth of our understanding in this area, there has been a bi-annual Academy of Consumer Research conference on gender, marketing and consumer behaviour. This is a significant landmark for gender based research from a business, as well as from a marketing, perspective (Costa 1991; Beetles and Harris 2005).

Alongside this growing interest in men and women as consumers is a relative absence of attention to gender issues in the academic marketing literature. When I started writing about gender and design back in the 1990s (Moss 1995, 1999), I was struck by the extent to which specialist marketing journals were ignoring the importance of gender as a segmentation variable and after some research, it became easy to understand some of the barriers.

One writer, for example, dismissed the category of demographic segmentation variables as 'poor predictors of behaviour and consequently less than optimum bases for segmentation strategies' (Russell 1981). This contrasted with my own research findings which highlighted the importance of gender as a segmentation variable through a study of the cognitive visual preferences of men and women. In the 1990s when I started this research, precious few research articles were investigating cognitive sex differences in relation to marketing messages, and where there was a focus on gender, this was in relation to sociological factors such as gender representation and lifestyle factors. For example, one piece of research focused on shopping patterns, finding that working women spent less time in the supermarket, made fewer shopping trips and spent fewer hours per day on housework than did housewives. This piece of work also revealed the fact that price was a less critical issue for working women than convenience and time-saving (Zeitham 1985). Another researcher focused on ways of portraying women, finding that modern and traditional groups of women favoured advertisements portraying women in roles that were consistent with the women's own sex-role orientation (Leigh et al. 1987) so that 'modern' women preferred advertisements that portrayed them in that light, while 'traditional' women preferred traditional advertisements. This was not exactly rocket science.

Other researchers (Jaffe and Berger 1994) found that a 'modern advertising positioning' (defined as an advertisement that presented women in a modern rather than traditional role) was essential for effective communication with women who scored high on masculinity. Low-masculine women, by contrast, could be tempted equally influenced by a modern or by a traditional positioning. Beyond these studies, there was little that took as its specific object the broader implications of sex as a variable. Few had looked beyond the economic and sociological questions to consider whether there were fundamental differences in the cognitive patterns of men and women.

Standard marketing textbooks were singing from a similar hymn sheet. Of three standard textbooks on marketing written in the 1990s, one failed to mention gender as a variable (Mercer 1992), one mentioned it purely as a means of defining the target market (Stanton et al. 1991) and one as a means of defining women's propensity to shop (Schiffman and Kanuk 1994). Moreover, this last book refers to 'male and female' traits as though these are attributes that males and females are equally likely to have and there is no suggestion in this or the other two textbooks that males and females may have traits that set them apart. There is, moreover, no suggestion that the cognitive processes of men and women may differ in any fundamental way and as a consequence, no discussion of the impact of gender on consumer behaviour.

Have textbooks changed in the last ten years or so? I revisited the text by Schiffman and Kanuk, only this time in the eighth edition version of the text produced in 2004. Here is what you will find in the paragraph dealing with men and women as consumers:

> 'Women have traditionally been the main users of such products as hair coloring and cosmetics and men have been the main users of tolls and shaving preparations. However, sex roles have blurred and gender is no longer an accurate way to distinguish consumers in some product categories.'
>
> (Schiffman and Kanuk 2004, 57)

How representative of research on marketing is this sociological perspective, focused here on sex roles? An answer can be found in a recent study of the gender issues appearing in top marketing journals over the period 1970–2002 (Wolin 2003). This study appeared in a well-respected journal, the *Journal of Advertising Research*, and revealed that the main focus in advertising research has been in five areas, with the proportion of studies in each category illustrated in parenthesis:

1. Gender role stereotyping (46.1 per cent).
2. Selectivity hypothesis findings. This includes research comparing the way men and women process information (7.9 per cent).
3. Spokesperson gender affects findings. This research examines reactions to spokesperson gender (5.3 per cent).
4. Gender advertising response findings. This includes research on reactions to music, preferences to length of advertising exposure, reactions to use of nudity in advertisements (38.1 per cent).

5. Gendered brand positioning findings. This includes acceptance of 'feminine' or 'masculine' brands (2.6 per cent).

As you can see, research on gender role stereotyping is the most popular by a long way, and this represents a further example of the sociological perspective. Schiffman and Kanuk's emphasis on it is therefore representative of the emerging body of research from the academic community. There is little emphasis in this body of research on differences in cognitive processes.

The reason for this neglect? According to Elizabeth Hirschman, Professor of Marketing at Rutgers University in the US, the general silence on these subjects reflects the fact that consumer research has been dominated by the masculine orientation and that this has failed to consider that there may be another one, that of the female voice (Hirschman 1993). It is not that there is nothing to say on the subject but rather that 'past and present consumer research makes visible and gives voice to only half the gender-based ways of knowing; it largely excludes experiences emanating from a feminine perspective' (Hirschman 1993, 540).

She may have a point. While research in the field of management and leadership has for some time been concerned with differences in the behaviour and performance of men and women (Rosener 1990; Marshall 1995; Eagly et al. 2003; Moss and Daunton 2006), concerns such as these are relatively new to the world of academic marketing. As Jonathan Schroeder, Professor of Marketing at Exeter University writes 'gender research remains in the closet in many consumer behaviour and marketing research circles' and 'rarely plays a central role in framing research, with notable exceptions, of course' (Schroeder 2003, 1). He refers to 'speculation that we live in a post-gender world' (ibid.) although, he personally takes the view that 'gender remains a central organizing feature of identity' (ibid.). He is not alone in this view. Two academics, Bristor and Fischer, take the view that 'gender is a pervasive filter through which individuals experience their social world' (Bristor and Fischer 1993, 519).

This book makes inroads into filling the gap and also offers explanations for the continued concentration on sociological factors. It is hoped that agreement or disagreement with the material presented here will engender (if you will pardon the pun!) further work on this most important of topics, and help take forward the process of presenting design and other marketing in an optimal fashion to markets of men and women. This is a vast topic and there will undoubtedly be omissions in what is presented here. For example, the emphasis is less on the philosophical, economic, political and sexual factors that make gender such a rich field (Schroeder 2003, 1) than on the behavioural and cognitive factors that impact on it. My aim has been to set the tone for a new direction of studies in consumer behaviour so that other researchers can pick up the torch and see what new areas it illuminates.

The central thesis of this book is that an exploration of the male and female production and preference continuum demonstrates the existence of opposing paradigms. In the view of some researchers, including myself, a great deal of the design and marketing that is currently available commercially is anchored at the male end of the aesthetic continuum. For example, Professor Craig of the University of North Texas has referred to the way that 'the man's woman … continues to be portrayed according to the rules of the patriarchy' (1992, 9). The notion of a specifically male set of values has also been developed by Professor Penny Sparke, a prolific writer and Pro Vice-Chancellor for the Arts at Kingston University. She writes in her book *As Long As It's Pink* (1995: 2–3) that 'women's tastes stand outside the "true" canon of aesthetic values of the dominant culture' and notes that architectural and design modernism imposed on goods and their design a stereotypically masculine aesthetic, not only because it was undertaken by men but because it was embedded within masculine culture.

My own book takes this thinking a step further by describing research that delineates the male and female design aesthetic and showing how partial each gender is to the aesthetic associated with its own gender. One of the questions raised by this evidence is the appropriateness of the widespread, and in some industries, near ubiquitous use of the male aesthetic. One of the reactions people often make on learning of the all-pervasive use of the male production aesthetic is to assume that it must be supported by massive market research. In fact, in my experience much market research is conducted using products and stimuli anchored at the male end of the continuum which means that respondents offer opinions on what is, essentially, a limited palette of choices, all coming from one end of the range of aesthetic possibilities. One of the central messages of this book is that there is another way of seeing at the other end of the continuum, and that design and marketing people would get rich pickings by expanding their focus on both ends of the continuum. Or, to use another metaphor, instead of fishing in a relatively small lake, they could have regular trawls in a series of inter-connected rivers and lakes.

I hope that you enjoy this voyage of discovery as the new waters come into view.

PART I

Setting the Scene

Chapter 1
Customer Demographics: Identifying the Target Market

Knowing Your Market

It was a summer's day, and the advertising agency was ready to unveil the concept pieces that would be at the core of its marketing campaign. This was a niche agency set up by advertising creatives with experience at some of the UK's top agencies. Informality was the order of the day and the young creatives sported open-necked shirts and trainers. Sitting on the other side of the room was the client, a natural energy producer who was backing wind turbines. This visionary had devoted his life to harnessing energy from renewable sources and everyone waited expectantly for the white sheets to be removed from the boards around the room.

Commanding the show was the advertising MD, a casually-dressed man in his early 40s, with sleeves rolled up. He stepped back while his assistant, a slightly younger man, took centre stage. 'We have sourced images which will impact strongly on the energy consumer,' he explained 'and our aim is to effect a significant consumer shift from regular energy suppliers to greener sources.'

The sheet from the first board was removed. It showed an image of the founder of the company gazing out at the grey wind turbines that stood immediately outside the window of his empty sitting room. The MD then moved to the second concept board. The sheet was ripped away to reveal a wave of energy decorated with numbers illustrating the Fibonacci sequence, the elegant mathematical formula that lies behind many of the structures of the natural world.

The MD then moved to the final image and a flourish of the hand unleashed a gasp from everyone in the room. All eyes were on a foetus with a gas mask, which was floating in the dark stratosphere encased in a bubble. This was the chilling future awaiting consumers if they did not buy into green energy.

'Any questions?' asked the MD as he looked around the room. My hand shot up. 'Yes, who are these ads aimed at?' Glances were busily exchanged as it became clear that this question was not anticipated in the briefing notes. As the seconds ticked by and the silence became burdensome, I asked myself how advertising messages could be created without a clear idea of the target market. Yet here was an advertising MD with an excellent track record feeling perfectly fine about presenting ideas which needed no external reference point. Is this acceptable practice or not? Is the creative an artist or a craftsman who adjusts his work to suit the desires of the customer?

The Importance of the Customer

If you asked that question of Michael Hammer, the brains behind the concept of Business Process Reengineering (BPR), he would be unequivocal in his answer. BPR taught businesses worldwide about the need to reconfigure their activities so that the customer was always centre stage, warning companies that business survival depends on shaping products and services around the 'unique and particular needs' of their customer (Hammer 1995). One of the results of BPR was to increase the salience of the customer in the eyes of business so Hammer might well have attempted to change the thinking of the solipsistic creative to become more customer centric.

This focus on the customer means that successful businesses are those that keep their customers in view and deliver products matched to their needs. The first step in this process is to identify who exactly is making the purchase decisions about a product, defining them as closely as possible. Traditionally, market research has defined the customer in terms of their social class, age and geographical location, but played scant attention to their gender. Now, after many years out in the cold, a fourth variable, gender, is receiving increasing attention. Some organizations are now taking an important step forward and asking whether their customers are men or women although (as we shall see later) much market research is still rooted in variables such as age, class and location.

Arguably to ignore a person's gender is to omit vital additional information and this explains why the first substantive plenary session of the 1999 Alpach European Forum on economic and social trends – a symposium attended by business leaders and politicians – was dedicated to the issue of 'gender differences'. According to many commentators, it is the needs and desires of women that increasingly drive the political and business worlds, and there is a move to try and understand these.

Examples? A crop of books has appeared examining how to sell to women. These include *Don't Think Pink* by Lisa Johnson and Andrea Learned, *GenderSell* by Judith Tingley and Lee Robert, Marty Barletta's *Marketing to Women*, Fara Warner's *The Power of the Purse*, Bernice Kanner's *Pocketbook Power* and *Eve-olution: The Eight Truths of Marketing to Women*, by Faith Popcorn and Lys Marigold. These authors, all American incidentally, consider that women constitute a sufficiently distinct market to make it worth giving considerable thought as to how best to target products and services at them.

Historically, there has been a range of views on whether women constitute a sufficiently homogeneous group to warrant being the focus of attention with many commentators taking the 'postmodern' view that the study of gender can be problematic (Bristor and Fischer 1993). There are several underlying factors, one of which is the lack of a clear understanding of the meaning of gender within the field of marketing with 'researchers working from very different theoretical perspectives … disagree(ing) on the meanings of the term' (Caterall and Maclaran 2002, 406). Interpretations can cover a vast range of understandings and we need to be prepared for different perspectives. At one extreme, we find the postmodern view that gender is an unproductive dichotomy rooted in cultural understandings of what it means to be masculine or feminine (Firat 1994), a tradition reflected in the work of post-structuralists such as Judith Butler, and which leads adherents to argue that gender has no place in consumer research and should be abandoned.

A word about Judith Butler. This Professor in the Departments of Rhetoric and Comparative Literature at the University of California, Berkeley, scored a publishing coup when her PhD thesis, *Gender Trouble*, was published as a book in 1990, selling over 100,000 copies internationally. The crux of her argument is that the coherence of the categories of sex, gender and sexuality is culturally constructed through the repetition of stylized acts in time. These stylized bodily acts, in their repetition, establish the appearance of an essential, 'core' gender. This is the sense in which Butler famously theorizes gender, along with sex and sexuality, as akin to a performance. This leads her to consider that 'woman' as a unitary category is a construct of psychoanalysis, 'giv(ing) a false sense of legitimacy and universality to a culturally specific and, in some cases, culturally oppressive version of gender identity' (Butler 1991, 330).

A middle position is adopted by so-called 'liberal feminists' who, according to Bristor and Fischer in their excellent review of feminist thinking on consumer behaviour (1993), argue that any inferred psychological male/female differences are not necessarily innate but can develop out of women's socially allocated roles. According to this way of thinking, sex differences are the simple manifestation of social inequalities and not the result of biological differences. Liberal feminists are not sympathetic to the notion that there is a biological basis to cognitive abilities but accept a causal link between social inequalities and sex differences. As a result, they believe that single-sex samples may lack validity for generalized consumer behaviour knowledge for as long as the social inequalities prevail. As inequalities are removed (so the thinking goes), observed psychological differences will diminish or disappear, and this will result in widespread androgyny (Jagger 1983). The reader may be interested to know that, in the early 1990s when Bristor and Fischer were writing, 'liberal feminists' were considered to be the 'most numerous' of the feminists.

At the extreme end of the continuum, opposing the postmodern view of gender as an irrelevant variable, is what Bristor and Fischer (1993) label the 'women's voice or experience' point of view. This perspective allows for the fact that there are more or less permanent differences between male and female experiences, and that female experiences constitute an equally valid basis for developing knowledge and organizing society (Calas and Smircich 1991). This way of thinking, in contrast to that of liberal feminists, does not consider men and women to be essentially the same. On the contrary, it tends to subscribe to the view that 'distinctions of gender, based on sex, structure virtually every aspect of our lives' (Jagger 1983, 85).

The reader needs to understand that within the 'women's voice or experience' perspective embraces two opposing points of view (Bristor and Fischer 1993). The first holds that differences between men and women are primarily or largely innate and linked to biology, a view that emphasizes the unique biologically based creative capabilities of women, suggesting that they form the basis for a distinctive female way of thinking. From there it is a small step to the evolutionary psychological perspective (Lupotow et al. 1995), which is gaining in popularity in several disciplines and which views sex differences as the bi-product of historical circumstances and affecting male and female success in the reproductive stakes. According to a review of gender in marketing this approach forms an 'influential, emerging paradigm that could have significant implications for the study of gender and consumption' (Caterall and Maclaran 2002, 417).

One should not perhaps be surprised by the less than enthusiastic support given to the evolutionary psychological approach. Dr Rick O'Gorman for example, an academic at Sheffield Hallam University, has argued that 'the social sciences have in large part been resistant to acknowledging that at least some aspects of human behaviour and cognition are likely due not primarily to socialization processes, ill-defined as these are, but due instead to a result of the phylogenetic and evolutionary history of Homo sapiens' (O'Gorman 1999, 96). This resistance has fuelled a concern to reject biological determinism and instead viewed gender as a purely socially constructed category, albeit one deeply embedded and rooted in real differences in life worlds. This is the second view within the 'women's voice' perspective.

Regardless of which of these two positions are adopted, a central concern of those adopting the 'women's voice or experience' perspective has been to eradicate the subordination of women by validating that which is associated with femaleness. As a consequence, androgyny has not been presented as an ideal that will help to achieve this goal (Bristor and Fischer 1993). On the contrary, most people who adopt this perspective argue, as a minimum for the importance of recognizing the ways in which knowledge is gendered and gaining legitimacy for that feminine knowledge that has been suppressed or marginalized.

One consequence of this way of thinking is the tendency of 'women's voice' feminists tend to identify theories and practices that are male-gendered and tend to contrast these with the female alternatives. For instance, definitions of moral development have been construed as male biased (Gilligan 1982) since they are based on the masculine tendency to assume a sharp distinction between the self and other. This contrasts with purportedly feminine notions of morality in which the boundaries between the self and other are thought to be more fluid (Bristor and Fischer 1993). Those adopting the 'women's voice or experience' perspective might also consider predominantly middle-class white male scholarly community has persistently studied the consumption of durables in a way that betrays a lack of understanding of female consumers. To rectify this, they might argue, experiments on consumer attitudes need to involve men as well as women.

You might be wondering where along this spectrum of attitudes this particular book lies? The answer is that it pretty unequivocally shares the 'women's voice and experience' perspective and so must, of necessity, it must come into conflict with the postmodern and liberal feminist perspectives. I make no apology for this and signal in advance that the gender differences described here are presented as having their roots in social *and* biological factors. However, this view is presented without a detailed discussion of the evidence and without this, such a position would be untenable.

Having now understood the main positions adopted by researchers investigating gender and consumer behaviour, we can look briefly at how the terms 'gender' and 'sex' are used in this book. The first term, 'gender', is a social concept referring to psychologically, sociologically or culturally rooted traits, attitudes, beliefs and behavioural tendencies, with a linked notion that gender is not fully determined by sex (Bristor and Fischer 1993). The term 'sex', on the other hand, is a biological concept that allows us to distinguish between males and females purely on the basis of physiological characteristics. Its influence beyond that is subject to question with Fischer and Arnold taking the view that biological sex per se does not predetermine behaviour … [but] has a profound influence on a person's socialization experience (Fischer and Arnold 1990, 519) and others holding that it can have a substantial impact on emotions and behaviours (Brizendine 2006). As one American team of researchers has put it, 'gendered differences are only sociologically inevitable' while 'sexual differences are largely biologically determined' (Gentry et al. 2003, 1). The term 'gender' is used in an unorthodox way in most of this book to connote both these meanings.

With positions and terms behind us, we can now move forward and examine the place that men and women occupy as consumers and decision makers. It is important to do this since, as we have seen there is a view that business strategies should be framed around customers. This takes us back to the story of the advertising campaign for green energy and prompts us to ask questions about the market for this type of energy. What does a typical customer look like?

The market for green energy

When I asked the organizers about the demographics of the market for green energy, there was a long silence until another question saved the day and spared the organizers the embarrassment of answering my question. Back in my office, I was eager to obtain information on the market for domestic energy, and green energy in particular. Within a short space of time I had some answers. Jan Pahl, an academic from the University of Kent and an expert on male and female expenditure patterns, established that the rather dubious honour of settling household bills falls largely to women (2000). Unfortunately, Pahl had not studied the question of energy decisions and it was only a Canadian survey conducted in 2002 by Daniel Scott of the Meteorological Service of Canada together with Ian Rowlands and Paul Parker of the University of Waterloo near Toronto, that came anywhere near an answer (Rowlands et al. 2002). This study showed that men and women were equally interested in green energy, a conclusion which, if it holds true worldwide, has vast ramifications for the £400 billion a year global electricity market. This market has been opened up to global competition and a detailed understanding of customer demographics offers competitors a distinct advantage.

So, casting our thoughts back to the advertising away-day, we might ask whether the advertising images presented to the meeting would appeal equally to men and women. Would men and women be equally swayed by pictures of a man, a baby in a gas mask and a mathematical formula spiralling through the galaxy? Or were these simply images that appealed to the male advertising creative, and that he then assumed others would like too?

If we analyse the images in light of the information presented later in the book, this appears to be a plausible explanation. For example, the fact that the only person depicted (apart from the unsexed foetus) was a man may link to the fact that the artist was a man and numerous pieces of research show that we tend to draw people of own gender. Furthermore, the starkness of the male figure and the fact that the foetus is used to project images of fear (filling us with foreboding as to the consequences of not purchasing energy efficient sources) could be linked to the separate finding by Majewski (1978) that boys have less of a tendency than girls to draw smiling faces.

Once you are acquainted with the body of the research, you will see that the male designers have left their fingerprints in other ways too. The high-tech features, for example, whether it is the gas mask, the wind turbines or the mathematical formula, could all be construed as tell-tale signs of male authorship. The evidence? Back in 1995, long before the spate of books exploring the impact of gender on marketing, I had conducted experiments comparing male and female designs and one of my findings was that men were much more likely than women to create designs with a technical look (Moss 1995). This was one of many features that characterized the male 'production aesthetic' and one reason why the finding of a distinct male aesthetic was so significant was because I subsequently discovered that each gender had a strong preference for the production aesthetic associated with its own gender. This finding emerged in experiment after experiment and helped show that the images displayed by the advertising executive might have greater appeal to an all-male than a mixed audience. In other words, for the demographics of the target market, these images may have been less than optimum.

Of course, this conclusion rests on the supposition that design and advertising preferences are not universal, but can be segmented. In fact, this way of thinking is still relatively new and so this book draws together for the first time the research from which a detailed understanding of segmented design preferences can be gained. As you read on, you will see, that this book draws on fields as diverse as psychology, art therapy, design and advertising, and since this is the first time the entire body of work has been presented, you cannot therefore blame the agency for not being aware of these points.

All the time that I was researching design preferences in the 1990s, the topic of diversity and visual preferences was not really on anyone's radar screens. As you read on, you will see how ill-advised this neglect has been. On a more positive note, you can now learn how your business could benefit from this new understanding.

Men and Women as Purchasers

Statistics offer us a glimpse not only of the relative importance of men and women as earners and potential spenders, but also of the way men and women divide the task of making decisions about the purchase of different items. These two topics are the subject of this next section.

Income of men and women

According to Lisa Johnson and Andrea Learned (2004), American women now earn one trillion dollars a year and their incomes over the last three decades have increased a dramatic 63 per cent after inflation while men's median income has hardly moved. These authors identify a number of factors that have contributed to this massive increase in women's wealth including greater access to education and greater opportunities in the workplace. A few statistics lay bare the massive changes that have occurred in the space of the last few years. Thus, in 1960, 38 per cent of adult women in the US worked outside the home whereas by 2000 the figure had risen to 61 per cent. Since 1960, the proportion of married women who worked outside the home has almost doubled from 32 per cent to 59 per cent (Rach 2003) and some of this work is in the context of self-employment, with American women owning 40 per cent of all US companies.

The result? In 1997, the US Census Bureau survey data indicated that 48 per cent of working wives provide at least half of household income, and that a high 27 per cent of US households were headed by a single female bringing in the entire household income and making all household decisions. According to data released by American Interep Radio Stores, women over 18 years of age control over half the investment value in the US and, moreover, women control 43 per cent of shares portfolios valued at over $50,0000 (PBS).

A similar snapshot of women's economic power comes from the UK. The Centre for Economics and Business Research which conducted a study in 2005 on women's finances for the Liverpool Victoria Friendly Society estimated that women in the UK have about 40 per cent of the country's assets (BBC Radio 4 Moneybox 2005).

Of course, part of the reason for women's increasing wealth is the rapid rise in divorce and inheritance payments but women's increasing penetration of the labour market and the growing number of female entrepreneurs are also factors. Thus in the UK, in the last six months of 2006, women started 38,000 businesses, an increase of 9 per cent over the same period the previous year (Barclays 2006). Where overall employment is concerned, the proportion of women in work has been increasing over decades with research showing the female employment rate rising from 42 per cent to 70 per cent between 1971 and 2004 (Clarke 2005). Women may still face a glass ceiling, with just one in twelve non-executive directors at Britain's 100 biggest companies being women, dropping to 4 per cent of executive directors (Lorenz 2003), but their increasing penetration of the market gives them greater independence in financial and purchasing matters.

In terms of their importance in purchasing, one article in *Web Designer* (24 February 2006) has women spending or influencing around 83p of every pound spent by consumers with the figure higher for holidays and new homes (over 90 per cent). In the US, it is said that women spend 85 cents out of every dollar spent and women's financial power spurred *The Economist* to coin a new phrase – 'Womenomics' – to refer to the amplified economic power of women worldwide (Barclays 2006).

It is not just in the UK and America that women have increased their economic power. In China, there were 337 million female employees by the end of 2004, accounting for 44.8 per cent of the total workforce (*Daily Mail* 2007, *The Economist* 2006). In France, women's place in employment is high, with 79 per cent of women aged between 25 and 49 in employment during 1998, compared with less than one in two in 1968 (Thévenon 1999). Across the age groups, 48.2 per cent of the female population in France are in full-time qualified permanent employment, a figure that compares positively with the EU average of 45.6 per cent. Moreover women are setting up increasing numbers of companies (up from 18 to 30 per cent in 15 years) for which the survival rate is higher than those set up by men (Thévenon 1999). Although no figures are available concerning women's share of national assets in France, women's growing activity rates would suggest more immediate access to disposable income.

However, although women in France are entering the employment market in big numbers, the glass ceiling is very much in evidence. Only 6.3 per cent of the management posts of the 5000 leading companies in France are held by women (Laufert and Fouquet 1997). In the public services, where 59.6 per cent of all jobs are held by women, only 10 per cent of them reach the top levels of the administration, there are only 5 women out of 109 prefects and 11 women ambassadors out of more than 150! (Council of Europe 2006).

Household Purchasing Decisions

Knowing who makes the money is one thing but knowing who makes the decisions as to how to spend it may be another. How are decisions about how to spend money allocated between men and women? Answers to this question can be found either in market research data on individual products or from researching the literature on purchasing habits in families. The family is frequently described as an important social unit in terms of decision-making and consumption (Foster and Olshavsky 1989; Assael, 1998; Commuri and Gentry 2005; Kubacki et al. 2007) and we will concentrate here on the research data on family expenditure. A first step in this is to define what we mean by a family.

According to the popular source, Wikipedia, a family is 'a domestic group of people (or a number of domestic groups), typically affiliated by birth or marriage by analogous or comparable relationships – including domestic partnership, cohabitation, adoption' and in recent years many societies have seen a shift away from marriage towards cohabitation and single parenthood. The statistics paint a clear picture. In France in 1999, 18.5 per cent of families were single-parent families compared with 10 per cent in 1982 (Institut national d'études démographiques). By 2005 in the UK, nearly 1 in 14 dependent children lived in a lone-parent family, an increase from the 1 in 4 which was the case in 1972 (Council of Europe 2006). In 2000 in the US, nearly 1 in 3 dependent children lived in a lone-parent family (US Census Bureau 2000) and the increasing proportion of single parents leaves women in a position where they are responsible for a larger proportion of consumption decisions. This exacerbates the tendency towards female control of family expenditures found in the more traditional household consisting of a man and a woman, a unit whose consumption habits have been the subject of extensive research. The findings make for very interesting reading.

Research on household decision-making

In the commercial sector, some organizations have not always been focused on the role of gender in consumption patterns, although some market intelligence services, while focused primarily on non-gender variables, have recognized the importance of understanding the influence and role of different family members on household purchases. For example, the marketing of men's toiletries and colognes tend to target their products at the female of the household since she tends to be the primary purchaser of these products in the household (Nielson 1997).

Household decision-making and the role and influence of individual household members have, by contrast, been intensively studied in the academic marketing literature. Some researchers have focused on the function of different household members on the household decision-making process, identifying such roles as 'initiator', 'gatekeeper', 'decider', 'buyer', 'user' (Speckman and Stern 1977; Wind 1976, 1978) and 'caretaker' (Price et al. 2000). Others have focused on the perceived influence and participation of individual household members on the various stages of household decision-making processes. For example, two researchers in the late 1970s (Szybillo and Sosanie 1979) developed models of group decision-making within households in relation to products such as sofa-beds, ski weekends and maid services.

Other researchers have focused on the way in which husbands and wives influence household decision-making. An early, landmark study by Harry Davis and Benny Rigaux (1974) investigating marital roles in decision-making processes in Belgian households concluded that there were not only products for which men or women were more likely to make decisions, but different stages at which men and women might get involved in the decision-making process.

Davis and Rigaux mapped the extent to which, on average, husbands and wives were dominant in certain product decisions, with a score of one on the continuum denoting a male-dominated decision, and a score of three a female-dominated one.

The most extreme scores they presented were a score for life insurance of 1.37 (showing that men were very active in decisions here) and a score of 2.91 for household cleaning products (showing that women were very active in decisions here). Other products at the high end of the continuum included kitchenware, wife's and children's clothes, food and non-alcoholic beverages, showing these to be wife-dominated purchase decisions. They identified, also, purchases that were made collectively (described in the research as 'syncratic decisions') as well as a more autonomous style of decision-making (described here as 'autonomic'). Examples of products attracting syncratic decision-making at all three phases included housing, furniture, toys, school, concerts, films, theatre and holidays.

In a second phase of analysis, the authors tracked the extent to which husbands and wives adopted these positions in each of the three phases of the decision-making process identified by David and Rigaux.. The first of these phases was identified as the 'problem recognition' phase, the second as the 'search for information' phase and the third as the 'final decision' phase. What they concluded was that, while 64 per cent of the decisions were positioned in the first two stages, there can be a shift in the final stage towards syncratic decision-making. Table 1.1 illustrates this tendency.

The figures tell an interesting story. What we can see across the three stages of decision-making is a tendency for husbands and wives to make decisions either jointly or in partnership. In fact, the proportion of decisions, at all phases, that are uniquely down to husbands is limited, and studies from the 1980s continue to show a shift away from husband-dominated decisions, a result possibly of societal changes (Belch and Willis 2002). Davis and Rigaux's study was conducted in the 1970s, but by the 1980s, studies in America were showing that women were taking a larger role in decisions to purchase insurance, cars and financial services (Chandler 1981). This shift away from husband-dominated decisions was highlighted further in a 1987 study which replicated Davis and Rigaux's landmark study, finding this time, ten years on, that decisions to purchase automobiles, televisions and financial planning had shifted from husband-dominated product decisions to joint

Table 1.1 Patterns of influence at three stages of the decision process

	Phase		
Pattern of influence	**Problem recognition**	**Search for information**	**Final decision**
Husband dominant	2	3	2
Autonomic	10	9	5
Syncratic	7	6	13
Wife dominant	6	7	5

decisions (Putnam and Davidson 1987). Moreover, final decisions to purchase stereos, financial planning, automobiles, carpet and living room furniture, many areas in which husbands had previously had an exclusive role in decision-making, were now all jointly made.

The move away from husband-decision-making was found also in studies outside America, with a 1993 UK study (Vogler and Pahl) distinguishing between five systems of resource allocation. These were as follows:

1. Female whole wage system. In this system, the woman is responsible for managing all household expenditure with the exception of the partner's personal spending.
2. Male whole wage system. In this system, the man is responsible for managing all household expenditure with the exception of his partner's personal spending.
3. Housekeeping system. Here, the woman is given a housekeeping allowance and her partner looks after the rest of the money.
4. Shared management system. The couple pool their resources and both partners share and manage household finances jointly.
5. Independent system. Here both adults keep their finances completely separate.

Analysing data contained in the 'Social Change and Economic Life Initiative', these researchers found that allocative systems were distributed in the proportions shown in Table 1.2.

These figures show that in 60 per cent of cases, men were likely to have some degree of involvement in the spending of household income, this being the aggregate of the 'male whole wage' and 'shared management' categories. Men, moreover, were likely to have sole control in just 12 per cent of cases. Women, by contrast, were likely to have some degree of involvement in as many as 88 per cent of cases, and sole control in 26 per cent of cases. This comparison of the male

Table 1.2 The allocation of income and expenditure in cohabiting couples (Vogler and Pahl 1993)

Methods of allocation of income	Per cent of couples in each system
Female whole wage	26
Male whole wage	10
Housekeeping	12
Shared management	50
Independent	2

and female figures showed that women's role in household spending was likely to be greater than or equal to that of men, a conclusion confirmed by a second study, this time conducted at the University of Essex in the UK.

The Essex study analysed data in the British Household Panel Survey of 1991 and 1992, revealing that as many as 83 per cent of women were likely to have some involvement in the spending of household income (Buck et al. 1995), a figure that compared with only 68 per cent in the case of men. The study showed, moreover, that approximately 24 per cent of women, as compared with only 9 per cent of men, were likely to have sole control over financial decisions. These figures highlighted what is often not revealed, namely that women have a decisive role in the way family income is spent. The results are shown in tabular form in Table 1.3.

While these last two studies looked at men and women's responsibility for spending decisions across the board, another UK study in the 1990s examined responsibility in relation to the purchase of specific products, finding that women were more influential in the selection of clothing and major appliances (for example, the washing machine) than men (Mohan 1995). A further study (Moss 1996b) studied marketing data produced by the Target Group Index (TGI) in the UK, and showed that there were significantly more female than male purchasers of chocolate, china and glass, electric kettles and furniture. Moreover, data from the Family Expenditure Survey (FES), an annual survey of 7,000 households in the UK, revealed that there were significantly more female than male purchasers of books, china and glass, cosmetics, kitchen equipment, jewellery, photographic equipment, small electrical goods, stationery and toys (Moss 1999). That's quite a list!

The dominant position of women as purchasers does not end there however. According to a former Marketing Director of Lever Brothers 'the bulk of our brands are targeted at women who still do the bulk of the shopping' (Batstone

Table 1.3 The allocation of income and expenditure in cohabiting couples under 65 years of age

	Both same working hours	Male main earner	Female main earner	Both employed
Female whole wage	23.5	26.4	26.3	27.5
Male whole wage	8.6	12.0	9.9	11.0
Housekeeping	3.2	13.7	7.0	11.2
Shared management	59.1	46.2	51.5	48.5
Independent	3.7	1.0	2.3	0.5

1994) and the female domination of the purchases in the grocery, book, china, small electrical goods, cosmetic and furniture markets is echoed in the car and housing markets. Amazing! In the UK, research has revealed that 60 per cent of women are either solely responsible for, or have had a significant influence in, the purchase of their household's car (Sutton 2008). Another estimate puts women's influence even higher, suggesting that they take the major decision or have an equal say in just under 70 per cent of car purchases (Cooper 1994).

Where house purchases are concerned, men have a decisive say in only 9 per cent of cases, according to a survey conducted by the National Association of Estate Agents (NAEA). Over 76 per cent of estate agents surveyed in the NAEA Market Trends report agreed that women were the key decision makers (Moss 1999). More recently, Clive Fenton of Barratt Homes has said that 'The overall influence of women in the market is massive. In couples and familes, women have invariably been the key decision makers in design, layout and location' (Norwood 2005).

By contrast, the UK's TGI survey revealed that there were significantly more male than female purchasers of computers, fridges, washing machines and SLR cameras. The Family Expenditure Survey showed a significantly greater number of men than women purchasing alcohol, diesel oil, garden tools, petrol, recorded music, sports goods and video cameras (Moss 1999). Moreover, men have traditionally dominated the traditionally masculine domain of DIY although, this now seems under threat. According to a YouGov survey of DIY and women (November 2004) more than 50 per cent of women are now doing DIY themselves. and of this number, more than two thirds are assembling and half putting up the furniture themselves. Not altogether surprising then that it is mainly women who account for the 33 per cent growth in the DIY market since the beginning of the millennium, a significant encroachment by women into a market worth £12.5 billion in 2004 (Lamb 2005).

Salli Brand, author of *The Girls' Guide to DIY* (2004) distinguishes that male and female priorities are different: 'My experience with women is that they are more methodical than men, and that they are more interested in the aesthetics. When she buys screws, she'll pick out the prettiest ones. He'll buy the strongest ones' (Marsh 2004, 29).

If we turn to the detail of current purchasing patterns in the US we find similar trends, with women playing the dominant role in household decisions. As Michael Silverstein, principal at Boston Consulting Group and author of *Trading Up: The New American Luxury* (2003), has said: 'Today's woman is the chief purchasing agent of the family and marketers have to recognize that'.

This is not a lone voice. Fara Warner in her book *The Power of the Purse* (2005) describes women as 'the majority market' (ibid. 5) and 'the world's most powerful consumers' (ibid. 6) accounting for $7 trillion in consumer and business spending and control. Marti Barletta, author of *Marketing to Women* (2006), quotes women as responsible for 83 per cent of all consumer purchases, 89 per cent of all new bank accounts and 80 per cent of healthcare decisions, with more than two-thirds of all health care spending being made by women. The list of female-dominant purchasing extends to the following too:

- home furnishings (94 per cent)
- holidays (92 per cent)
- houses (91 per cent)
- home improvement decisions (80 per cent)
- cars (influence, 90 per cent and purchases, 60 per cent)
- computers (66 per cent)
- consumer electronics (55 per cent)
- investment decisions (53 per cent).

This list could be extended to other product areas in which women have a significant role as purchaser, for example, jewellery where women's partners are as likely to buy it for them as they are for themselves (Heilman et al. 2006). Moreover, where business travel is concerned, a report by the Travel Industry Association of America in 1996 estimated that women accounted for 40 per cent of business travel, with 17.2 million women making 67 million business trips during that year (Rach 2003).

Many of these statistics may come as a surprise, but none more so than the figures for car purchases. According to several websites (http://www.roadandtravel.com and http://www.dealix.com):

- Women purchase more than 65 per cent of all new vehicles (an $83 billion market) and 53 per cent of all used vehicles.
- Women influence more than 95 per cent of all automotive purchases in US households.
- Women spend $300 billion annually on used car sales, maintenance, repairs and service.
- Women buyers are the fastest growing segment of new and used car buyers today.

So much for car purchases. It is only fair to point out that while some purchases show a shift towards more female-only decision-making, some show a move towards joint decision-making by men and women. For example, a study in 1982 by William Qualls found a profound shift toward joint decision-making for children's education and housing. A later study (Phipps and Burton 1998) found likewise that while some purchases are made with separate incomes (for example, restaurant food, clothing, child care), some are made with pooled incomes. This was found to be the case with housing and donations to charity for example.

Signs of a greater role in purchasing by men also arose in a 1992 study (Zinn) which found that American men were purchasing a quarter of household groceries, an increase of 17 per cent from 1987. Moreover, the study revealed that 80 per cent of men were doing some major food shopping every month (ibid.).

The picture in Asia

For a picture of shopping patterns in Asia we have to rely on an in-depth study of men's and women's roles in shopping in Singapore. The author, Francis Piron, Senior Lecturer at Nanyang Business School, Nanyang Technological University, investigated the relative involvement of men and women in grocery shopping decision-making and purchasing in Singapore (2002). He measured people's involvement at all stages in the decision-making process – as 'initiator', 'buyer' 'influencer', and 'decision-maker' (Speckman and Stern 1977; Wind, 1976, 1978) – in the purchase of household products (fruits, vegetables, meat, canned food, toiletries, cleaning and dairy products and drinks). He found that, overall, decision-making was the realm of women, who dominated all stages in the decision-making process. The only product category that served as an exception, with a tendency for decisions to be made jointly across the phases, was beverages.

Conclusions and Practical Lessons

This chapter has discussed men and women's role as purchasers and decision-makers and shown that women have a decisive say in a high proportion of purchase decisions. It has shown too that, conversely, there are relatively few markets in which the same could be said of men.

This is a stark reality which many organizations may not yet grasp. Remember how green energy was being marketed without reference to the person making the purchase decision? Companies should avoid this mistake by clearly identifying the customer and purchaser (often, but not always, the same person) and shaping the product around their preferences. How successful have they been in the past? This is the subject of the next chapter.

Chapter 2
Marketing to Men and Women

The Failure of Marketing

If you hadn't been studying how firms design and market for men and women you might be surprised to hear the view that 'Marketing to women is a big and echoing void' (Popcorn and Marigold 2001, 9). The discipline of marketing has, after all, been around in its present form since at least the 1940s and so you might expect the science of advertising to be well developed. Why 1940? That was the year that television was introduced, with audience figures soaring in the 1950s, and it was advertising that paid for the popular new shows. This helped support the growth of advertising, marketing and PR agencies and soon television far surpassed radio as an advertising medium.

Bill Bernbach, founder of Doyle Dane Bernbach in New York City, Leo Burnett, founder of the Leo Burnett agency in Chicago, Illinois and David Ogilvy, founder of Ogilvy and Mather in New York City, all came to prominence in the late 1950s and 1960s and led what has been called the 'creative revolution'. Bernbach's agency captured the spirit of the new age. He believed that advertising had to be creative and artistic or it would bore people and that respect for the public's intelligence was the starting point for good advertising. The advertisements his agency created were understated, sophisticated and witty.

Marketing entered the popular psyche when Vance Packard wrote his best seller *The Hidden Persuaders*. Published in 1957, it sold over a million copies – a stunning achievement then for a work of non-fiction and still a pretty impressive figure for pop sociology. In *The Hidden Persuaders*, Packard revealed that marketers had discovered myriad ways of selling using motivational research and other psychological techniques, including depth psychology and subliminal techniques to manipulate expectations and induce desire for products, particularly in the American postwar era. The extent to which opinion could be manipulated was explored by Edward Bernays (1955) who referred to his scientific technique of opinion-moulding as the 'engineering of consent'.

In marketing terms a landmark year was 1959, the year Jerome McCarthy distilled the elements of the Marketing Mix into the four elements that will trip off the tongue of most marketing students – price, promotion, product and place (distribution). Just a couple of years later in 1961, Albert Frey (Smith and Taylor 2004) distilled the essence of marketing into just two categories, namely factors relating to the 'offering' and those relating to the 'process'. Where the 'offering' is concerned, this relates to factors such as the product, service, packaging, brand and price. While, the 'process' relates to activities such as advertising, promotion, sales promotion, personal selling, publicity, distribution channels, marketing research, strategy formation and new product development. The reference to 'new product development' puts one in mind of design and although design is not explicitly referred to in these models, later commentators have defined it as one of the elements in the marketing mix that shapes a person's overall reactions to a product (Roy and Wield 1989). It is the ubiquity and importance of design which explains the central place it occupies in this book.

Missing from these early typologies is an explicit reference to people, whether as customers or staff. Perhaps this is the reason why Philip Kotler, the S.C. Johnson and Son Distinguished Professor of International Marketing at the Kellogg School of Management at Northwestern University, believing that 'marketing must help the company deliver more value to the customer' (1999) offered a typology based this time around the four 'Cs' (C standing for customer). As you can see, his typology has a greater customer focus:

- Customer Benefits = product.
- Cost to Customer = price.
- Convenience = place.
- Communications = promotion.

The lack of any explicit reference to people was put right in 1981 by Mary Jo Bitner and Bernard Booms who added 'People' to their seven-part Marketing Mix, thereby formally putting the human element on the marketing map. The strategic importance of this cannot be understated and the importance of giving consideration to the needs of the customer and satisfying those needs is the driver of much that is discussed in this book.

In focusing on the needs of the customer we are seeking to understand the factors in design and marketing that can make a product offering 'seductive' as one academic has elegantly put it:

> 'Beyond the principle of utility, it becomes more and more important to associate a principle of pleasure to the value. The useful must be linked to the beautiful, the rational to the imaginary, the indispensable to the superfluous … it is imperative that the image be seductive.'
>
> (Craig 1992, 10)

To bring this about, design and advertising agencies must 'acquire knowledge of consumers' symbolic meaning-systems in order to invest the … development process with its culturally meaningful potentiality' (Hackley 2002, 215–16). To assist in our understanding of consumers' meaning-systems, the focus in this book will be on design and marketing and the way that gender influences what people produce and prefer – what we call here the 'design production' and 'design preference'.

Of course, as we saw in the previous chapter's discussion of men and women's role as decision-makers, there is already some awareness of the importance of gender in the Marketing Mix. What we saw underlines the view that women make 80 per cent of consumer decisions (Johnson and Learned 2004) and this has been translated into marketing speak with David Ogilvy, founder of one of the world's largest advertising agencies, when he said that, 'The consumer is not a moron. She is your wife' (Wikipedia). In the same vein Tom Peters, author of *In Search of Excellence* and *The Circle of Innovation,* predicted that women will be the future primary purchasers of almost every good and service (Tingley and Robert 1999, 111).

These kind of sentiments are vividly echoed in Paco Underhill's book *Why We Buy (*1999) when he says, 'Shopping is still and always will be meant mostly for females. Shopping *is* female'. He goes on to say that, 'Women are capable of consigning species of retailer or product to Darwin's dustbin if that retailer or product is unable to adapt to what women need and want'. The consequence, portentously evoked by Underhill, is 'like watching dinosaurs die out' (ibid. 113).

Some retailers, to give them their due, have awoken to the fact that women do most of the shopping and are the main decision makers for a high proportion of products. Marks and Spencer, in recognition perhaps of men's role as reluctant shoppers, initiated the male crèche, a shopping-free sanctuary complete with sofas, DVDs and toys such as Scalextric sets (McCormack 2004). This is one way of adjusting the offering to the target market, but according to Faith Popcorn (Popcorn and Marigold 2001), organizations still have a long way to go.

Where are they going wrong? According to Faith Popcorn, firms keep on marketing to women 'in the same old way' (Popcorn and Marigold 2001). Judi Bevan, author of a fascinating history of the UK high street retailer Marks and Spencer, describes the firms customer base as being largely female, yet paints a picture of a system in which most strategic business and marketing decisions are made by men (Bevan 2007). She does not specifically blame Marks and Spencer for leaving key decisions to men, but shows us how male-dominated the organization is and how ill-conceived some of their decisions have been. A few examples will serve to illustrate the point.

After the original Marks and Sieff families relinquished control of the company the top job was held by men from outside the family, including in recent years Rayner, Greenbury, Salsbury and Vandevelde. Profits reached their apogee under Greenbury who engaged in furious cost cutting exercises to take profits over the billion pound mark. Soon, however, the fall-out from the drastic measures taken to reach this target led the Dutch Vandevelde to be joined at the helm by the young and dynamic Roger Holmes in 2001. What was it that had led Verdict, the retail research firm, to speak of a fall in the value of the Marks and Spencer market share from 13 per cent to 10.5 per cent between 1996 and the end of 2000? What had happened between 1997 and 2000 to create a 67 per cent decline in shareholder value, a bigger drop in shareholder value than had been experienced by any other FTSE company in that period?

Judi Bevan describes Roger Holmes's impressions on first joining the firm in 2001: 'I was struck by how inwardly focused the company had remained … Nobody seemed to be asking how many customers coming into the stores were actually experiencing a difference' (Bevan 2007, 235). Absence of a customer focus appears to have been a distinguishing feature of the period from the mid 1980s to the 1990s, when Lord Rayner was chairman of Marks and Spencer. One of the decisions he made was to expand overseas and buy Brooks Brothers, a store which sold clothing aimed at men of his own age and taste. This 47-store Brooks Brothers chain was, as Bevan puts it, somewhat old-fashioned and formal, legendary for its slow and courteous service and it rather sounds as though the features that attracted Rayner to the chain were features that mirrored his own personal preferences. Perhaps this personal resonance explains how Rayner could be persuaded to pay a cool $750m for a chain of stores estimated by some to be worth half that amount. Unfortunately for Marks and Spencer, despite continuous investment, the American chain never made a respectable return on capital.

During the reign of his next successor but one, Peter Salsbury, the proportion of the Marks and Spencer budget devoted to advertising and marketing was increased from a modest 1 per cent of sales to a massive 3 per cent. This led to a flurry of marketing campaigns, one of which featured a larger sized naked woman. This advertising campaign met with a lot of opposition, particularly from women who aspired to a smaller figure and when asked who he thought the typical customer was, the then Marketing Director replied that there was no such thing. He said that there were 11 types of customer, hardly the clearest or most dynamic of marketing messages.

By contrast, the founder's son, Simon Marks, had always emphasized the importance of getting the product right, and Roger Holmes returned to Simon Marks' passion for the product. 'We needed to get back to a passion for product' he said (Bevan 2007, 235). One of the first things Holmes did was seek customers' views on Marks and Spencer stores. From there, his strategy for revitalizing women's clothing sales was to use the organization's clothing talent to target the core customer – women between the ages of 35 and 50. This strategy, coupled with the sale of overseas stores, paid off. In 2001, Marks and Spencer shares rose by 75 per cent over seven months, making it the best performing FTSE share over that period.

What Roger Holmes appears to have appreciated instinctively was the importance of targeting the market and shaping the product around the needs and wants of the consumer. This can be contrasted with the actions of Sir Derek Rayner, who when he took over the American Brooks Brothers stores assumed other people would like what he liked himself. Perhaps one of the lessons from this unfortunate episode (as we saw Rayner paid vastly over the odds and the chain was sold a few years later) is that one should not use one's own tastes to guide decision-making since what we like may be very different from what appeals to the customer. Given this, we need to make a concerted attempt to get inside the mind of the customer and should not be surprised to find that what appeals to them may be very different from what appeals to decision-makers.

This may sound like an obvious enough conclusion and you may be wondering why it even needs to be stated, but the example of Marks and Spencer shows how easily it can be overlooked. Incidentally, we do not want to single out this British company for any particular opprobrium, especially since observers suggest that service quality and customer satisfaction are generally in decline (Frow and Payne 2007). This shows that the dangers of neglecting the needs of the customer could have been illustrated with reference to many other companies.

Of course, the neglect of customer needs is not confined to the annals of corporate strategy and in the space of a week I encountered several in the field of architecture. The stories came from Germany and the UK, and you may have your own stories to add to this catalogue of neglect.

The first of these stories concerns the UK's British Library, the much vaunted national library that replaced the famous Reading Room at the British Museum (this was where Karl Marx wrote *Das Kapital*). This new building is approached by means of a large, open public space and with security in mind, there is a rule stipulating that readers must deposit their personal effects in the cloakroom in the basement before proceeding to one of the reading rooms. Inevitably, there are long queues at the cloakroom and while standing in line, it is difficult not to notice the pattern of behaviour that transpires each time someone offers up their belongings. The stalwart cloakroom attendant greets the customer at the counter, picks up heavy bags and coats (particularly cumbersome during the winter months), traverses a long open space before reaching the hanging area and then retraces their steps across the long area to give the customer a counter.

If you were to conduct a time and motion study, you would say that the cloakroom design was sub-optimal in terms of the effective use of the attendant's time and energies. How could the architects have allowed this to happen?

I fell into conversation with one of the attendants one day and he told me that he had worked for the old British Library before transferring to this new art building. 'But didn't you talk to the architects about what you thought was necessary to ensure that the space was optimized from a working point of view?' I asked. 'I tried to get to speak to an architect' was the answer 'but they weren't interested'. The long queue is one of the results.

If only this was an isolated case of the failure of architecture to factor in the customer. In the same week, I met two people involved in the design of high prestige university buildings. One was in the UK and one in Germany and although these people's paths had never crossed their stories were remarkably similar. In the UK case, the building was to be made entirely of glass and this meant that academics would have to work in an open plan office without shelving for books or private offices into which to retreat for private reflection or meetings with students. The overarching concern was the external appearance of the building which took priority over all other considerations.

British madness? Not especially since in Germany, the architects had created such an immensely long building that it would be difficult for people at one end to communicate with those at the other. There was no talking the architects out of this and it was only by dint of a great deal of persuasion that the architects abandoned plans to lay a stone floor in the library (imagine the clicking of women in stilettos!). The architects had tried their best to press their case, even urging the installation of sound-absorbent curtains to absorb the noise!

So in all these cases, whether in the UK or Germany, the creatives had pursued a vision that took little account of the needs of the user, something that could be particularly serious where female customers are involved. For the shopping guru Paco Underhill, noticed that whereas a man will breeze through the produce section of the grocery store, pick up the head of lettuce on top of the pile and fail to notice the brown spots and limpid leaves, a woman will 'palpate, examine and sniff her way past the garbage, looking for lettuce perfection' (Underhill, 1999, 116). Not surprising to find him suggesting that 'Women demand more of shopping environments than men do and take pride in their ability to select the perfect thing whether it's a cantaloupe or a horse or a husband' (ibid.).

Recently I examined the relative strength of men's and women's preferences and, with statistician Dr Rod Gunn, quantified men's and women's preferences for web design. The results prove Underhill to be absolutely right – women's preferences are much stronger and more polarised than the men's (see Chapter 6).

The lessons we can learn from the mistakes made at Marks and Spencer highlight the importance of becoming acquainted with the users and purchasers of a particular product and getting to grips with their preferences. As the executive president for merchandising and marketing at the American home improvement store, The Home Depot, said, as a retailer: 'we need to understand these people [women] ... and how the evolving demographic structure of society is affecting them' (Warner 2006, 28).

A good example of the benefits of effective targeting comes from Eastman Kodak a company that often came last in the battle for market share until it got to grips with the demographics of the digital camera market. Initially when digital cameras were introduced, many camera makers assumed that the core target would be largely men because of their 'early adopter' status in technology but in fact research showed (for example the Consumer Electronics Association noted in its 'Five Consumers to Watch' study 2004) that 30 per cent of women surveyed considered themselves to be 'early adopters' of technology such as the digital camera. Kodak took advantage of data highlighting the fact that many couples shop for cameras together and that women are a prime target for cameras, to make a digital camera that delivered the technical fundamentals to men, while signalling to women that this camera was for them. This careful targeting led Kodak to create technology that was easier to use, at a time when most competitor companies focused on increasing the complexity of their products. The result of this precise targeting was that Kodak posted a 40 per cent surge in digital sales in 2004 (Warner 2005).

Unfortunately, as we have seen, organizations often do the reverse to targeting and neglect to consider the detailed needs of their customers and users. If what you offer customers is from the pool of products that *you* like, or that your designers like, then you still may be fishing in a goldfish bowl rather than the equivalent of an ocean. My own research on male and female design aesthetics has shown that men and women often have a preference for designs produced using the production aesthetic of their own gender and that these designs are often very different to those of the other gender. For example, he uses and likes a sparing use of colours while she uses and likes a greater number of colours; he creates and likes a technical appearance while she prefers less technicality, and so on. Yet when you examine the products available on the market – you could be talking about websites, kettles, computers, televisions or cars – you often find that these are produced using a masculine production aesthetic.

How does this come about? Several factors are likely involved but one which can help explain the fact that a lot of design is anchored in the male paradigm is the fact that market research, though 'ostensibly' design to increase the range of options, often presents respondents with versions of a design all of which are anchored in a single paradigm, often the male paradigm. To use a fishing metaphor, this is akin to fishing intensively in one particular pond, the male pond rather than putting a toe in the water of the female pond and comparing consumers' reactions to products that cross the two ponds. You will pardon the fishing metaphor I am sure, but you can appreciate that if the owner of a fish restaurant is always buying fish from a trout farm, they will have only limited fare to offer their customers, whereas if they also buy from a coastal fishery, they will satisfy more tastes by being able to offer cod, haddock, plaice and tuna as well as trout. The same lesson applies to design. A large proportion of organizations are currently selecting designs from within the male design paradigm (the trout farm) and ignoring the new waters available through the female design paradigm.

In a sense, businesses cannot be blamed since they are probably not aware that there are different ponds to choose from and that aesthetic tastes extend far beyond the preferences of senior male executives. When once you explore the preferences of a more diverse group, then you discover the extent to which a large proportion of products are produced within a narrow band of aesthetics, largely at the extreme male end of the gender production aesthetic. In fact, there does exist a whole way of seeing outside of this, at the female end of the gender production aesthetic, but a relatively small proportion of products appear to be produced at this end of the continuum. One of the purposes of this book is to bring the existence of these differing aesthetics to a larger audience so that, in time, the way products, services and shop interiors are presented can be transformed.

Narrow Marketing Paradigms

As we have said, a lot of marketing and design is using concepts from an extreme end of the aesthetic continuum and real choice is not being offered across a whole raft of product areas. 'You can have any car so long as its black' was the Ford mantra, and today you can imagine it replaced by 'You can have any car so long as it's produced using the masculine design aesthetic'. You could just as easily substitute the words 'web design' or hi-fi station for 'car' and you would still come out with a factual statement. Many products are designed and marketed with the illusion that they will appeal to a wide variety of tastes but in practice this is not always the case.

Look at car websites, for example, whether they are Ford's, Nissan's, Volkswagen's or Renault's, and you will see the same dark backgrounds and horizontal framing. Later it will become apparent, when we look at the sort of design that men and women produce, that what you are looking at here are features that are typical of the way men design. By contrast, if you look at female-produced websites you would see something rather different. What would greet you would be lighter, brighter colours, more detail and fewer straight lines. Unfortunately, you will find very few examples of this in a commercial setting since the female way of seeing is not 'on the map' or at least, was not when the research reported in this book got underway.

Interestingly, the man described as the father of Public Relations, Edward Bernays, wrote in his 1928 book *Propaganda* that 'Our minds are molded, our tastes formed, our ideas suggested … largely by men we have never heard of.' At the time, he may not have meant the term 'men' to be used in a literal sense but reading it today, in the context of our present discussion of male and female tastes, this literal reading sheds light on the problems and opportunities faced by the world of design and marketing. Businesses keen on appealing to markets consisting of a mixture of women and men need to ensure that their products, services and shop interiors take account of the tastes of both genders.

The need to expand the aesthetic repertoire in which products are created is challenged by the need to create economies of scale and this need can encourage a narrowing rather than expansion of interests. The music business is a case in point with a merger in July 2004 resulting in just four companies now owning 80 per cent of the global music market. Two of these – Universal and the newly merged Sony BMG – each have about 25 per cent of the market, with the other two companies (Warner Music and EMI) having the remaining share. In order to streamline its offering and presumably reduce costs, EMI in March 2004 was reported to be cutting one fifth of its recording artists, including niche artists.

The forces of globalization compose the kind of threat to diversity lamented by G.K. Chesterton in his references to standardization's 'flat, wilderness' (Simms 2005). You might think of this when hearing television advertisements in the Philippines marketing nose pegs that can be inserted in nostrils to produce a more European-shaped nose (Simms 2007, 47–8), or when you hear of plastic surgery procedures in Japan which widen the eyes of Japanese women so that they achieve a more Western appearance (ibid. 47).

It is true that the homogenization of some aspects of life seems inevitable, especially where technology has the upper hand. For example, in the UK, there used to be local variations in the time of day registered, but the growth of railways and the need for consistent timetabling that forced a move to synchronize clocks (ibid. 37). However, where taste is concerned, you could argue that an expanded market creates a greater imperative to ensure a match between the product aesthetic and that of the market. So, if you know that more than half your customers are female (the case of car companies today), you might want to ensure that cars and the marketing that goes with them please both men and women. As we shall see later, the exteriors of cars are still designed by men and there is no knowing what, in the absence of the 'engineering of consent', women might prefer visually. Potentially, there is great competitive advantage for the company that tries to find out.

Why a narrow paradigm is suboptimal

Why does it matter if firms restrict the look of their products to a narrow paradigm? Research conducted in 2007 by a firm of market researchers, using eye-tracking to follow eye movements, found some answers. It sought reactions to posters abd found that spontaneous recall for those who liked the poster was 17.3 per cent, while for those who did not recall was 10.3 per cent. This showed that if people like something, they will spend more time looking at it (Maughan et al. 2007). This is an important finding since the greater the emotional load of an image and the longer the exposure to it, the better the image is remembered. Having discovered this, the next important question for the researchers concerned the nature of the relationship between increased number of fixations and increased preference for an advertisement.

This is an important question since answers would help ascertain which was the cause and which the effect. The researchers wanted to understand the direction of the causality and whether people look more because they like something, or like something because they have looked at it more and gained increasing familiarity. Answering this question has vital lessons for businesses trying to gain the attention of consumers.

The researchers outlined the implications for marketers. Firstly, the fact that a person pays more attention to an ad when they like it implies that marketers should maximize the likeability of their product and its presentation. To do this implies knowing the target market and understanding how variables such as age, gender and personality affect preferences. Secondly, the fact that familiarity can also have an impact on preferences shows that the frequency and saturation of advertising material may also shape preferences. In fact, the market researchers concluded that, most plausibly, *both* directions of causal influence exist so that prior preferences as well as familiarity-induced preferences will play a role in consumers' responses to advertising material.

This conclusion is backed up by other findings which show that products perceived as pleasurable are preferred (Yahomoto and Lambert 1994), purchased more often (Groppel 1993; Donovan et al. 1994) and used more frequently than those not perceived as pleasurable (Jordan 1998). So substantial business gains can be made from ensuring that products and retail environments (including websites) appeal to customers. This emphasis on the product takes us back to the thinking of Simon Marks, the son of the founder of Marks and Spencer, who used to say that the product is what really matters. A revitalized emphasis on the product was part of the vision of Roger Holmes who said that 'We needed to get back to a passion for product' (Bevan 2007, 235).

Preferences

We have seen the importance of factoring in customer preferences and it is unfortunate that many academics and business executives fail to appreciate is the extent to which people's preferences may differ. Businesses often look for a one-size-fits-all solution, without realizing that tastes vary enormously and that what the director of marketing and his team like may be different from what the customer likes. An example comes from the Dutch electrical consumer firm, Philips, whose slogan since 2004 has been 'Sense and Simplicity'. The Philips brand was relaunched that year with a box floating down the Amstel river in Amsterdam and since then, the slogan has underpinned the company's advertising and marketing thinking.

A passionate talk by a Director of the Philips Marketing team laid bare the company's thinking. He explained that the company was making the transition from a company rooted in technology to one rooted in people and that the key to making the change was understanding the customer. He went on to describe Philips as a company where 'people come ahead of products, and where we deliver to people what matters most to them'. I sat up in my chair when I heard this and when the lights went down and the corporate marketing video started up, I made sure that I had a clean page on which to note down this company's people-centred vision.

The first woman to appear on the screen spoke eloquently about the importance of getting up on time in order to get the children to school. Next was a young girl hoping that she would look as good as her mother when she reached her age; after that, a woman talked of the importance of ensuring her photo album was up-to-date, followed by another proclaiming the importance of arranging the family's washing. This line-up of women was followed by a man lauding the merits of coffee on a long-haul business flight.

This was the pioneering, people-centred approach to product development of one of the world's leading consumer electronics producers and what we were witnessing was a vision of men and women's social roles that had scarcely shifted since the 1950s. The vision was enshrined in an expensive corporate video and in specially constructed houses which used live actors to act out scenes involving the company's products. One of these showed a woman giving her child new concept toys, while another showed her admiring a picture frame with a changing photographic image. Was this really the revolution in customer perception that we were promised?

The company's website (Philips.com) confirmed the company philosophy of 'Sense and Simplicity', and like the launch on the river Amstel, used the image of a box to illustrate the concept of simplicity. This time, it was an unadorned, white, moving box and I wondered whether the company had any inkling if the research findings that women prefer rounded shapes to linear ones, and detailed surfaces to plain ones? This is particularly important in the case of Philips since many of their products are targeted at women.

Philips' emphasis on simplicity took a lead from John Maeda's book *The Laws of Simplicity* (Maeda 2006) and anyone attending one of Philips' opulent Sense and Simplicity events would have found a copy of Professor Maeda's books in their going-home bag. There, the MIT professor sets down his ten laws of simplicity which are the following:

1. The simplest way to achieve simplicity is through thoughtful reduction.
2. Organization makes a system of many seem few.
3. Savings in time feel like simplicity.
4. Knowledge makes everything simpler.
5. Simplicity and complexity need each other.
6. What lies in the periphery of simplicity is definitely not peripheral.
7. More emotions are better than less.
8. In simplicity we trust.
9. Some things can never be made simple.
10. Simplicity is about subtracting the obvious and adding the meaningful.

Looking at this list, I pondered the basis for elevating these thoughts to the level of laws. How would an object of beauty such as a Fabergé egg fit into this schema, for example? Fabergé, produced an egg a year for the Russian Tsar, producing a total of 57 eggs which are widely regarded as great works of art. How well would the concept of simplicity fit with these? Take the 1897 'Coronation' egg for example. Here is the description of it taken from a website describing Fabergé eggs:

> 'This superb red gold egg enamelled translucent line yellow on an engraved field, is enclosed by a green gold laurel leaf trellis-work cage mounted at each intersection by a yellow gold Imperial double-headed eagle enamelled opaque black, and set with a rose diamond. A large portrait diamond is set in the top of the egg within a cluster of ten brilliant diamonds; through the table of this stone, the monogram of the Empress is seen. Another, smaller, portrait diamond is set within a cluster of rose diamonds at the end of the egg, beneath which the date is inscribed on a similar plaque.

> Concealed inside this elaborate shell is an exact replica of the Imperial coach used in 1896 at the Coronation of Nicholas and Alexandra in Moscow. In yellow gold and strawberry coloured translucent enamel, the coach is surmounted by the Imperial Crown in rose diamonds and six double-headed eagles on the roof; it is fitted with engraved rock crystal windows and platinum tyres, and is decorated with a diamond-set trellis in gold and an Imperial eagle in diamonds at either door.'
>
> (http://www.geocities.com/Paris/Rue/4819/felist.html)

Does this represent simplicity? Or again, the Madonna Lily egg from 1899, described thus:

> 'This egg takes the form of a clock with a revolving dial. The four-coloured gold egg is enamelled translucent daffodil-yellow, and is richly set with diamonds. It stands on an onyx platform decorated with coloured gold scroll mounts, rosettes and the year in diamonds, and is designed as a vase with red gold scrolls serving as extra supports at either side. The belt of the dial which divides the egg is enamelled opaque white with diamond set numerals and the hours are pointed by the head of an arrow in a drawn bow. The gold rim of the vase is chased as a cluster of roses; a bunch of Madonna lilies carved from quartzite and each set with rose diamonds emerges from the vase.'

You can probably see that the attempt to create a single set of laws to define the way people's visual preferences cross time, cultures and gender may be a difficult, if not fruitless task. Maeda writes that 'Complexity implies the feeling of being lost; simplicity implies the feeling of being found' (2006, 61) but would this sentiment be echoed across all periods of history and culture, and would everyone react in this way?

The material presented to you in the rest of this book will suggest that it makes sense to move away from a one-size fits all approach to design and marketing and work instead with an array of paradigms to suit different situations. The book will argue that the best design emerges from an appreciation of the varied nature of design preferences and that rather than prescribe an overarching design principle such as 'simplicity', it would be more constructive to adopt an approach that has, as its first step, the identification of the target market and the preferences of that market. The design and marketing task would then consist of honing the product or marketing message around the preferences thus identified.

The Homogeneity Principle

It is appropriate at this point to introduce the 'homogeneity principle' in which a person of one type is attracted to another person of similar type. In a recruitment context, it is referred to as the 'self-selecting' tendency since it is widely recognized that people tend to prefer other people similar to themselves. People are said to be using 'self-reference criteria' – the use of their own perceptions and choice criteria to determine what is important – and sometimes the process of doing this is unconscious. This means that people are often not aware that they are using 'self-reference criteria' and, in the context of aesthetic evaluations, may not appreciate that aesthetic value does not inhere in objects but is the product of empathy between object, perceiver and artist. Instead, they make the mistake of assuming that the criteria they employ are applied universally.

There is, to give commentators their due, some awareness that it may be less than optimum to use universal criteria of excellence. For example, the business guru Michael Hammer, father of the concept of Business Reengineering, spoke of the need for products to be shaped around the 'unique and particular needs' of the customer (Hammer 1995, 21), and for products and services to be 'configured to' the needs of customers (ibid. 21). In the field of branding, similarly, an academic, Karande, has expressed the view that there should be congruence between the brand personality and the consumer's self-concept on the basis that purchases are thought to offer a vehicle for self-expression (Karande et al. 1997).

This has led to a search for an understanding of the factors that influence congruence. This is a prize worth fighting for. Much retailing research is driven by the notion that the physical form of a product is an important element in its design and that it creates certain effects in buyers.

As we saw earlier, it has been found that products perceived as pleasurable are preferred and that the perception of beauty correlates highly with the rating of a product as 'interesting', of 'good design' and 'imaginative' (Lindgaard et al. 2006). Moreover, where correlations with perceptions of usability are concerned, a preliminary study found that 53 per cent of participants (with a sample base of 100) 'showed a significant positive relation between beauty and their assessment of usability' (Hassenzahl 2007, 293). This led to speculation that beauty and usability may correlate as a consequence of a 'halo' effect, leading to a tendancy to infer a higher quality of the product from its beauty (ibid. 294).

What is this perceived higher quality worth? In one study (Bloch et al. 2003), participants saw and rated pictures of two different toasters which, while equal in terms of function, differed in terms of beauty. Participants were asked to state their willingness to pay for both toasters, and their answers demonstrated a willingness to pay a premium of around 55 per cent for the beautiful toaster. In further studies the premium individuals have been prepared to pay was found to be influenced by individual and situational aspects. Where individual aspects are concerned, it has been found that the so-called *centrality of visual product aesthetics* (CVPA) is an important moderator of beauty's value and affects the premium that individuals are prepared to pay for beauty. In the toaster study, high CVPA individuals were willing to pay a premium of 66 per cent for the beautiful toaster while low CVPA individuals were prepared to pay a premium of only 40 per cent (Hassenzahl 2007).

Where situational aspects are concerned, it was found that the value of beauty is dependent on the context in which the product was used. Where the product has high task-related context, beauty played only a minor role; by contrast, where the context emphasized self-presentation or personal identity, beauty assumed greater value (ibid.).

Moreover, it was found that the perception of beauty, in the right context and presumably with the appropriate CVPA, was mediated by greater attention. This latter finding emerged, as we saw earlier (p. 27) from an interesting study conducted in 2007 by researchers at a market research organization, Bunnyfoot. Using eye-tracking to monitor responses, they noted the fixations of respondents to bus shelter advertisements and recorded the relationship between fixations and whether the stimulus was liked or not. According to the study:

> 'The most significant finding, from a marketing perspective was the discovery of a robust correlation between the number/duration of fixations a person makes while looking at an advertisement and whether or not they liked the advertisement.'
>
> (Maughan et al. 2007, 341)

In this way, of the participants who were neutral about an advertisement or disliked it, only 20–24 per cent fixated 15–20 times, whereas 60–67 per cent of those who liked the advertisement fixated 15–20 times.

As we can see, not only do products that are liked receive greater attention, but those that are perceived as pleasurable are used more frequently than those not so perceived, leading to enhanced purchasing. As we shall see later, what people like is often a mirror image of what they actually produce themselves.

This brings us back to the notion of congruity, one which finds parallels in other fields. In the field of communications, for example, it translates into the notion that persuasiveness can be enhanced by similarity between source and receiver (Brock 1965). In social psychology, it translates into the 'matching hypothesis' or 'similarity-attraction' paradigm according to which increased similarity leads to increased attention and attraction (Byrne and Nelson 1965; Berscied and Walster 1978). In other words, the person you like is the person who mirrors your own thoughts and views, and may possibly even mirror your looks and behaviour.

Findings continue to emerge about the importance of congruence (or 'rapport' or 'mirroring' as it is sometimes called). At California State University, Sacramento, a study of psychotherapists' successes with their clients showed that those therapists who achieved the best results had the most emotional congruence with their patients at meaningful junctures in the therapy. These mirroring behaviours showed up simultaneously as the therapists comfortably settled into the climate of the clients' worlds by establishing good rapport. When reporting these effects, Psychiatrist Dr Louann Brizendine referred to them as being observed exclusively among female therapists and she also referred to 'mirror neurons' that allow women not only to observe but also to imitate or mirror the hand gestures, body postures, breathing rates, gazes and facial expressions of other people (Brizendine 2006). The processes that make this possible have been brought to our attention by brain-imaging studies that show how the act of observing or imagining another person in a particular emotional state can activate similar brain patterns in the observer, with females being especially good at this kind of emotional mirroring. Sometimes, in fact, women's mirror neurons can overwhelm them, especially when it comes to experiencing the pain of another person.

The impact of the mirror neurons on women was amply illustrated by an experiment involving men and women at the Institute of Neurology part of University College, London. Researchers placed women in an MRI brain scanning machine while they delivered brief electric shocks (some weak and some strong) to their hands. The hands of the women's romantic partners were then hooked up for the same treatment and the women told whether strong or weak signals were being passed to their partners. The results showed that even though the women could not see their partners, the pain areas of the women's brains (activated when they had received the shocks themselves) lit up when they learned of their partners' shocks. It seems that the women were just feeling their partners' pain, or as Dr Brizendine puts it, 'walking in another's brain'. Interestingly, she claims that researchers have been unable to elicit similar brain responses from men and that there may be more mirror neurons in the human female brain than in the human male brain.

If this emotional mirroring can give psychotherapists the edge, it may do the same for designers and marketers since the need to shape products or services around the 'unique and particular needs' of the customer (Hammer 1995) places a premium on what one might call an interactionist as against a universalistic approach. This means that instead of seeking solutions or laws that will apply to *all* situations, we should seek out solutions that work in *particular* instances, an approach to problem-solving known in the field of Human Resources as a 'contingency approach'. It took 60 plus years of treatises on leadership style and books on management methods by thought leaders as diverse as Henri Fayol, Alfred Sloan, James Thompson, Jay Galbraith, March and Simon, Lawrence and Lorsch and others to come to the realization that there is no single best way to lead or manage an organization, and that organizations will arrive at the best solutions after mapping the key factors affecting the business. These factors include environmental variables (uncertainty, risk and competitive players are leading ones) as well as organizational ones (capital intensity of the industry, age of the organization and maturity of the major markets are key dimensions here) and these are usually mapped on a continuum.

A flavour of the findings in the field of Contingency Theory are obtained by taking a glance at the thoughts of two commentators, Jay Galbraith and Richard Scott. Writing about organizations, Jay Galbraith states that: 'there is no one best way to organize' (1973, 2) and Richard Scott adds that 'the best way to organize depends on the nature of the environment to which the organization relates'. He goes on to say that 'Contingency theory is guided by the general orienting hypothesis that organizations whose internal features best match the demands of their environments will achieve the best adaptation' (Scott 1981, 97).

One struggles to find a similar strand of thinking in the field of marketing since, as we have seen, the preference seems to be for prescriptive, one-size-fits-all solutions. Having said that there have been some dissenting voices, a case in point being that of Elizabeth Hirschman, an American Professor of Marketing. In 1993 she noted that women as a constituency were largely absent, indeed excluded, from consumer research and she described the dominant ideology in consumer research as masculine. This lead her to express the view that 'the feminine perspective has been excluded from all but a small proportion of current consumer research' (Hirschman 1993, 550).

Hirschman is not alone in her views and she quotes fellow American academic Sandra Harding, Professor of Social Sciences and Comparative Education at UCLA Graduate School of Education and Information Studies as saying that 'Traditional social science has begun its analyses only in men's experiences ...Defining what is in need of explanation only from the perspective of bourgeois, white men's experiences' (Hirschman 1993, 539). A similar observation has been made by Morris Holbrook, Professor of Marketing at Columbia Business School, and it is interesting that this sentiment comes from the pen of a man. He observed 'how completely the field of consumer research has been dominated by the masculine orientation' (Holbrook 1990, 12–13) and wrote that if we deny the feminine voice, then 'we can only succeed in falsifying the reality that confronts at least half the population'. A similar notion comes from Marcia Westcott who suggests that if feminine ways of seeing are excluded from consumer research, then our knowledge will always remain partial and incomplete (Hirschman 1993, 551).

Elizabeth Hirschman called for consumer research that would lay bare these 'excluded knowledges' and this call must be answered if the homogeneity principle is to be put into effect. For if the only perspective offered by consumer research reports is that of the male customer, how are people to understand the needs of different sets of customers? We saw in the first chapter how important women are as consumers (some people put women as controlling 80 per cent of purchasing decisions) so an important question concerns whether women's needs as consumers differ from men's and if they are, how they can be met by organizations. The process of answering these questions is very much at the heart of this book.

A number of questions remain to be answered. Do managers, brand managers, designers and other managers leave footprints of themselves in their *performances* – designs or management behaviours – and relatedly, do segmentation variables such as gender, personality and nationality elicit common patterns of response? A linked question concerns the extent to which *preferences* (whether for designs or management behaviours) are influenced by these variables and, if they are, then a final question concerns the relationship between *performances* and *preferences* and whether the influence exerted by segmentation variables on performances act in a parallel fashion on preferences. If so, then the performances of a particular personality, gender or nationality are likely to be preferred by people of the same personality or gender.

A finding of segmentation variables having a parallel influence on performances and preferences would have a number of implications for the management of *performance* and *preference* issues. Where *performance* issues are concerned, it would have implications for the recruitment, appraisal and promotion of creatives and marketing managers and offer insights on how to achieve or avoid recruitment in one's own image (Byrne and Neuman 1992; Dipboye and Macan 1988). It would also, significantly, have implications for marketing and design issues, offering guidance on how to achieve the congruity between product and customer self-concept that we saw advocated in the marketing literature. This interactive perspective links with the empathy principle according to which aesthetic value inheres not in objects but in the empathy that can exist between object, perceiver and artist (Dipboye and Macan 1988) and a focus on interactive rather than universal principles would have implications, in turn, for notions of equality and diversity. We will return to many of these points in the final chapter, but meanwhile is more detail about the implications for equal opportuntities and diversity.

Equal Opportunities and Diversity

In the 1960s and 1970s, Equal Opportunity (EO) policies were introduced in the UK and other parts of the world to complement anti-discrimination and equal pay legislation and to equalize opportunities and outcomes in the workplace. EO policies were predicated on the assumption of ontological equality, a belief in the fundamental sameness of individuals (Miller 1996; Gagnon and Cornelius 2000). Where gender was concerned, the EO mindset produced an acceptance that white, non-disabled, heterosexual men's experiences and interpretations of organizational life were universally applicable (Alvesson and Billing 1997). This led to organizational analyses that 'occurred through a lens which is primarily white and male' (Cianni and Romberger 1997, 116) producing organizational cultures constructed around a 'white, male norm' (Kirton and Greene 2000, 288–9). A practical consequence was that minorities were required to adopt the norms and practices of the majority (Nkomo 1992). 'Success was, for instance, all about having women at senior levels of the company – even if none of them had children and they all behaved exactly like men. The message seemed to be: If they want to join us, they can, but they need to fit in and play by our rules' (Schneider 2001, 27).

The accumulated critiques of the notion of sameness implied within EO policies gave way to initiatives emphasising the positive features of difference (White 1995) and this has led to a focus on diversity rather than equality. However, it should be noted that where gender is concerned, discussions of diversity at a group level have been held back by a fear that the discussion of differences would be used, as it arguably has in the past, to reassert inferiority and exclusion (Webb 1997). This, conceivably, had the effect of maintaining the power of dominant groups (Liff 1996) and 'drastically underestimating the difficulties and obstacles typically encountered by members of disadvantaged groups compared to others' (Barmes and Ashtiany 2003, 291).

Managing diversity within an organization

The body of work presented in this book advances our understanding of diversity by exploring the research evidence for gender-specific criteria of excellence in design and marketing. As we have saw earlier, the emphasis will be on the visual aspects of design and marketing, but passing reference will be made to the use of language too. Bringing this body of work together is a first in the field of marketing and design, and may set a precedent for work in other disciplines too.

Why should we be looking at the way that different people's preferences vary? The answer is simple. Evidence for the operation of group criteria of excellence is too important to ignore, particularly as there is evidence (Eden 1989) that managers may be involved in the psychological, rather than simple objective, construction of the world, leading them to, singly or collectively, produce different cognitive maps. We have a situation, then, in which managers in organizations are creating new products and second guessing customer preferences, judging solutions through the distorting prism of their own lenses. They are imposing their own values on the brand, whether through the decisions they make about it, or through the decisions they make concerning the personnel who should work on it.

It is not difficult to grasp the connection between a firm's recruitment process and the quality of their product and see how a firm's recruitment process will impact on customer satisfaction. Those involved in the recruitment of creatives and marketing and design managers need to be mindful of the extent to which people select others in their own image and, in the field of design, the extent to which people prefer designs created by people of their own gender. I am not for a moment suggesting that these acts involve conscious or direct discrimination, but merely that people may exercise an unconscious bias of which they are unaware. The key question then becomes how to break free of the homogeneity principle which will predispose decision-makers to select people whose style mirrors their own preferences. If this happens, what may get edged out in this whole process are the preferences of the customer, and this is particularly likely where the customers' preferences are at odds with those of the managers of organizations.

We will look in more detail in the last chapter at the organizational implications of the homogeneity principle, but it would be helpful if the reader could at this stage absorb how powerful a force it can be. In an ideal world, its power would be used to attract customers but its strength may in fact prevent this happening. One of the messages of this book is that only an awareness of its power can lead organizations to take steps to counteract its effects *within* the organization and ensure that what the organization produces is in line with customer preferences. In doing this, the organization is taking steps to ensure that the homogeneity works its magic in relation to the *external* rather than internal market.

So, one of the objectives of this book is to increase the awareness of the impact of the homogeneity principle on organizations and the importance of making this work in favour of an organization rather than against it. In doing this, it sets out to rectify some of the deficiencies present in other books on gender and marketing.

For example, these can quote research without discussing new and contradictory findings (this is particularly the case with discussions of linguistic differences for example); they can also completely ignore the subtle differences in visual preferences that we discuss at length here (differences in preferences for shape, colour, detail and technicality); and, last but not least, can completely ignore the obstacles that stand in the way of implementing change in organizations. This is a big mistake since it is not enough to know about the differences but you need to be forewarned of the difficulties and have a strategy for dealing with them.

Unfortunately it is not just small organizations that fail to deliver products that match customer preferences but large ones too, for example when Peter Salsbury took over the reins at Marks and Spencer in 1999 and made marketing decisions in isolation of customer preferences. In simple terms, an organization needs to consciously map *internal* and *external* preferences against each other and see if they mirror each other. If they do, the organization is likely to be on a winning streak: if they don't, it's time to go back to the drawing board!

Lack of marketing diversity in different industries

A number of industries may benefit from greater diversity in their approach to customers. In the case of the car industry we saw earlier that the majority of car purchasing decisions involve women and yet, according to the media research director of Conde Nast, car makers are not communicating well with women. 'You are not really speaking to us. You are not saying anything that will actually make us go out and buy your cars'. She emphasizes her point by saying that: 'We are making the decisions and we are half your market. Start talking to us' (McGowan 1996).

A failure to acknowledge diversity could also be said to relate to car showrooms. According to Dealix (Dealix 2006; http://www.roadandtravel.com/newsworthy/newsandviews04/womenautostats.aspx), the market expert and leader in automotive Internet marketing services in the US, 39 per cent of women would rather deal with women in the car showroom whereas in fact the actual proportion of female car dealer sales staff is 7 per cent of the total dealership workforce, 4.2 per cent of new car sales and 2.1 per cent of used car sales professionals. There is clearly a sizeable diversity gap to be bridged.

A similar realization that there was a gap in terms of targeting the customer came from the field of consumer electronics where, according to a 2003 report by the Consumer Electronics Association (CEA) (CNN.com 2004) women actually spent more on technology than men, contributing 57 per cent of the $96 billion annual spend. The report on small electrical goods entitled '*What Women Want and How it Differs from Men*', based on telephone interviews with 1,002 US adults, showed that women are increasingly interested in gadgets from DVD players to digital cameras, whether for themselves or for their families (CNN.com; Consumer Electronics Association 2003), but a meagre 1 per cent of women thought that manufacturers had them in mind when creating products. The women were also unhappy with the way that products were sold to them, with nearly three-quarters of women in the survey complaining about being ignored, patronized or offended by sales people when shopping for electronics and 40 per cent claiming to be treated better when accompanied by a man.

Perhaps typical of these comments are those of Brenda Myers, a retired customer service manager of a fibre-optics cable maker, who said that 'Every time you go to these places, they think women don't know anything, and they don't tell you the same features as they would when my husband goes with me.' Even worse, she added, 'some of them talk to your husband even though you're standing right there, too'. She was angry at the unequal treatment she felt when she shopped for a new television set last year at a national electronics retail stores. 'I was ticked off,' said Myers. There was also unhappiness in the survey from more than half of respondents who said that advertisements for electronics were confusing, though half the men surveyed felt the same way (CNN.com 2004).

The same might be said of the DIY market in which women buy 61 per cent of major home improvement products. This is a market worth $70 billion in the US (RethinkPink) yet, despite this, these products have been traditionally marketed to men rather than to women. Given the increasing importance of women in the DIY market (see p. 15), this failure to factor in the diversity of the target market does not make sense. This is particulary problematic given that, according to author Salli Brand, author of *The Girls' Guide to DIY* (2004) distinguishes that male and female priorities are different: 'My experience with women is that they are more methodical than men, and that they are more interested in the aesthetics. When she buys screws, she'll pick out the prettiest ones. He'll buy the strongest ones' (Marsh 2004, 29).

Similar charges of ignoring women can be made of the sportswear industry since in 2001, revenue from sales to women at market leader Nike hovered at less than 20 per cent of sales at $1.5 billion. This was despite the fact that the market in women's sports-wear had been skyrocketing and that, according to the NPD Group, women's sportswear had generated sales of more than $15 billion in 2001 – nearly $3 billion more than men's sportswear. Nike was missing substantial proportions of this market and the sales figures showed that for most of its history, the company was focused on the male end of the sportswear market. How could Nike could have 'failed so miserably with women'? (Warner 2007).

One answer was simply the failure to recognize that women's needs might be different from men's. For example, even the President of the Nike brand, Mark Parker, concedes that for most women, high performance isn't about sports; it's about fitness. 'We never appreciated the whole world of the active lifestyle,' he says (Warner 2002, 124). Another blind spot concerned the shop interiors of Niketown which were designed with greater appeal to men than women and which were 'known to be a turnoff to female customers' (ibid. 124). Warner directs her critical gaze on the San Francisco Niketown which has a women's section on the fourth floor and no direct was of getting there since at each floor women have to wade through displays of basketball, golf and hockey to catch the next escalator up. What is more 'the feel of the store is dark, loud and harsh – in a word, male' (ibid. 124).

It is not just the worlds of consumer environments and products that have failed to find favour in the eyes of women. Several pieces of research have shown that women are more likely than men to find advertisements sexist (Wolin 2003) and a 1,000-respondent study by Greenfield Online for Arnold's Women's Insight Team (Van der Pool 2002) found that a massive 91 per cent of women did not think advertisers understood them. Even worse, the majority of women were angry at how advertisers portrayed them, with far greater levels of dissatisfaction from women than men (58 per cent as against 42 per cent). This indicates a chasm between the female consumer and the marketer's understanding of her. Which, according to Marti Barletta is explained by the fact that 'many marketing and advertising truisms … are actually rooted in male gender culture' (2006, 44).

Marti Barletta spends a lot of her book *Marketing to Women* outlining the main elements that she thinks make up male and female gender cultures and the main ones are highlighted in Table 2.1. Clearly, if one accepts the evidence for even of a portion of these differences, can see how one way of presenting products could be acceptable, broadly, to one gender but not to the other. This may account for some of the dissatisfaction that customers are experiencing in different sectors.

Table 2.1 Main differences between the attitudes of men and women (Barletta 2006)

	Men	**Women**
Individualistic/collectivist	Individualistic – men's perspective is the 'I'. Results in report talk	Collective concerns – women's perspective is the 'we'. Results in rapport talk
Object or people centred	Object centred	People centred
Approaches to tasks	Accomplishes a single task at a time	Multi-task (when shopping, will try and accomplish as many tasks as possible)
Attitude to priorities	Will focus on the top priorities	All points will be priorities
Detail	Likes minimal details about a product	Likes copious information on a product and will not buy until her wish list is satisfied. She is a perfectionist
Product features/benefits	Interested in how product features work	Interested in what product features do

You might think that this is a doom and gloom message but Marti Barletta sees 'an enormous opportunity for the marketer who crosses that chasm' (2006, 44) with so few companies doing serious marketing to women, any company that exerts itself enough to make a determined effort can expect to capture a disproportionate share of the women's market' (ibid. 136). How can this success be achieved? Barletta speaks of persuading and motivating people, talking to them about things they care about – 'what they cherish, what they're proud of, what they enjoy' (ibid. 8), it means getting under the skin of customers and seeing the world through their eyes. As we have seen, many organizations have missed opportunities in the past but some are seizing the new opportunities with relish!

In the rest of this book we will focus our attention on the visual since this is the area that has largely been overlooked in earlier reports on marketing diversity and examine the evidence for gender differences in visual productions and preferences (drawings, painting, graphic, product and web designs). We will also look briefly at some of the evidence on attitudes and language differences.

Conclusions and Practical Lessons

We have seen that organizations are not always very good at thinking their way into the mind of the consumer and that even some of the biggest companies such as Nike and Marks and Spencer have managed to take their eye off the market. Instead, the senior staff have allowed their own preferences to guide what they offer to the consumer and this attitude ignores the impact of diversity on customer preferences. Organizations that hope to meet customer expectations need to ensure that their vision is attuned to that of the target market.

Understanding Marketing Diversity

In the chapters that follow, we will look in more detail at the way that a person's gender influences the type of products that they produce (the 'production aesthetic') and that they like (the 'preference aesthetic'). We will start by studying the 'production aesthetic' and the way that this is shaped by a person's gender and personality.

PART II
Theoretical Background

Chapter 3
Drawings and Paintings: Production Aesthetics and Gender

The focus of this book is design and marketing, but when I started researching this topic in the early 1990s there was precious little research comparing men and women's output and preferences. At the same time, there was an extensive literature highlighting the connectedness of different art forms whether graphic design or art and if this literature was reliable, it meant that information on gender and its impact on output and preferences produced in one area of graphic expression (say, drawings and paintings) could be extrapolated to another area such as design and advertising. The argument as to the inter-connectedness of different graphic forms would open up the evidence base considerably so it was critical to find out how extensive and convincing were the arguments concerning the inter-connectedness of different forms of graphic expression.

We are fortunate insofar as discussions on the connectedness of different art forms have been pursued since antiquity revisited in more recent times. In the 1950s, for example, it was taken up by Herbert Read (1953) in his book *Art and Industry* in which he argued that any distinction between art and design was largely the creation of the machine age. His argument is both historical and aesthetic since he shows how, in the pre-Renaissance period, the so-called fine arts (architecture, sculpture, painting, music and poetry) were not explicitly named, nor recognized as separate disciplines and that in classical Greece, a single word 'techne' was used to cover pure and applied art. He argues, moreover, that the applied arts (that is, objects designed primarily for use) appeal to aesthetic sensibilities in the same way as abstract art and that in both cases, there is an intuitive as well as a rational element that allows them to satisfy the canons of beauty.

This ancient debate has been taken up more recently by another academic, Buchanan, (1995), who refers to Read's work as a 'standard text' in the US and Britain and 'an exceptionally influential introductory work on design for general readers' (ibid. 51). Buchanan considers that one of the three elements that contribute to the development of design in the contemporary world is an awareness of the aesthetic appeal of forms and he sees no contradiction between the notion of design as a cognitive and expressive skill. In fact, in his words, 'expression *is* design thinking' (ibid. 46) and he quotes approvingly George Nelson's vision of design as 'communication and of the designer as artist' (ibid. 54) and makes a persuasive case for design as an expressive skill. To quote from his work:

> 'Leonardo da Vinci's speculations on mechanical devices were simply another expression of his poetic and visual imagination …'
>
> (ibid. 33)

> 'Walter Gropius's goal was to "provide a concrete connection between artistic exploration and practical action".'
>
> (ibid. 37)

> 'Most designers recognise that the appearance and expressive quality of products is critically important not only in marketing but in the substantive contribution of design to daily living … .'
>
> (ibid. 45)

> 'Expression does not clothe design thinking; it is design thinking in its most immediate manifestation, providing the integrative aesthetic experience which incorporates the array of technical decisions contained in any product.'
>
> (ibid 46)

Read and Buchanan's sentiments show that there is nothing in the finished work of design that sets it apart *per se* from the work of 'fine art' and the discipline of 'visual culture' is similarly founded in that it blurs the boundaries between different visual disciplines. Why this way of thinking? Rogoff (1998) offers one explanation for the emergence of this unified approach to the visual arts:

> 'Images do not stay within discrete disciplinary fields such as "documentary film" or "Renaissance painting" since neither the eye nor the psyche operates along or recognises such divisions.'
>
> (ibid. 26)

Some might still take issue with Buchanan, arguing that the functional nature of design sets it apart from painting and drawing. However, while it may be true that most designers will be more constrained than most fine artists this is a difference purely of degree and a detailed design brief, offering some constraints, will not prevent a designer from producing an individual response. As Buchanan (1995) says:

> 'The subject of design is not given … The subject matter of design is radically indeterminate, open to alternative resolutions even within the same methodology.'
>
> (ibid. 24)

> 'There are many constraints on the work of a designer but the consideration of constraints is only a background for the invention or conception of a new product.'
>
> (ibid. 25)

The notion that the artist themself, in the work they produce, applies to the other forms of graphic expression too, for example handwriting. If you think about it, most literate individuals, when taught to write, are given a uniform set of instructions, the 'copybook', on how to write, and yet each person's handwriting is distinct from that of another. These departures from the copybook are what defines the individual nature of a handwriting, and so you can think of the copybook as analogous to the design brief insofar as it sets the parameters but still leaves room for movement. One has only to consider signatures and the way that these are admitted as evidence of a person's individual identity to realize how defining a mark of individuality these are.

So the copybook or design brief may place limits on the writer or designer but ultimately they will always leave room for self-expression. A common objection to this view is that design work, unlike painting and drawing, is produced in a team and leaves little room for self-expression. It is true that nowadays design work is often more team-based than fine art, but there are cases today, as there have been in the past, when fine art was created by teams and many cases today when designs are created by individuals rather than teams. So this point is, again, not a fundamental difference separating design from fine art.

We have been arguing for the relatedness of art and design at a theoretical level but there is also empirical research showing that links exist between the kind of drawings or doodles someone produces and the other forms of graphic expression. Some of this empirical research is explored in the next section.

The Connectedness of Graphic Expression

The acts of drawing, painting and handwriting all involve the use of the hand to make an impression on another surface and you might ask whether these acts are consistent with one another. Two attempts have been made to answer this question, the first in a 1933 study by Allport and Vernon (reprinted in 1967) and the second in a 1948 study by Wolff. We will take a brief look at these two publications.

Allport is well known for his 'influential personality' theory (Fancher 1979) and his 'great' 1937 book *Personality: A Psychological Interpretation* (Koch and Leary 1992). Just a few years before then he researched with Vernon the extent to which features of different motor acts inter-correlated (Allport and Vernon 1933), basing their findings on experiments involving 25 male subjects. These were asked to draw the following six shapes:

1. Circles drawn on paper, with the right hand.
2. Circles drawn on paper, with the left hand.
3. Circles drawn with crayon, right and left hands.
4. Squares drawn on blackboard, right hand.
5. Squares drawn in sandbox, right and left feet.
6. Parallel lines drawn on paper, right and left hands.

For the reader interested in the details of this experiment, subjects were given an A4 writing surface with a pencil or crayon and told to draw a series of six figures which were subsequently measured, but not in the presence of the subjects. In the third stage, a roll of paper 20" wide was hung on a blackboard (the initial exposed surface was 30" but the subject could extend it) and the subject drew six circles with a black crayon, later repeating the exercise with the left hand. In stage 4, on a large blackboard extending the length of the room, the subject drew three squares with diagonals, using only the right hand. In stage 5, a wooden box 3' × 2' × 4' was two thirds filled with moistened sand via a screw attached to the subject's foot, the subject drew one square with diagonals using the right foot and one using the left foot.

Intercorrelations between these six items were examined in respect of:

1. The average area of figures.
2. The total areas occupied by the figures.
3. The proportion of unoccupied space.

The intercorrelations between these factors are shown in Table 3.1 and you can see that they exceed 0.5 which is the minimum level for this number of subjects at which the results are significant at the 0.01 level. This is a high level of significance and if you take the different shapes drawn as examples of 'graphic expression' then these results successfully demonstrate the presence of similarities between the different forms of graphic expression os a single person.

Further research to establish whether different forms of graphic expression have unifying features in the work of one person was carried out by Wolff, a psychology professor (1948). The focus was on handwriting and doodles and Wolff asked twenty female subjects to produce handwriting and shapes in four different conditions – using right and left hands and then with eyes open and then closed. They were asked to produce a number of shapes – a horizontal line, a vertical line, a circle, a triangle, a square, a normal signature, signatures that were smaller and larger than usual and a disguised signature.

Each form was produced in four settings and, according to Wolff, the chance probability of the four variations appearing in identical form in these four settings

Table 3.1 Intercorrelations between the features contained in different forms, excluding the drawings done just with the left hand (the most difficult task subjects had to perform) (Allport and Vernon)

Average area of figures	Total area occupied by the figure	Proportion of unoccupied space
0.87	0.74	0.71

was no more than 10 per cent. Despite this, Wolff detected identical forms across the four settings in 54 per cent of cases, in other words in five times more cases than chance would lead one to expect. Wolff received similar results with male students and he went on to repeat the experiment a week later, with the consistencies this time appearing in 46 per cent of the four settings. This led Wolff to conclude that there was 'a constancy of graphic expression under various unfamiliar conditions' (ibid. 22) and an 'intricate relationship of consistencies' (ibid. 23–4).

Wolff's results appear to offer convincing evidence in support of this final claim and they seem to corroborate Allport and Vernon's findings of a correspondence between different forms of graphic expression. However, a word of caution is called for. Wolff refers to 'consistencies' between shapes and forms but nowhere defines this term. As a consequence, there is no explanation as to precisely how similar shapes and forms must be before they are deemed to be 'consistent'. For this reason, the results of his experiment cannot be accepted uncritically.

Fortunately this was not Wolff's only experiment, since he went on to question whether the consistency of graphic expression could be the result of imitation, learning and training rather than individual expression. One of the questions he posed was whether writers can disguise their handwriting and in order to test this one group of three subjects was asked to write a phrase in 'the usual' and in a 'disguised' way, as well as in capitals. A further group of three subjects was given the handwriting samples and asked to try and match the phrases to a single person. The results showed that subjects were able to distinguish the original writings from the disguised ones in 70 per cent of cases which shows that the personal impulses behind graphic expression cannot easily be disguised. It also shows that even where people begin by being taught a copybook method of writing, they normally depart from it and create their own handwriting. The individual nature of people's handwriting led Wolff to conclude that graphic expression is a personal expression of cognition.

A further experiment by Wolff illustrates this in a vivid way. Wolff asked three subjects to produce handwriting ('Example A') as well as doodles ('Example B'). He then gave Example A to ten people and asked them to produce descriptions ('Set A') of the expressive qualities that the handwriting contained. Another ten people were given Example B and instructed to produce similar descriptions ('Set B'). A further group of people were given Sets A and B and asked to match them so that a description related to Set A could be paired with a description from Set B. According to Wolff, the matchings of Sets A and B were correct in 70 per cent (0.7) of cases, where chance would have produced matchings in only 15 per cent (0.15) of cases. This second experiment of Wolff's demonstrates, as does that of Allport and Vernon, that different forms of graphic expression are consistent with each other.

So we can see that the studies conducted by Allport and Vernon and Wolff invite two conclusions. The first is that graphic expression carries the mark of its maker, and the second is that different forms of graphic expression are consistent with each other. This second point implies that the features contained in someone's graphic expression – whether it be handwriting, doodles, drawings, paintings or designs – will always be internally consistent. This means that one can look to any of these disciplines for information about gender differences and could also expect that the findings made in one field (say, drawings) will find support from the findings made in another field (say, designs). This opens up the field from which the impact of gender on graphic expression can be studied.

The Impact of Gender on Graphic Expression

How is graphic expression related to the person who created it? There is a vast and disparate body of research that explores the links that bind art and design works to their creators and this work is summed up by Alfred Tunnelle's view that the artist is someone who sees things not as they are but as he is (E.F. Hammer 1980, 8). Tunnelle's remark appears in a book on projective drawings and this is no accident since there is a body of research that views the process of drawing or designing as one of projection in which the drawing or design serves as an X-ray of its creator.

To study the impact of gender on a person's graphic expression is to move into an area in which opinion is deeply divided. Where the concept of gender is concerned, some commentators are described as denying its impact on human actions (Caterall and Maclaran 2002), arguing that gender is an unproductive dichotomy (Firat 1994). Others, by contrast, accept the impact that gender can have on human action, and speak of a specific 'feminine sensibility' (Mainardy 2001) and a 'profound difference in the sense of space in the two sexes' (Erikson 1970, 100). By analogy, Jane Cunningham, an advertising planner, told the advertising magazine *Campaign* that: 'men and women are hardwired differently. They process information differently and have different behavioural default settings' (M. Jones 2007).

The position adopted in this book is consistent with a Diversity approach insofar as it acknowledges the coexistence of a wide range of realities, and views differences as strengths rather than weaknesses (White 1995). In seeking to identify the extent to which there may be separate male and female styles of graphic expression, we are in fact standing outside a patriarchal system in which 'Art by women is judged according to norms and expert constraints that are not their own' (Heide 1991). At the same time, acknowledging that gender may be a productive dichotomy leaves the door open to an acceptance that gender differences may be a product of socio-cultural and/or innate differences, with increasing popularity focusing on the role of evolutionary psychological factors (Lupotow et al. 1995). According to recent commentators, such an evolutionary approach should not be overlooked by consumer behaviourists, even if it restricts the possibilities of social and cultural change (Caterall and Maclaren 2002).

A brief word on our use of the term 'graphic expression'. We have seen how artificial the distinctions between fine art and design can be, and this makes it legitimate to research the whole field of graphic expression for initial clues as to the differences that might emerge from a study into gender differences in design. The phrase 'graphic expression' is used in a broad sense to include drawings and paintings, and this chapter will initiate our study of the male and female *production* aesthetic by comparing the drawings and paintings of children and young adults. We also bring into the field a study of handwriting since this is another manifestation of graphic expression and in the next chapter move away from a focus on *productions* to a consideration of the *preferences* of men and women.

In the third part of this book the focus will shift from handwriting and fine art to those forms of graphic expression that are the central concern of this book, namely design and marketing. A similar process will be followed there insofar as we will first compare the *productions* of males and females (this time concentrating on graphic and product designs) and then in a second stage, compare their *preferences*. In Chapter 7 we will examine production and preference aesthetics in relation to web design, and then examine some of the explanations for the differences highlighted in these chapters. Chapter 9 will conclude the book with a broader look at the implications of these findings for design and marketing.

We will begin by looking at the evidence concerning handwriting.

Handwriting and Gender

In the early twentieth century there was considerable interest in establishing whether male and female handwriting could be differentiated and both Binet (1904) and Downey (1910) conducted studies in which subjects were asked to sort 200 samples of handwriting (50 per cent male and 50 per cent female) into those by men and those by women. The results are shown in Table 3.2.

A decade or so later, in one of those academic ding-dongs that characterizes scholarly debate, another academic, Newhall (1926) questioned the validity of these results. His ammunition? He pointed to the small sample of people acting as judges and repeated the experiment using no fewer than 92 judges. This time, the range of correct answers dropped to within 0.55–0.60 – a result barely better than chance although he did find that the older judges achieved a probability of

Table 3.2 Percentage of times the sex of a writer can be estimated (Binet 1904 and Downey 1910)

Results (judges)	Mean correct	Range	N
Subjects of Binet	69.8	65.9– 73.0	10
Subjects of Downey	67.3	60.0–77.5	13

correctness that was 'comparable to the results of previous investigations'. His results therefore left things rather in the air although they served in part to confirm previous findings.

Two further attempts were made to resolve the issue. The first, by Kinder (1926), involved 200 judges and 100 samples of handwriting. Kinder found that on average 68 per cent of judgements were correct with regard to the sex of the writer, with correct responses ranging between 58 and 76 per cent of judgements. A further investigation by Broom et al. (1929) verified Binet and Downey's findings and led them to conclude that: 'It is apparent ... that there are sex differences in handwriting and that it is possible to determine sex of writers correctly roughly two times in every three judgements' (ibid. 166). More recently, a study by McCollough (1987) achieved very similar results to these studies and Table 3.3 brings these results together.

Looking across these results, it makes it apparent that it is possible to recognize reasonably accurately whether a piece of handwriting is by a man or by a woman and you might be wondering what the features are that characterize the handwriting of men and women. Various attempts have been made to describe the differences with Downey (1910) describing male handwriting as 'bold, careless, experienced, and individual' and female writing as 'colourless, conventional, neat and small'. A more detailed analysis by Muller and Enskat (1961) is shown in Table 3.4.

How useful are these classifications? On the minus side, some of the terms are not clear. For example, the terms 'compliant', 'passive', and 'confused' are not terms with a clear meaning and not terms which are normally used in graphology. On the plus side, as we shall see, the Muller and Enskat analysis throws up differences which parallel those found in comparative studies of male and female paintings and drawings which are the focus of our attention in the next section.

Table 3.3 A comparison of studies showing whether the sex of a writer can be identified from handwriting

Author of study	Date	Mean % correct	Range	N (judges)
Binet	1904	69.8	65.9–73.0	10
Downey	1910	67.3	60.0–77.5	13
Newhall	1926	58	55.0–60.0	92
Kinder	1926	68.4	58.0–76.0	200
Broom	1929	70.0	65.0–74.0	24
McCollough	1987	67.8	62.0–74.0	1

Table 3.4 Comparison of features of male and female handwriting (Muller and Enskat 1961)

Handwriting trait	Male handwriting	Female handwriting
Movement	Dynamic Strong rhythm Deliberate Strengthened Definite Regulated Sure Rigidity	Gentle Weaker rhythm Compliant Passive Natural Confused
Form	Hard Angular Sharp Sober Cool Precise Emphasis on form Original forms Lack of uniformity	Soft Rounded Colourful Warm Natural Emphasis on movement Fewer original forms Uniformity

Summary: Handwriting as a reflection of sex

Six studies have investigated whether in 'blind' tests a person's sex can be inferred from their handwriting. These studies indicate that it is possible to do this in about 70 per cent of cases which shows that sex can, to a significant extent, be inferred from handwriting. A further study analysed some of the features which characterized male and female handwritings and since according to Allport and Vernon (1933), handwriting is a form of graphic expression and one that is consistent with other forms of graphic expression, it may offer clues as to differences between the output of males and females in other areas of graphic expression (for example, such as drawings, paintings and designs).

Drawings, Paintings, Constructions and Sex

When I first embarked on this topic, I was keen to discover what research had been conducted comparing boys' and girls' drawings and paintings. Extensive desk research revealed the existence of a substantial and disparate literature comparing the work of males and females, much of it comparing the work of boys and girls. As we shall see shortly, it is normal practice in work on gender to look at the behaviour of children as well as adults, so a focus on children is not seen as problematic. It should also be noted that the literature spans a period of just over a hundred years, so the standard of the studies is variable. In reviewing this literature, we will divide it between research comparing the form and colour in the drawings and paintings of males and females, and studies comparing the subject matter used.

A word about the age of the subjects used in the experiments reported in the literature. As we mentioned the experiments used children from nursery age up to adolescence as well as young adults, and the reader might want reassurances about the relevance of studies involving children's work to an understanding of adult design. In fact, in the psychological literature, it is standard practice to make inferences about adult cognitive behaviour from the cognitive behaviour of children. By way of example, Professor Simon Baron-Cohen of Cambridge University argues for the intrinsic nature of a sex difference from its presence in childhood alone. To quote some instances from his book *The Essential Difference* (2006), in a chapter entitled 'The female brain as empathizer: The evidence':

> 'The female agenda seems to be to enjoy an intimate, one-to-one relationship. Young girls, on average, are reported to show more pleasure in one-to-one interaction. For example, girls are more likely to say sweet things to one another (things you hardly hear between boys), or caress or arrange each other's hair…'
>
> (ibid. 46)

> '… boys show more solitary pretence ... their pretence often involves a lone superhero engaging in combat. Mortal combat ... . This male preoccupation with power and strength again suggests that males are less concerned with a sharing of minds and more interested in social rank.'
>
> (ibid. 49)

> 'It has been suggested that boys' talk tends to be "single-voiced discourse". By this it is meant that the speaker presents their own perspective alone. In contrast, it is suggested that female speech tends to be "double-voiced discourse". The idea is that whilst little girls still pursue their own objectives, each also spends more time negotiating with the other person, trying to take their wishes into account.'
>
> (ibid. 51)

> 'Males more often use language to assert their social dominance…here's how Eleanor Maccoby puts it: "Boys in their groups are more likely than girls in all-girl groups to interrupt one another…"'
>
> (ibid. 52)

> 'Practice may partly explain why the sexes diverge in their skills with age, but problematic for this view of the origin of these differences is the fact that the male superiority in throwing accuracy is present even in children as young as two years old. At this age, we can safely assume that there has been little difference in opportunities to practice, and yet the two-year-old boys clearly outstrip the girls.'
>
> (ibid. 93)

Since work on gender differences regularly extrapolates from children's studies to adults, we follow the same pattern here.

Work focusing on form and colour

Opinions are divided as to whether there are consistent differences between the artistic work of males and females. Some argue against a specific 'feminine sensibility' (Harris and Nochlin 1976) with others agreeing with Erik Erikson (1970) in speaking of a 'profound difference in the sense of space in the two sexes'. Which view is correct? In this section, the studies of a more quantitative nature will be taken first (Section A) and those without a quantitative basis, or at least with only a limited one, will follow (Sections B–D). The discussion of these studies is organized here chronologically.

(A) Kerschensteiner, Franck and Rosen, and Majewski Kerschensteiner (1905) compared the drawings of boys and girls in different forms in Germany, and one of the points the study focused on was the extent to which the boys' and girls' drawings showed a concern to represent reality. On a measure of 'true to appearance', he found that the boys insisted on greater realism in their pictures than the girls, as can be seen from Table 3.5. Kerschensteiner also remarked that the girls' drawings seemed to avoid perspective representations and that they appeared more 'primitive' than those of the boys.

The next quantitative study appeared several decades later in America when the authors, Franck and Rosen (1949) asked 250 psychology students in the USA to complete 60 different abstract shapes in any way they liked. When the male and female completions were compared, 36 of them yielded significant differences (at the level of $p < 0.05$) in the manner in which the men and women had completed them. In a second test, these 36 stimuli were shown to a further 150 male and 150 female students and three independent scorers scored their completions as to whether they were 'masculine' or 'feminine' in appearance. The criteria used in assessing whether a completion was masculine or feminine were derived from the first test with two sets of criteria relating to formal and content respectively (see Table 3.6). The inter-rater reliability scores ranged from 0.84 to 0.90 which was an acceptable level of reliability.

A scoring system was used to rate the completions with minus points awarded to male categories and plus points awarded to female categories. The range of potential scores covered the range from 0 (which would signal that all items had been completed in a masculine manner) to 36 (which would signal that all items had been completed in a feminine manner). Applying this scoring system, the results revealed a mean score of 14.4 from the male subjects and 19.6 from the female subjects and the researchers used these results as further evidence for the fact that the female subjects produced more female-type completions than the male subjects.

Table 3.5 Percentage of girls' and boys' representations of horses and houses which were 'true to appearance' (Kerschensteiner 1905)

Form in school	House		Horse	
	Boys	Girls	Boys	Girls
2	–	–	1	–
3	1	–	1	–
4	5	2	2	2
5	6	2	2	–
6	18	3	–	1
7	28	7	9	1
8	32	8	17	–

Table 3.6 Characteristics of completions by men and women as used in scoring criteria (Franck and Rosen 1949)

Masculine – formal categories	Feminine – formal categories
Closing of stimulus	Stimulus left open
Expansion from stimulus outward	Internal elaboration
Stimulus built up	Stimulus built down
Stimulus made sharper	Stimulus made blunter or enclosed
Protruding single line	Protruding single lines reinforced or supported
Oneness	Two-somes
Profiles	Frontal faces, figures, stick figures, flowers, fruit, animals
Skyscrapers, towers	Houses, rooms, windows, vases, lampshades, staircases
'Dynamic' objects (those that move under their own power)	'Static' objects (movable by an external force only)

Several decades later, again from America, came a PhD study into the relationship between the drawing characteristics of children and their sex (Majewski 1978) and the subjects this time were 121 children from the first, fourth and seventh grades. The researcher arranged for their drawings to be rated against 31 characteristics and of the 31 characteristics used, significant differences emerged on nine. One of these related to the shape of the lines (rectilinear v. circular) and Majewski found that there was a divergent trend at all three levels in the girls' preference for circularity as against the boys' preference for rectilinearity. This difference was statistically significant ($p = <0.05$).

How valid are the results of these three studies? Kerschensteiner's study suffers from the fact that he did not use independent raters and did not explain the basis for his choice of constructs and so his results are of anecdotal significance only. The studies of Franck and Rosen and Majewski, on the other hand, used more systematic methods both in terms of the methods used to select the criteria against which works were to be judged (Majewski found these in 'the writing of experts' and Franck and Rosen agreed the constructs as a result of an earlier test) and in terms of using independent raters to judge these qualities. This second point was important since, in some cases, there was a subjective element to the judgement.

For the sake of completeness, I provide details of the other studies I found that compared the use of form and colour in male and female drawings and paintings. I have separated these studies from those we have described earlier since they do not provide quantitative findings.

(B) Ballard, McCarty and Neubauer Ballard (1912) looked at the drawings of nearly 20 000 London children aged 3–15 and while most of his findings (see pp. 57–66) relate to the children's choice of subject matter, he does occasionally remark on the stylistic features that distinguish the boys' and girls' work. He remarks, for example, that the reason girls draw decreasing numbers of houses (after the age of 12) is that 'the perspective baffles them ...The perspective is bad all through'. He also remarks that girls 'resist the claims of realism more steadily than boys' although, unlike his findings on subject matter, this particular one is not backed up by statistical analysis.

Interestingly, a later study by McCarty (1924), comparing the drawings of four- to eight-year-old boys and girls, also noted that the boys tended to excel at perspective, and observed furthermore that the girls' interests veered towards the aesthetic rather than the mechanical aspects of painting. This was a point noted by Neubauer (1932) who commented that girls were more concerned with the formal aesthetic qualities of a piece of work than boys.

(C) Alschuler and Hattwick, Fisher, Lark-Horovitz and Luca, and Erikson From the 1940s to the 1960s come a series of studies which produced interesting results but, unfortunately, little by way of quantification. An influential book, *Painting and Personality* by Rose Alschuler and LaBerta Hattwick, appeared in 1969 and discussed the drawings and paintings of 150 children aged 2–5. These were studied over the period of a year and the data was extensively analysed in an attempt to show how children's experiences are often reflected in their paintings and drawings. One of the authors observations was that girls used colour more intensely than the boys and it is unfortunate that there are no statistical analyses to back up this claim.

From the 1960s comes a study by Fisher (1961) in which he noted that males tended to draw straight lines, while females drew more circular shapes. A few years later the psychologist Eric Erikson (1970) reported in his book *Childhood and Society* on a fascinating experiment that he conducted in 1937. What he did was set up a play table and a random selection of toys, and invite the 150 pre-adolescent children involved in the experiment to imagine that the table was a film studio and the toys actors and sets. The children were asked to create an exciting scene on the table and, in all, about 450 scenes were constructed. Although he did not quantify his results, Erikson spoke of distinctive differences in the way that the boys and girls arranged the blocks and described these as follows:

- Males – built towers and structures pointing upwards. They emphasized the exterior elaboration of buildings and rarely focused on enclosing space or representing people inside houses.
- Females – built low, circular structures and emphasized the openness and peacefulness of house interiors.

A few years later, a study on children's art by Lark-Horovitz et al (1967) noted that the pictures drawn by girls tended to be pretty in a way that the boys' were not but unfortunately they did not present the evidence on which this conclusion was based.

(D) Lippard and Chicago Lucy Lippard is a journalist and American art critic whose book *From the Centre* (1976) provides a collection of her writings on women artists. The book includes a foreword to a catalogue of the work of ten artists and this includes a description of the elements, in her view, characterising women's work. These include 'overall texture, sensuously tactile and repetitive preponderance of circular forms, central focus, inner space, indefinable looseness or flexibility of handling, a certain kind of fragmentation; a new fondness for pinks and pastels' (ibid. 49). Judy Chicago (1982) identified patterns that she had observed in women's art and these included repeating and circular forms.

(E) Japanese studies Exciting studies have been conducted in Japan in 2001 by Megumi Iijima of the Department of Pediatrics at the Juntendo University School of Medicine in Tokyo and three academics from other Japanese institutions. They offer fascinating parallels to the Western studies of children's drawings we have looked at earlier.

One of the Japanese studies compared the organizing features in the free drawings of 168 boys and 160 girls (aged 5 to 6) and found that the most common compositional device used by 74.4 per cent of the girls was to arrange motifs in a row on the same plane, a device used by only 20.4 per cent of the boys. The boys, on the other hand, were much more likely to draw motifs arranged either in piles, three-dimensionally or from a bird's eye view, arrangements that were found to be an 'exceptional' occurrence in the girls' drawings.

In a further study by the Japanese team, a comparison was made of the extent to which boys and girls used up different colour crayons. In order to do this, researchers compared the colour crayon usage of 146 girls and 143 boys aged 5–6 and found that boys used up more blue and grey that the girls. The girls, on the other hand, used up more warm colours like red and pink. The measurements tell the story eloquently with the girls using up 10 millimetres of pink as compared with the boys' 3.5 and 15 millimetres of red as against the boys' 10 millimetres. The conclusions of this study are in line with those of an earlier study by one of the authors (Minimato 1985) and show the extent to which girls use warmer colours (pink and red) and boys cooler colours (blue and green). Iijima et al. also noted differences in the way that the boys and girls apply colour, noting the fact that girls tend to use more colours per drawing than the boys and that, while boys tend to use one or more specific colour(s) in one area, girls use each colour rather diffusely.

Summary – formal aspects of male and female paintings and drawings We have looked at a number of studies which examined whether the formal aspects (form and colour) of the drawings, paintings and constructions of males and females differed. Despite the uneven quality of the research and the fact that it was carried out in a variety of geographical locations (spanning the USA, Japan, Germany and the UK) and over a long period of time (just under 90 years) there was a surprising degree of unanimity in the researchers' conclusions. These are summarized in Table 3.7 and researchers whose findings appear to be both valid and statistically significant are marked with an asterisk.

Work focusing on subject matter

Having examined the formal features of men's and women's work it is appropriate to see whether there are differences in the area of subject matter as well. In order to do this, the work of a number of researchers is reviewed in the next section and, as in previous discussions, the studies with quantitative results will be taken first (Section A), followed by the more general studies (Sections B–D).

(A) Ballard, McCarty, Hurlock, Majewski, Hargreaves and Iijima The first important study was by Ballard (1912) whose extensive study we looked at briefly earlier (see p. 55). Where subject matter is concerned, he found that there was a large difference in the extent to which the boys and girls in their sample of 20,000 drawings drew ships and plants. Stratifying by age, he found that between the ages of six and ten, more than 20 per cent of the boys' drawings were of ships, as compared with no more than 9 per cent of the girls' drawings. Between the ages of 7 and 15, more than 36 per cent of girls' drawings were of plants, as compared with only 16 per cent of the boys'.

This is one of the earliest studies of subject matter and it throws up consistent differences (in the sense of differences manifested over a period of five years at

Table 3.7 Summary of research findings on the form and colours used in male and female drawings and paintings

Male	Female
Vertical line Alschuler and Hattwick, Fisher	**Rounded lines and structures** Alschuler and Hattwick, Erikson, Lippard, Majewski*, Chicago
Angles Franck and Rosen*	**Blunt lines** Franck and Rosen*
Structures built up Franck and Rosen*, Erikson	**Stimulus is built down, low** Erikson
Realistic Kerschensteiner	**Less realistic** Kerschensteiner, Ballard, Lippard
Sharp perspective McCarty	**Loose perspective** Kerschensteiner, Ballard
Concern with function	**Concern with aesthetics** Neubauer, Lark-Horovitz
	Pinks and pastels/more intense, warmer use of colour Alschuler and Hattwick, Lippard; Minamato; Iijima et al.

least) as well as large differences (of 10 per cent or more) between the work of the boys and the girls. In common with many of the other studies, however, it does have methodological weaknesses. For example, Ballard generated the categorization system himself and he does not justify his choice of categories. Neither did he use third parties to rate the subject matter contained in the pictures against these criteria. Despite these drawbacks, this is an interesting study.

The next major study was carried out by McCarty (1924) in the USA and analysed the drawings of 31,239 children aged four to eight. McCarty compared the drawings of the boys and the girls, and found that boys were more interested in vehicles than the girls, and girls more interested in flowers, furniture, household objects and design than the boys. She also found that 'the girls tended toward the aesthetic' whereas 'the boys tended toward the mechanical or scientific aspects of life' (ibid. 26). McCarty highlighted the disparities in choice of theme by showing those items in which one sex differed more than the other by 20 per cent or more and converting the absolute percentages into the per cent which the smaller number differed from the larger. Her figures are shown in Table 3.8.

There are echoes here of the findings in Ballard's study, but although there are similarities between the conclusions of the two studies (boys preferring to draw vehicles, and girls plant life, furniture, children and babies), a major difference concerns the extent of the differences. So, if McCarty's results for four- to eight-years-olds, for example, are compared with Ballard's results for the same age group, it becomes apparent that although both studies indicate a preference by males to draw more vehicles and fewer plant themes than females, the size of the male/female difference is greater in Ballard's work than it is in McCarty's. The figures on which this conclusion are based are shown in Table 3.9, indicating the mean percentage difference between the boys' work ('B') and that of the girls ('G').

Table 3.8 Proportion of boys and girls drawings that use certain themes (McCarty 1924)

	Boys (%)	**Girls (%)**
Vehicles and tools	100	22
Public buildings		50
Special characters		53
Adult human beings		66
Animal houses		67
Flags		70
Animals		73
Sky, clouds and geographical conceptions		76
Miscellaneous buildings		77
Scribbling		80
Flowers	42	100
Furniture and household objects	58	
Design	67	
Children and babies	70	
Toys	72	
Fruit and vegetables	78	

Table 3.9 A comparison of Ballard's and McCarty's results

Subject matter	Average % of Bs' drawings on given themes		Average % of Gs' drawings on particular themes		Mean % of excess of Bs' use of themes over Gs'	
	Bal'd	**McCt'y**	**Bal'd**	**McCt'y**	**Bal'd**	**McCt'y**
Vehicles	14	10.2	3	2.6	11	7.6
Ships	21	–	9	–	12.0	–
Plant life	10	13	27	20	17.0	7.0

How can the differences between Ballard's and McCarty's studies be explained? In many respects, the two experiments are comparable since they both used large samples, both included the work of children aged four to eight, and both gave their subjects the option of drawing whatever they liked. However, whereas McCarty's subjects were instructed to 'draw anything you wish', Ballard's had a text read to them with suggestions of the sort of items that they could draw and were then asked to draw whatever they liked 'from memory'. Ballard did this in order to counteract the influence of recent drawing lessons and any suggestion that Ballard's list actually constrained the children is countered by the divergent choice of themes selected by the boys and the girls. In fact it is possible that Ballard's 'memory drawings' produced more spontaneous drawings than McCarty's 'draw anything you wish' did.

Another factor that makes it difficult to compare these two studies is that McCarty's and Ballard's categories are not necessarily identical. For example, Ballard's category of 'plant life', is nowhere defined and it is impossible to know whether this included all or some of the items (such as trees, flowers, fruit and vegetables) measured individually by McCarty. The same difficulty arises in respect of Ballard's 'vehicle' category since Ballard's definition includes cars, buses, balloons and aeroplanes, whereas McCarty's excludes the balloon but adds wagons, trucks, boats, sledges and even dolls' buggies. You can therefore see that the 'vehicle' categories of the two authors are similar but not identical.

The next major study, conducted by Elizabeth Hurlock of the Department of Psychology at Columbia University (1943), examined the spontaneous drawings of children and adolescents aged 15–20, with the majority by adolescents in the 17–20 age range. It should be noted that unlike the other studies we have looked at, the drawings used in this study were not produced in response to a specific request but were produced incidentally, and then collected by teachers and students. Of the 1,451 pictures collected 462 were specifically identified as the work of males or females, and this was the sample targeted for study (of these 462 pictures, 291 were by boys and 171 by girls). Using this smaller sample, Elizabeth Hurlock then set about comparing the drawings of the two sexes.

A number of differences came to light. Firstly, it transpired that 22 per cent of the girls' drawings, and only 1 per cent of the boys', consisted of geometric figures and stereotyped patterns, what she termed 'conventional designs'. Then, whereas only 2 per cent of the girls' work showed caricatures, a massive 33 per cent of the boys' drawings did with the majority (56 per cent) showing male figures with only 7 per cent featuring females. This was not to say that the girls were not drawing human figures since the results showed that 36 per cent of the girls' drawings showed human forms, as against only 18 per cent of the boys', but the girls tended to avoid the use of caricatures and favoured their own sex in their drawings.

Another major difference occurred in the use of the printed word with 30 per cent of the boys' drawings, as against 19 per cent of the girls', using letters in a printed form. Moreover, the way the boys and the girls treated the printed word varied with the girls tending to ornament their letters and the boys concerned to 'duplicate the work of a professional'. Elizabeth Hurlock's findings are summarized in Table 3.10.

How do Hurlock's findings compare with the earlier studies, for example that of Ballard? A comparison of the two studies involves removing categories which are either not defined or included in both studies and this means removing the category 'boat' (not defined by Hurlock) as well as the three categories of 'the printed word', 'caricatures' and 'conventional designs' since these categories are not used in the studies. Removal of these categories leaves us with four categories, namely 'human forms', 'sports', 'animals' and 'houses' and if we compare

Table 3.10 Percentage differences in the subject matter chosen by a sample of girls and boys (Hurlock 1943)

Subject matter	Male pictures (N= 291) %	Female pictures (N = 171) %
Printed words	29.9	19.3
Caricatures	32.9	2.3
Human forms	18.2	35.7
Conventional designs	1.3	22.8
Sports	7.5	1.1
Animals	2.0	6.4
Houses	0.0	1.7
Boats	3.1	0.0

these, we see that on the last three categories, the studies agree on the size of the differences. Where they diverge is with regard to the size of the difference on 'human forms', with Ballard finding evidence of minimal differences between the male and female drawings and Hurlock finding that females draw twice as many human figures as the boys. How can these differences be accounted for?

It is important to realize that the categories Hurlock uses in Table 3.9, although presented as discrete, are in fact overlapping since a careful reading of the study reveals that the category labelled 'caricature' is in fact made up (100 per cent) of caricatured human figures. If we factor this into the equation and aggregate the percentage of drawings in the categories of 'caricatures' and 'human forms', then we arrive at the figures shown in Table 3.11. This shows that there is not as great a disparity between the two studies in the proportion of males and females drawing the human figure as one might have imagined. If a difference exists, it is not so much in the proportion of males and females who draw human figures, but rather the proportion of males (as opposed to females) who poke fun at the human form and draw caricatures. A further difference relates to the greater proportion of boys and girls drawing males and females respectively.

There are two other important studies. The first, by David Hargreaves (1977), involved a study of the graphic productions of 135 school children (71 boys and 64 girls) with a mean age of ten-and-a-half years in Durham, in the north of England. These children were asked to carry out the circles test (a test in which subjects are confronted with 35 circles and asked to sketch objects or pictures which have a circle as a major part). The objects which the subjects drew were then classified according to a six-fold categorization of subject or type and then categorized according to whether they were drawn by males and females:

1. Life. All representations of an animal being or their parts
2. Nature. Inanimate, naturally occurring objects or their parts, for example, planets, spiders' webs, fruit and vegetables.
3. Sports-games. Objects used in sports and games, for example, balls, racquets and targets.
4. Mechanical-scientific. Man-made instruments and machines, for example, aeroplanes, bicycle wheels, trains, dials.
5. Domestic. Objects found in a home, for example, plates, tea pots, buttons, clothes.
6. Abstract. Signs and symbols, for example, letters, numbers, musical notes.

The themes which the subjects chose fell into the categories shown in Table 3.12. As you can see, four of the categories used (life, nature, mechanical and abstract themes) yield statistically significant differences between the relative concern of the males and females to depict these categories. Unfortunately, since the categories that Hargreaves uses are different from those used by Ballard, McCarty and Hurlock, it is not possible to compare their findings. But his conclusions are nevertheless still important because he shows that boys produced

Table 3.11 Hurlock: proportion of males and females drawing caricatures and human forms

% of males (m) and females (f) drawing 'caricatures' and 'human forms'	% of all M pictures	% of all F pictures
	51	38

Table 3.12 T-tests of male and female differences in the forms of male and female completions (Hargreaves 1977)

Subject matter which formed the basis for the completions	Boys (N=71) Mean	Girls (N=64) Mean	T-test results and significance of the difference between male and female results
Life	5.46	7.33	2.85** $p < 0.01$
Nature	2.17	1.52	3.30** $p < 0.01$
Sport	2.31	2.16	NS
Mech-Sc	3.01	1.50	4.76*** $p < 0.001$
Domestic	4.14	4.81	NS
Abstract	0.55	1.00	2.22* $p < 0.05$

*** highly significant ** moderately significant * significant

significantly more mechanical and scientific drawings than the girls, a finding which corroborates Ballard's findings as to boys' interest in ships and vehicles.

Another important study at this time was by Mana Majewski (1978), a researcher we encountered earlier when examining the way colour and shape are used in the paintings and drawings of children. Dr Majewski also examined differences in the subject matter used, finding that the girls drew a significantly larger proportion of pictures of the environment than the boys (a difference which was significant at the p = <0.02 level) and that the girls drew a significantly higher proportion of happy faces (significant at the p = <0.001 level). While boys, by contrast, tended to draw males, a tendency which was significant at the p = <0.05 level. These are all high levels of significance.

Majewski's finding that each sex has a statistically significant tendency to depict people of their own sex chimes with the findings of several of the earlier studies we referred to (summarized in Table 3.13). As Cox (1993, 94), the author of a study of children's drawings tells us, 'studies have found that most children

Table 3.13 Percentage of boys and girls drawing their own sex first

Study	n	Age range	% boys	% girls
Weider and Noller (1950)	153	8–10	74	97
Weider and Noller (1950)	438	7–12	70	94
Knopf and Richards (1952)	20	6	80	50
Knopf and Richards (1952)	20	8	80	70
Jolles (1952)	2,560	5–12	85	80
Tolor and Tolor (1955)	136	9–12	82	91
Bieliauskas (1960)	1,000 Drawings	4–14	71	73
Tolor and Tolor (1974)	232	10–12	91	94
Papadakis-Michaelidas (1989)	507	2; 6–11; 5	73.4	78.6
Aronoff and McCormick (1990)	109	Undergraduates	High proportion	High proportion

prefer to draw their own sex first in a free drawing task'. She quotes research conducted by Heinrich and Triebe (1972), which reviewed 19 studies, all of which described a tendency for children to draw someone of their own sex.

The findings that each sex had a tendency to depict people of their own gender is an interesting one and in the decade that followed, several studies were conducted which produced similar findings. This is potentially strong corroborative evidence of a tendency to depict people of ones own gender and so, we will have a quick look at 11 of the studies conducted between the 1950s and the present day. The first of these, by Weider and Noller (1950 and 1953) revealed that 70–74 per cent of primary school boys and 94–97 per cent of girls drew their own sex first, a tendency which was unrelated to socio-economic status. A second study by Jolles (1952) found that around 80 per cent of children aged 5–8 drew people of their own sex and in the same year, two studies by Knopf and Richards found a tendency for 80 per cent of boys to draw someone of their own gender. In 1953 Mainord concluded that this tendency to draw someone of the same gender continued into adulthood but with a smaller proportion of women than men drawing a figure of their own sex first. The studies did not stop there, since 1955, Tolor and Tolor found that 82 per cent of boys and 91 per cent of girls drew someone of their own sex and in a 1958 study, out of a massive sample of 5,500 adults consisting of college students, high school students and psychiatric patients, 89 per cent drew their own sex first. Excluding those who were patients in hospitals, 72 per cent drew their own sex first (Hammer 1980).

The finding that people tend to draw someone of their own gender emerged from four later studies. One in 1960 by Bieliauskas was based on the analysis of 1,000 drawings by children aged 4 to 14 and concluded that both sexes favoured their own sex when drawing a person, but that the tendency to do this increased with age, particularly after the age of nine, although the developmental pattern was more stable for boys than for girls (Cox 1993). A second study by Tolor and Tolor (1974) revealed that more than 90 per cent of girls and boys produced drawings of people of their own gender and two more recent studies produced similar conclusions. The first of these, by Papadakis-Michaelides (1989), found that over 73 per cent of boys and 78 per cent of girls drew their own sex, while an analysis by Aronoff and McCormick (1990) of the drawings of 109 undergraduates found that males (and masculine persons) drew males first while females (and feminine persons) tended to draw females first; androgynous persons were found to be equally likely to draw a male or a female first.

From this, it can be seen that several researchers or groups of researchers have found a significant tendency for people to draw a person of their own sex first and it is extremely tempting to seek the factors that lie behind this. One theory is that the sex of the figure drawn reflects the sex role identity or sexual orientation of the artist (Aronoff and McCormick 1990), although Brown and Tolor (1957) in an extensive review of the literature, doubt that choice of sex in figure drawing reflects the drawer's psychosexual identification or adjustment. An alternative theory advanced by a number of scholars, is that the image drawn of the body is a configuration or gestalt of ones own body and that when an individual draws a person they may reflect the impression that they have of their own body or, if not of the body, then of a projection of aspects of themselves. As we saw earlier, Alfred Tunnelle declared that 'The artist does not see things as they are but as he is' (E.F. Hammer 1980, 8) and this explanation could underpin much of what we have observed. For example, if graphic expression communicates information about the person who has created it, this could be precisely because a person projects aspects of themselves into the graphic work they create.

If we now try to draw together the findings of the quantitative studies, it would appear that there are similarities between the subject matter used in the drawings of young children (as shown by Ballard's study) and those of young adults (as shown in Hurlock's study) and that the relative importance of certain themes in the work of males and females does not appear to alter over time. Summarizing choice of themes, it would appear that:

1. Females show a greater tendency than males to draw females and happy faces.
2. Males show a greater tendency than females to draw males.
3. Females show a greater tendency than males to draw plant life and objects from nature.
4. Males show a greater tendency than females to draw ships and moving objects.
5. Males show a greater tendency than females to draw caricatures.
6. Males show a greater tendency than females to use the printed word.

Coming pretty well up to date is the work in Japan of Megumi Iijima and three academic colleagues (2001). One of their studies compared the drawings of 124 boys and 128 girls from six separate kindergartens and found several differences in the type of objects depicted by the girls and the boys. Girls were found to be significantly more likely to feature flowers, butterflies, the sun and human motifs, especially girls and/or women. Boys, by contrast, were much more likely to draw moving objects such as vehicles, trains, aircraft and rockets. These objects rarely appeared in the girls' drawings and there are striking and obvious similarities between these conclusions and those from Western studies.

Having examined the quantitative studies, it is now possible to move on to look at some of the more qualitative work and the studies will be reviewed in chronological order.

(B) Ivanoff, Gesell and Franck and Rosen Early studies by Ivanoff (1908, Katzaroff 1910) examined the drawings of children from the public schools of Geneva. A total of 2,062 drawings were examined and Ivanoff found that whereas boys tended to choose their objects from a wide range of subjects, girls took theirs from the immediate environment, drawing more landscapes, flowers and geometrical forms than the boys.

Fast forward a few decades and Gesell (1940) examined the drawings of five-year-olds and concluded that at this age boys began to show a preference for drawing boats, flags, merry-go-rounds and elephants. While girls preferred drawing horses, ladies and dolls. At around this time, Franck and Rosen (1949), whose study we examined earlier in this chapter when examining the influence of gender on formal features such as shape, also found an influence of gender on subject matter. Thus, whereas male subjects drew faces in profile, female subjects drew them in full frontal position and whereas the males drew skyscrapers, towers and dynamic objects which had the ability to move under their own power (such as cars and steamers), the females drew static objects which could only be moved by an external force (such as sailing boats). This distinction between the static and the moving, as well as between the self-propelling (for example, a steamer) and the propelled (for example, a sailing boat) is one which helps explain Ballard's findings that ships were more important to boys than to girls. Frank and Rosen also found that female students tended to draw objects from nature such as flowers, fruit and animals and containers of all kinds (such as houses, beds and vases).

(C) Erikson and Lark-Horovitz Eric Erikson's study (1970) has already been mentioned (see p. 58) and it is worth noting that as well as revealing differences in the way males and females used space, this study also revealed differences in the use made of subject matter. Thus, while the boys used toys as part of violent and dangerous scenes, the girls used toys as part of a static arrangement, thereby backing up Frank and Rosen's findings regarding gender differences in prference for movement.

Just a few years later, Lark-Horovitz et al. (1973) gave a detailed account of the differences in the drawings of boys and girls based on original research as well as on the work of others. He concluded that, where figure drawing is concerned, boys almost never draw women (in fact only 1 per cent of their drawings are of women) and girls seldom draw men (again, only 1 per cent of their drawings). In terms of other subject matter, he found that boys are concerned with technology and vehicles as well as machines and objects that depict power and heroic, happy or unusual actions. By contrast, he found that girls preferred to depict horses and still life themes.

(D) Feinberg, McNiff and Boyette, and Reeves The last five studies reviewed in this section were carried out in the 1970s, 1980s and 2001 and they bear out many of the findings of other studies as well as presenting some interesting new ones.

Feinberg (1977) carried out a study in which she found that boys' drawings reflected aggressive, destructive themes whilst those of the girls were 'devoid of the notion of encounter and aggression' (ibid. 64) and McNiff (1982), carrying out research in the USA, drew similar conclusions. She collected 1,800 drawings from 26 children aged six, seven and eight and these were all spontaneous productions, produced with no guidance from adults as to content or form. Of these drawings, 839 (47 per cent) were by girls and she concluded that there are 'striking contrasts in the interests and thematic work of boys and girls' (ibid. 280). For example, she found that the subject of plants and other images of life dominated the girls' pictures and that the boys' interests were consistently different, for example focusing on themes of violence and disaster such as battles between opposing groups (animals, humans or machines), disasters, whether natural or man-made and machines such as racing cars and motorcycles where the focus was on power and force. She also found differences in the treatment of a single theme, for example space, with the girls drawing people in space and the boys focusing on the machinery and the technology.

Unfortunately, some of McNiff's data lacks comprehensiveness. For example, she tells us that '80 per cent of the plant drawings' (ibid. 280) were by girls but since she does not supply details of the total size of the sample there is no way of knowing therefore whether the plant category of drawing was a large one or not and no way of gauging the importance of this category of drawing.

By contrast, she does provide us figures to illustrate her claim that the boys in her sample are more interested in conflict and machines than the girls (see Table 3.14) and McNiff interprets these differences as indicating that the boys are motivated by an interest in power and are consequently competitive and attracted to conflict, while the girls are socially aware and connected physically and emotionally to their surroundings, being responsive to changes in the natural environment and attracted to living things with aesthetic or emotional appeal.

The next important study was conducted by Boyette and Reeves (1983) in the USA and examined 126 drawings by 110 children aged 9 and 12. In terms of the subject matter for the drawings, this was left to the children and once the

Table 3.14 McNiff: incidence of the use of themes of conflict and machines in boys' and girls' drawings

Use of theme	Boys' pictures		Girls' pictures	
	Number	As % of work	Number	As % of F work
Conflict	264	27	3	0.3
Machines	157	16	9	1.0

pictures were collected, a content analysis of each of them was performed by three independent observers. Their conclusions were that 'boys are less likely to depict domestic scenes than are girls, and are more likely to depict activity, angular shapes, humans in profile and violent scenes than the girls' (ibid. 325). Unfortunately, since the authors report very little of the relevant quantitative data it is difficult to evaluate the significance of this part of the work.

Summary – subject matter contained in male and female drawings We have examined a number of studies investigating whether the subject matter in male and female drawings and paintings differed in systematic ways. Many of the less quantitative of these studies contained methodological flaws, for example, it was not uncommon to find that the principal researcher had decided the criteria against which works would be judged without adequately explaining why those criteria were chosen. Moreover, in the more quantitative studies important data was sometimes missing.

Despite the uneven quality of the research, and the fact that it was carried out in a variety of geographical locations (spanning the USA, Japan, Switzerland and the UK) and over a long period of time (just under 80 years) there is a surprising degree of unanimity in the researchers' conclusions. These similarities are all the more striking in that many of the subjects focus on the behaviours of young elementary school children who, by virtue of their youth, will have had less exposure to societal influences than older children or adults. The differences are summarized in Table 3.15 and work which appears to be statistically significant and methodologically sound is marked with an asterisk.

Conclusions and Practical Lessons

We have surveyed a literature on male and female drawings that spans more than a hundred years and which I first brought to the attention of a marketing audience in an article in 1996. This information has now been presented in more detail and highlights differences in the way that males and females use colour and shape as well as differences in their thematic choices. Tables 3.7 and 3.15 summarize these

Table 3.15 Comparison of the themes used by males and females in drawings and paintings

Males	Females
Vehicles and self-propelling objects (ships, cars, aeroplanes, trucks, flying saucers, spaceships, rockets) Ballard*, Lark-Horovitz, Gesell, McCarty, Franck and Rosen*, Majewski*	**Static objects (plants, flowers, still lives, furniture, landscape)** Ivanoff, Ballard, Iijima et al*
Printed word Hurlock*	**Not printed word (pictorial)** Hurlock*
Standard typography Hurlock*	**Decorated/non-standard typography** Hurlock*
Males Hurlock*, Majewski*	**Females** Gesell, Hurlock*, Lark-Horovitz*, Majewski*, Iijima et al*
Not females Lark-Horovitz	**Not males** Lark-Horovitz
Human form: caricature Hurlock*	**No caricature** Hurlock*
Human form: profile Franck and Rosen*	**Human form: frontal** Franck and Rosen*
	Human face: smiling Majewski*
Skyscrapers and towers Franck and Rosen*, Erikson	**Houses, windows and rooms** Gesell, Franck and Rosen*, Hargreaves*
Technology and machines McCarty, Lark-Horovitz, Hargreaves*	
Violent themes McNiff	**Themes related to life** McNiff

differences showing that where shape and colour are concerned, females use a different palette from males and more rounded and lower forms. Where themes are concerned, the research shows that males favour the use of tall buildings, technology and machines, moving objects, violent themes, male figures, standard typography and caricatures. The penchant of the females, by contrast, was to prefer the use of low rise buildings, static objects, female figures, smiling faces and non-standard typography.

The significance for designers and marketers lies in the consistency of different forms of graphic expression (whether drawings, doodlings, design or paintings) and the fact that one could expect many of the differences we have noted in these studies of drawings and paintings to emerge in the designs and advertisements that men and women produce. The significance does not end there, for we will see in the next chapter how men and women's *preferences* match their *productions* with the result that the features that distinguish the graphic output of males and females will also be features that men and women prefer. The experiments on drawings and paintings therefore have a lot to offer marketers and designers in terms of understanding what designers are likely to produce and what they, and separately customers, are likely to prefer.

For example, one might suggest that male designers are more likely to illustrate their work with moving objects, technical objects, the printed word, caricature and males, and that these images would have more appeal for men than women. Female designers, by contrast, might be more likely to illustrate their work with static objects, plant life, smiling faces and females, and one might anticipate that these images would have more appeal for women than man. Whoever said that there was nothing new under the sun needs to examine these fascinating studies. They have much that is original to offer to designers and marketers.

Chapter 4
Drawings and Paintings: Preference Aesthetics and Gender

In the last two chapters we looked at research findings concerning the factors influencing peoples graphic productions and in the last chapter looked specifically at the influence of gender in one form of graphic expression, drawings and paintings. In this chapter the focus will move from productions to preferences and we will look at what has been written, in a general and specific sense, on the factors that influence people's preferences for drawings and paintings. Key questions will focus on whether people's aesthetic responses are homogeneous and if not, what the research literature tells us concerning the variables that influence people's preferences. In Part III of this book, we will move on to ask similar questions of the applied sector, including design. Meanwhile, we will look at the earlier literature on preferences for the non-applied areas of graphic expression, such as drawings and paintings preferences.

The Perception of Aesthetic Value

Broadly speaking, there are two opposing views on the factors that lead people to perceive aesthetic value in an object. There is, first, the 'universalist' or 'normative' view that aesthetic value is inherent in an object and is not contingent upon the way a beholder reacts to the object. This way of thinking rests on the assumption that the aesthetic value of an object can be assessed objectively, a view shared by the philosopher Kant (1978) who claimed that the judgement 'this is beautiful' would be universally held insofar as (in his view) every normal spectator would acknowledge the validity of the statement in relation to a particular object or work of art. In his opinion, aesthetic preferences are based on objective appraisals of objects and are not influenced by individual notions of good taste. This means that, in his view, aesthetic judgements behave universally, just as if beauty were a real property of the object judged. This is a view that (as we shall see) the psychologist Eysenck was later to test empirically.

The second view stands in stark contrast to this universalist one since it holds that aesthetic value is not inherent in objects but is bestowed on them by the beholder. According to this way of thinking, the assessment of value is subjective rather than objective, making it likely that people will perceive beauty in different places. Many will recognize this way of thinking in the words of the Scottish philosopher David Hume (1987) who wrote in the middle of the eighteenth century that: 'Beauty is no quality in things themselves: it exists merely in the mind which contemplates them and each mind perceives a different beauty'. For Hume, the decisive test of beauty, as of colour, is a psychological one, and the important question is whether or not the object 'excite(s) agreeable sentiments'. According to this way of thinking, deciding whether or not something is beautiful is not susceptible to objective analysis through a process of measurement and calculation but is best decided by gathering the views of individuals.

This so-called 'interactionist' or 'judgemental' approach (Hassenzahl 2007) to aesthetics, popularly summarized in the phrase 'beauty is in the eyes of the beholder', has a long history in fact. It is encountered in the fifth century BC writings of Protagoras who considered that all values – whether related to truth, beauty, good, even existence – were dependent upon the human observer. This was radical relativism of the kind we have to wait thousands of years to see re-emerge which it does, in some feminist research. It will be useful to look briefly at a couple of examples to illustrate the point.

The approach taken by Schroeder and Borgerson (1998) illustrates this, the interactionist way of thinking insofar as they acknowledge that the advertising universe is one in which the ideal spectator is male and standards are measured in relation to reactions from this segment. Similar recognition of the non-hegemonic nature of preferences and the way certain values can assume greater importance than others, appears in the writings of Carol Duncan, Associate Professor and Chair of the Department of Religion and Culture at Wilfred Laurier University in Waterloo, Canada. She is well known as one of the pioneers of a new socio-political approach to art history, and her books include *The Pursuit of Pleasure: The Rococo Revival in French Romantic Art* (1975) and *The Aesthetics of Power: Essays in the Critical History of Art* (1993). In this last book, she argues that:

> 'art embodies quality for someone when it meets his or her wants – to be entertained, flattered, enlightened, charmed, awed and any of the other things people value in art. We may value a work because we find its colours pleasing, or because it reminds us of our childhood home, or makes us feel tension or joy or surprise (or because) it will enhance our social standing or because it gives us back a piece of our experience in the world in a heightened form.'
>
> (ibid. 175)

Carol Duncan in this way, explored the subjective nature of artistic experience and the factors that impact on preferences, issues that we will explore in more detail in the rest of this chapter. We will finish the chapter by homing in on the subject of this book, namely gender and examine the small amount of research that focuses on gender and reactions to form and colour.

The Direction of Preferences

What direction do people's preferences normally take? Do opposites attract, or do preferences generally follow a pattern of like attracting like? We adopted a scatter-gun approach and explored the literature on social preferences as well as preferences for paintings and drawings.

Where social preferences are concerned, there appears to be opposing evidence, with on the one hand, the view that similarity makes for the best social relationships, and on the other, the view that opposites attract. The first view was expounded by George Kelly, originator of Personal Construct Theory and expounded in his two-volume work: *The Psychology of Personal Constructs* (1955, 7): 'Man looks at his world through transparent templates which he creates and then attempts to fit over the realities of which the world is composed'. He went on to say that one can develop a relationship with someone to the extent that the other person has a similar way of looking at the world, what he famously calls the 'construct' system.

Other commentators have reached similar conclusions. Two researchers, Griffitt and Russell Veitch of Bowling Green State University, for example, paid 13 males to spend ten days in a fallout shelter, and found that those with similar attitudes and opinions liked each other most by the end of the study, particularly if they agreed on highly salient issues (Gross 1991). In the same way, Steve Duck of the University of Iowa found that when people used similar cognitive constructs to describe other people, there was a strong likelihood that people would like each other (ibid.). In a third study, Kirton and McCarthy (1988), from the UK, found that people work well in environments in which their own cognitive patterns are matched by those of people around them, a match which they termed 'cognitive fit'. According to these three studies, personality plays an important part in shaping social preferences and if the personalities of those interacting are *alike* then the relationship will prosper, otherwise, it will not. In other words, these researchers believe that like attracts like.

It should be said that there are other researchers who take a contrary view, believing that successful social encounters are defined not so much by similarity of personality as by difference. According to these researchers, relationships are successful if personalities are *unlike* in certain specific ways. How valid is these opposing view?

Despite presenting evidence for the notation that opposites attract, the author of a 'classic' psychology textbook now in its fifth edition, Richard Gross (1991), emphasized the weight of evidence backing up the similarities hypothesis. Similarly, a psychology textbook by Zick Rubin and Elton McNeil (1987) of Brandeis University, now in its fourth edition, argued that although diversity is valuable and enriching, people with fundamentally different approaches to life are unlikely to become friends. As they say, 'our friends tend to be people who are similar to us' (ibid. 448) since 'people with fundamentally different approaches to life are unlikely to become best friends' (ibid. 462). So in terms of social relationships, it seems that the evidence supports the finding that people of one type attracts other similar types. In terms of aesthetic preferences, one might ask whether, likewise, like is attracted to like, or rather whether it is a question of opposites attracting. This will be the subject of our next section.

Aesthetic Preferences

When it comes to aesthetic preferences does like tend to attract like, or do opposites attract? When I first posed these questions back in the 1990s it was difficult to find answers since the existing research literature had not addressed these questions through empirical work. There was, however, work of a theoretical nature as well as empirical work from which one could infer certain answers. It is worth reviewing this earlier literature here so that readers have an idea of what it revealed.

Where theoretical literature is concerned, I came across a reference to the direction of people's preferences in *Taste and Temperament* (1939) by scholar and art critic Joan Evans. There she wrote that:

> 'men of each psychological type tend to admire the art produced by artists of the same type.'
>
> (ibid. 47)

> 'A man will always tend to have a primary attraction towards the art produced by men of like temperament with himself.'
>
> (ibid. 64)

So much for a theoretical view. Joan Evans had attended St Hugh's College, Oxford, from 1914, graduating in archaeology, and was elected the first woman President of the Society of Antiquaries in 1959, holding the post until 1964. This was something of a family affair, since both her father, Sir John Evans, and her half brother by more than forty years, Sir Arthur Evans, best known as the excavator of the Bronze Age archaeological site of Knossos, had also held the post.

As far as empirical work is concerned, there had been a trickle of studies focusing on personality and its possible effects on aesthetic preferences, and it seemed worthwhile, using knowledge of personality types and the artistic work associated with these, to infer whether the artefacts for which people express a preference tend to be the creations of people of *like* type or *opposite* type to themselves. This information provides a preliminary taste of the direction that people's preferences take when modelled against personality.

A note about the studies. Through literature searches and searches in books on aesthetics, I located a small number of studies, some of them dating back decades, that examined the effect of personality on aesthetic choices. If we accept the assumption of personality as something that can be measured at a single point in time (Hampson 2000) and accept that the methodologies of the studies were sound, then we can attempt to establish a preliminary hypothesis (and we make no claims to it being any more than that) as to whether these preferences illustrate a 'like attracts like' or 'opposites attract' tendency. In each case we will need information about the type of personality associated with the preference for a particular form of art, and the type of personality associated with producing this type of work. The next section attempts to provide you with just this.

Empirical Studies on Preferences and Personality

(A) Eysenck

The British psychologist, Hans Eysenck (1981) examined the pictorial preferences of introverts and extroverts, finding that introverts preferred old masters to bright modern types of pictures, and extroverts, the reverse. In an earlier study (1941), Eysenck had found that extroverts preferred brightly coloured pictures and bright colours to subdued colours.

Direction of preferences: It is not possible to ascertain from Eysenck's later experiment whether this illustrates a 'like attracts like' tendency or not since there is no data on whether the personalities associated with the production of 'old masters', and 'bright, modern types of pictures' are extrovert or not.

(B) Barron

Barron (1963) identified the personality types of subjects and then the sort of art-work that they preferred. His findings are shown in Table 4.1.

Direction of preferences: Waehner (1946) interpreted the painting of realistic landscapes and paintings as a sign of conventionality and since Barron (1963) finds that these are the types of painting preferred by people with 'conservative' personalities, there would appear to be a direct correspondence between the personality of the beholder and the painter whose work they like. This, then, is an instance of 'like attracting like'.

Table 4.1 Preferences associated with particular kinds of personality (Barron 1963)

Personality characteristics of subjects	Type of paintings they prefer
Conservative, serious, deliberate, responsible	Portraits, landscapes and traditional themes
More emotional, temperamental and pessimistic	Experimental, sensual and primitive work

(C) Welsh

Welsh (1949) found that conservative and conventional personalities had a preference for simple and symmetrical objects, while anti-social/dissident personalities had a preference for complex, asymmetrical pictures.

Direction of preferences: Waehner (1946) associates that the production of symmetrical drawing with a conventional personality, and therefore the preference that conservative types have for symmetrical objects seems a further instance of 'like attracting like'. Unfortunately, Waehner said nothing about the personality likely to produce asymmetrical images, but if it is the opposite of the type that produces symmetrical images, then the dissident personality's preference for a symmetrical images is another instance of a 'like attracting like' tendency.

(D) Honkavaara

Honkavaara (1958) investigated the relationship between a person's emotional state and the type of picture they preferred and the results revealed that 'form reactors' (defined as people who are realistic, socially secure, conforming and realistic) demonstrated a preference for realistic pictures, whilst 'colour reactors' (defined as people who internalize their feelings, are irrational, affectionate and individualistic) showed a preference for poetic pictures.

Direction of preferences: The form reactors' preference for realistic pictures would appear to be a clear case of a 'like attracts like' tendency and similarly, the colour reactors' preference for poetic pictures (presumably an expression of an emotional personality) is likely to be a manifestation of the same tendency.

(E) Knapp and Green

Knapp and Green (1960) created an abstract art test and found that a preference for clear geometric principles was associated with extroverted types, while a preference for fewer geometric principles was associated with introverted types.

Direction of preferences: Since Herbert Read (1958) associates the production of geometric forms with intuitive extroverts, this may be a further instance of a 'like attracts like' tendency although we have to bear in mind that Read's work lacked any methodological rigour.

(F) Knapp and Wolff

Knapp, this time with Wolff (1963), found that preferences for abstract art were associated with intuitive types and preferences for representational art with sensing types.

Direction of preferences: Herbert Read (1958) and Burt (1968) both associated the production of abstract art with the intuitive maker and the production of representational art with the sensing maker. As a result, Knapp and Wolff's study appears to offer a further instance of the 'like attracts like' tendency.

(G) Knapp

In a further study, Knapp (1964) established, by administering a well-known personality instrument, the Myers Briggs Personality Type Inventory (MBTI) that:

- Preferences for realistic paintings were associated with 'extroverted' and 'sensing' types.
- Preferences for geometric paintings were associated with 'thinking' and 'judging' types.
- Preferences for expressionist paintings were associated with 'introverted' and 'intuitive' types.

Direction of preferences: Since the production of 'realistic' pictures is associated by Read (1958) with 'extrovert' and 'sensing' types, and since Knapp's findings are that 'extroverted' and 'sensing' types prefer realistic paintings, this appears to be an instance of 'like attracting like'. Moreover, since the production of 'expressionistic' paintings (a subjective view of reality) is associated by Read with introverted types, and since Knapp's findings are that introverted types prefer expressionist paintings, this would appear to be a further instance of 'like attracting like'.

(H) Jacoby

Jacob Jacoby (1969) showed that 'cautious and conservative' individuals favoured small cars while 'confident explorers' favoured large cars. E.F. Hammer (1980) and others took the view that large objects are produced by aggressive, confident personalities while small objects are produced by people with less confidence. If these views are correct, then this study also illustrates the tendency for 'like to attract like'.

(I) Birren

Birren (1973) an expert on colour, claimed that colour attributes mirrored the personalities of those drawn to them, as his ensuing statement shows:

- Those who dislike colour will not have an agreeable rapport with the outside world and will be introspective and inhibited.
- Those who like colour will have an agreable rapport with the outside world, have outward directed interests, and be emotionally responsive.

- Bright and warm colours (the red end of the spectrum) represent an attraction to a stimulus.
- Softer illumination and cool colours (for example, the blue end of the colour spectrum) represent a withdrawal from the outside world.

If Birren's claims are well founded, this is further evidence of a 'like attracts like' basis to people's colour preferences

The Directions of People's Preferences

A review of nine studies has shown that in eight cases the characteristics of the paintings or colours that people preferred were those associated with the people expressing the preference. This is a preliminary indication that there may be a 'like attracts like' direction or what one might call a 'self-selecting' tendency to people's aesthetic choices, suggesting that people of a particular personality type favour work originated by those of a similar personality to their own

This conclusion must remain tentative, however, for while some of the studies on the basis of which painterly traits were translated into personality types had reasonable validity and reliability (for example, the work of Waehner (1946)), others (such as the studies by Read (1958) and Alschuler and Hattwick (1947)) were lacking any such reliability and validity. This means that the evidence for self-selection coming out of studies B and C quoted above may be more valid than the evidence coming out of studies D, E, F, G and I.

Having said that, however, there is sufficient evidence here on which to build a working hypothesis that people of a particular type will favour paintings or colours that mirror aspects of themselves, a hypothesis that is consistent with what we saw earlier of the homogeneity principle (in Chapter 2). In the context of design and advertising, it would imply that people respond positively to finished products created by people similar to themselves and before reporting in Chapter 6 on the empirical work we have conducted to test this hypothesis, we will review the literature regarding the theoretical impact of a person's gender on their aesthetic preferences.

The Role of a Person's Sex in Preferences for Shapes, Colours and Dynamic Movement

A small number of studies have been carried out that touch indirectly on the question of male and female visual preferences. These studies do not concern paintings (treated earlier on in this chapter) or designs (treated later in Chapter 6) so they have been reserved to the end of this chapter.

Responses to colour and shape

In 1932, a researcher at the Cambridge Psychological Laboratory conducted experiments to ascertain whether certain personality characteristics were associated with those who noticed form above colour, and vice versa with colour. The researcher, Oeser (1931–1932a), flashed a single image (labelled MF) and then flashed a series of images, all arranged in a circle. The images were removed and the subjects (19 female and 13 male students) were asked to describe the image which in their own view resembled the MF. Oeser recorded the features that people described, and then classified these responses into one of four categories:

1. Form dominant responses. If the subject had correctly identified only a feature concerning form, OR had correctly identified a feature concerning form while at the same time incorrectly identifying its colour, the response was labelled 'form dominant' (F).
2. Colour dominant responses. If the subject had correctly identified only a feature concerning colour, OR had correctly identified its colour while at the same time incorrectly identifying its form, the response was labelled 'colour dominant' (C).
3. Form/colour responses. If both form and colour were correctly identified but form was the first feature to be mentioned, the response was labelled 'form colour' (FC).
4. Colour/form response. If both form and colour were correctly identified but colour was the first feature to be mentioned, the response was labelled 'colour form' (CF).

Oeser found that a higher proportion of male than female subjects produced responses which were either 'form dominant' (F) or 'form colour' (FC) in type. Conversely, a higher proportion of women than men produced responses which were 'colour dominant' (C) or 'colour form' (CF) in type. Her findings are shown in Table 4.2.

As can be seen from Table 4.2, the percentage of women who had form as their primary focus (that is, adding the F and FC scores together) is 47.4 per cent compared with nearly 70 per cent for the men. Conversely, the percentage of women who had colour as their primary focus (that is, adding the C and CF scores together) is 53 per cent, compared with only 31 per cent for the men. This shows that a higher percentage of male than female subjects had responses which were form-dominant, while a higher percentage of the women than men had colour-dominant responses. The differences between these two sets of responses is statistically significant at $p < 0.02$.

Oeser's study concerns perception and the visual features that people notice so you have probably realized that this is not a study about preferences. However, since the visual features which make an impression on somebody will affect their preferences, and since Oeser's study shows that women are less likely than men to

Table 4.2 Classification of responses to Oeser's test of form/colour perception

Type of response	Women (%)	Men (%)
F	21.1	23.1
FC	26.3	46.2
Totals (F + FC responses)	**47.4**	**69.3**
CF	36.8	23.1
C	15.8	7.1
Totals (F + CF responses)	**52.6**	**30.8**

notice the shape of an object and more likely to notice its colour, women are more likely to be interested in, and show a preference for colour, than men. Moreover, since, as we have seen, female-produced designs place a greater emphasis on colour than do male-produced designs (with these emphasizing form rather than colour), we can see a mirroring here between what men and women produce and what they notice.

Oeser's experiment takes us a little way down the road of understanding male and female preferences, but only insofar as it tells us something about the elements that men and women notice: it, obviously, does not tell us anything about what men and women might finally prefer. The same is true of a piece of research conducted in 1987 by two academics, Richard Harshman and Allan Pavio, both at the Department of Psychology, University of Western Ontario. Their concern was with the nature of men's and women's mental imagery and their research is described in the next section

Mental imagery

Harshman and Pavio administered the Individual Difference Questionnaire (IDQ), a measure of self-reported imagery, to a sample of 401 male and 328 female students taking an introductory psychology course, and also gave it to a sample of 226 male and 80 female geography students. The questionnaire contained over 80 questions and the authors discuss the way that the results can be interpreted. They suggest that if chance fluctuations were to be the root of differences between the male and female responses then:

> 'We would expect two to three items in each sample to show significant sex differences at the .05 level, with, at most, one of these being significant at the .01 level. We would not expect the same items to show significant sex differences across samples.'
>
> (Harshman and Pavio 1987, 292)

Instead of this:

> 'We found that (in the large psychology sample) 36 items were significant at or beyond the .05 level with 17 of these beyond the .005 level. Furthermore, the differences fell into content related patterns that were consistent both within and between samples; the sex differences seemed both systematic and generalizable.'
>
> (ibid. 292)

One of the differences concerned the extent to which reference was made to moving or static mental imagery and the responses revealed that men relied more than women on dynamic mental representations, while women relied more on static mental imagery than men (Hampson 2000).

Preferences for shape

If we move back in time again, we come across an experiment that is unique in seeking to determine men and women's preferences for different shapes. The researcher, McElroy (1954) asked 779 Scottish children to record their preferences as between 12 pairs of line drawings that McElroy had in fact drawn himself. In drawing them, he hoped to produce shapes that were typically male or female and in order to do this, gave his 'female-shapes' curved features while the shapes that he thought were typically male had phallic properties.

The results? A greater proportion of boys than girls recorded preferences for 'female' configurations, while a greater proportion of girls than boys recorded preferences for the 'masculine' configurations (see Table 4.3).

Unfortunately, since he had produced the shapes himself, respondents were not reacting to genuine examples of male and female work, but merely to McElroy's notion of what masculine and feminine work looked like. McElroy's test cannot

Table 4.3 Male and female preferences for 'masculine' and 'feminine' configurations (McElroy 1954)

Sex of the subjects	Mean number of preferences for the masculine configurations	Mean number of preferences for the feminine configurations
Male	4.00	8.00
Female	4.57	7.43

therefore be seen as an accurate test of preferences for male and female work and new experiments, conducted using valid stimuli, need to be conducted. These are discussed in the next section of the book dealing with design and advertising.

Preferences for colour

The long history of colour preference studies has been described as 'bewildering, confused and contradictory' (McManus et al. 1981) but according to a recent piece of research, 'there is conclusive evidence for the existence of sex differences in colour preference' (Hurlbert and Ling 2007). This last piece of research was methodologically sound, used a large sample of Western and Chinese students and claimed to find significant evidence of sex differences in colour preferences. When the findings appeared in *Current Biology*, they created quite a splash in the world's media and so they are worth considering here.

Professor Anya Hurlbert and Yazhu Ling, both academics at Newcastle upon Tyne University in the UK, conducted a robust cross-cultural study in which they showed pairs of colours to 208 volunteers aged between 20 and 26 and the volunteers had to select which they preferred by clicking with a computer mouse. The main population (171) was British white Caucasians (79 male), with a sub-group of 37 who were Chinese (19 male). The majority of the Chinese had left China for the UK within the previous year.

What the authors found was that while both males and females shared a preference for 'bluish' contrasts, the female preference for 'reddish' contrasts was significantly greater than it was for the men. This finding was robust across national cultures even though in China red is the colour of 'good luck'. Interestingly, it was found that hue preference curves do not vary significantly for different lightness and saturation levels.

Conclusions and Practical Lessons

We have now reviewed all the experiments we could track down that dealt with artistic preferences as well as preferences for shape, colour, and movement. As we have seen, this is not a single body of work, but is scattered across academic journals and brought here (like the studies examining the drawings and paintings of males and females in Chapter 4) for the first time. Some of the studies were conducted in the early decades of the twentieth century (and are no less sound for that) and one was conducted just before this book went to print. What do they reveal?

Nine early studies of artistic preferences were reviewed and in eight of these we saw that the painterly traits of the paintings that people prefer are frequently traits produced by people of a similar personality disposition to themselves. This is a preliminary indication that there may be a 'like attracts like' nature to people's aesthetic choices, suggesting that people of a particular personality type favour work done by people of a similar personality, a finding consistent with the homogeneity principle (see Chapter 2). In the context of design and advertising, it would imply that people like finished products created by people similar to themselves.

We also looked at experiments on colour, shape and movement and in an experiment on the relative perception of colour and shape by Oeser at Cambridge in the 1930s found that a higher proportion of male than female subjects produced responses to images which were either 'form dominant' (F) or 'form colour' (FC) in type. Conversely, a higher proportion of women than men produced responses which were 'colour dominant' (C) or 'colour form' (CF) in type and these results would appear to suggest that the shape of an object has greater importance, relative to colour, for males, and vice versa for women.

Where colour preference is concerned, we have seen that the extensive early research is 'bewildering, confused and contradictory' and so have not chosen to delve into this. Instead, we reported on a recent British study of cross-cultural colour preferences in which women were found to have a stronger preference for reddish contrasts than men. Finally, we reported on a Canadian study of mental imagery that suggested that men were more likely to self-report using dynamic imagery, and women using static imagery.

In Chapter 6, we move on to the applied arts – design and advertising – and examine the research conducted in those fields on gender and preferences. Before doing that, however, we will have a quick look at the literature on gender, language and attitudes since we cannot overlook language in a study concerned with design and marketing.

Chapter 5
Attitudes and Language

Designs and advertisements rely on concepts and language as well as visuals, and it is reasonable to ask what research has been carried out comparing male and female language usage and preferences. In fact, unlike empirical work on design which (apart from my own studies) is pretty sparing, research comparing gender differences in concepts and language has been abundant. In fact, the topic of whether men and women use language and concepts differently has been the subject of several books and research articles and we will try to give a flavour of this work in this chapter.

A cautionary word about some of the popular books and articles on gender differences. Many of these tend to offer clear-cut views on the ways in which men's and women's attitudes differ. For example, Marti Barletta (2006) writes with confidence of men's and women's relative abilities to multi-task (with women showing more agility than men); of their relative preference for product details (saying that men like fewer detail and women, more); of their concern to focus on a few (men) or many (women) priorities when shopping; of their interest in how product features work (with men very interested and women less so). However, the reader should note that it is difficult to find rigorous research to back up these findings. The same is true of thoughts about men's and women's attitudes to purchasing (Carrabis 2006) on the website of Joseph Carrabis, the founder of a consultancy called NextStage Global. Idea after idea tumbles out concerning men and womens product expectations but there is no hint as to what the source for these ideas might be. As a consequence, it is difficult to know how much weight to attach to his utterings. Here is a sample of his ideas:

Serviceability

Joseph Carrabis claims that women are more concerned about the long-term serviceability of a product and men about the short-term serviceability and this lead him to state that 'Women, it seems, are more aware of servicing needs through time than men are'. The consequences in his view? 'If you know your target market is women, don't sell them on now, sell them on now (the near bars) and again (the middle bars) and yet again (the far bars), or make sure they buy enough so that what they buy is useful again and again and again. If your target is men, make them happy now.'

Sense of Time and Space

A further claim by Joseph Carrabis is that the female sense of time extends through time while the male time sense might be fixed on the now or near-now. In contrast to this, he writes that the female concept of space has a strong boundary, and that boundary is (metaphorically) within arm's reach. He contrasts with men whose spatial concept he says extends as far as the eye can see.

In what follows, we will track some of the more rigorous academic research work exploring differences in men's and women's attitudes and use of language.

Attitudes

Lesser vs. greater originality

In 2007, a study by Dr Rod Gunn of Glamorgan University, Sylvana Azzopardi and myself reported on the advertising preferences of business people in Malta. A questionnaire was distributed to members of professional and business organizations in Malta, with a target response rate of 1 per cent from the 50,000 members and this was achieved, with a total of 510 responses, 27.7 per cent from females and 72.3 per cent from males. The results showed statistically significant differences between the type of bank advertisements favoured by men and women with men preferring simple factual and rational information (results were highly significant at the $p < 0.01$ level) and women preferring original advertisements (this tendency was statistically highly significant at the $p < 0.001$ level). Interestingly, when dealing with advertisements with a reasonable level of originality, the men in the sample appeared to have greater difficulty understanding the message than the women (the difference between the sexes was significant at the $p < 0.05$ level).

Individualism/collectivism

Do men and women share the same views as to the relative attractions of an individual as against a collective identity? According to the findings of some researchers (Hofstede 1980; Kashima et al. 1995; Triandis 1995; Verkuyten and Masson 1996; see also Cross and Madson 1997; Madson and Trafimow 2001) women are more collective, allocentric or interdependent than men, and men are more independent or individualistic than women.

A word about two of these studies. The oldest of them, a study of IBM cultures in 50 countries by the respected Dutch researcher, Professor Geert Hofstede (1980), reported that men varied significantly more in their value orientations across cultures than did women. While women, he found, tended to be more similar in value orientations across cultures. This conclusion, if valid (and there have been criticisms of Hostede's methodology) would suggest that designs and advertising can more easily use a single message for global products aimed at women than for those targeted at men.

In the more recent experiment quoted above (that by Laura Madson and David Trafimow of the Department of Psychology at New Mexico University), a questionnaire was administered to psychology students to assess gender differences in self-concept. The test was the 'Twenty Statements Test' (TST) in which participants write 20 statements that complete the stem 'I am' (Kuhn and McPartland 1954). This was administered to 317 introductory psychology students (183 women and 134 men) and on the basis of earlier work by David Trafimow (Trafimow et al. 1991), the TST statements were classified into three types. Firstly, there were what were termed '*private self-cognitions*', classified as statements referring to personal qualities, traits, characteristics, beliefs, or behaviours that do not relate to other people (for example, 'I like to play basketball'). Then there were what were termed '*collective self-cognitions*', defined as statements referring to demographic groups, in-groups, or other people with whom one shares a relationship with a sense of 'common fate' (for example, 'I am a woman' or 'I am a Cubs fan'). Finally there were what were termed '*allocentric cognitions*' which were statements implying interdependence, responsiveness to others, friendship, or sensitivity to the viewpoints of others (for example, 'I am kind to others').

Where did the responses of the men and women sit in this survey? As predicted by the earlier literature, the women made greater use of allocentric cognitions (these stressing interdependence, friendship and sensitivity to others) and reported a higher proportion of collective cognitions than the men. These, by contrast, were more likely than the women to describe themselves in terms of their own unique abilities and traits and taken together, there results suggest that the women thought about themselves more in terms of their relationships with others (both personal relationships and group identities) and accessed collective and allocentric selves were more readily available than the men.

In case you are wondering, the differences between the male and female responses were extremely high from a statistical point of view. The extent of the difference in use of allocentric cognitions (with women using these more than men) was at the $p < .003$ level while the extent of the difference in use of collective cognitions was at the $p < .001$ level, and in use of private self-cognitions (with men using these more than women) at the $p < .001$ level. These are extremely high levels of significance which suggest that the opportunities for the results to be chance events are very low.

As we have seen, there are a number of studies producing evidence of a greater interest in the collective on the part of general women than of men and in the specific case of marketing, research has also brought to the fore women's greater interest in the collective and men in individualism. For example, Bakan proposed in 1966 an agentic–communal dichotomy of gender differences, and Myers-Levy (Myers-Levy and Sternthal 1991) explored male–female differences in information processing using this dichotomy. Their conclusions were that females, in fulfilment perhaps of a greater communal orientation (for example, affiliation orientation), tended to process information comprehensively, while males, in fulfilment perhaps of agentic roles (for example, achievement orientation) tended to process information selectively.

Numerous commercial implications ensue, some of which were explored in a further study by Ved Prakash (1992). He suggested that men were more likely to purchase a brand when shown an advertisement depicting competition against others as against a self-competition, while women were likely to have an equal preference as between the two types of scenario. In terms of the group size that men and women prefer to see depicted, it seems that men prefer large groups while women are happy with large as well as small groups. These conclusions suggest that the male preference could be the default option for women since women are equally happy with either option. These findings led Prakash to infer the following two rules for advertisers and designers:

1. *Designing appeals for males* If the target market for a product consists predominantly of men, then:

   > 'it would be best to show males socializing in large groups, participating in competitive activities, especially sports-related, and in scenarios of traditional sex-roles of male–female interaction. Some good examples of this type of advertisements are Busch, Miller and Miller Lite, Budweiser and Bud Light beers. Such advertisements tend to portray a sense of mastery, self-assertion, confidence, and camaraderie, thus appealing to the achievement-oriented roles of the males.'
   >
   > (Prakash 1992, 49)

2. *Designing appeals for females* If the target market consists predominantly of females:

   > 'the advertisements should portray women socializing in competitive circumstances, but preferably in non-sports activities such as scientific research, journalism, space exploration, or business management. Women could also be shown in non-competitive situations working by themselves or in some intimate settings with other females or males. Women could be shown socializing either in large groups or small groups. This flexibility provides fulfilment of the affiliation-oriented roles for women.'
   >
   > (ibid. 50)

Other consequences are highlighted in a study by Sanjay Putrevu (2004). which argued that men have had a significant preference for advertising messages with a comparative appeal (that is, an advertisement highlighting the benefits of one product over another) while women show a preference for advertisements featuring harmonious relationships. This sense on the part of women of being part of a collective unit suggests that designs and advertising targeted at women should depict people in a collective rather than individualistic situation. The opposite would be the case for advertisements and designs aimed at men.

Concern with people/objects

When it comes to the relative perception of people as against objects, the finding that females perceive people whereas men perceive objects is surprisingly robust across different studies. An interesting study by Professor Simon Baron-Cohen and his colleagues at Cambridge University exposed one-day-old newborn babies to the face of a woman and a rounded mobile and found out that girls looked for longer at the face and the boys at the mobile (Connellan et al. 2001).

The bias in girls towards the personal shows up in other experiments too. In one, a group of boys and girls were invited to look through a pair of binoculars which showed the left and right eyes two different images at the same time, one of an object and the other of a person. The children were shown exactly the same images but when asked what they had seen, the boys reported seeing significantly more things than people, and the girls more people than things (Moir and Jessel 1989).

Conceivably, this greater interest in the personal on the part of the girls helps explain the finding reported earlier (see Chapter 3) for girls to draw fewer caricatured portrayals of the human figure, since caricature is acknowledged to be a way of creating distance between perceiver and the object of their perception and a way of encrusting something mechanical on the living (Bergson 1999, Cohen 1989). Extrapolating to marketing would suggest a need to downplay the personal in adverts directed at men, but to do the opposite in adverts directed at women.

Detail vs. comprehensive processing

It has been suggested that when encoding advertising claims, men encode fewer claims (Gilligan 1982) and prefer simple advertisements that concentrate on no more than one or two features (Putrevu 2004). These item-specific processing skills lead men to prefer advertisements focused on single-attribute (ibid.) which make it possible to process focused information. Women, on the other hand, are thought to be more comprehensive processors, attempting to assimilate all available information before rendering judgement and are also thought to interpret verbal and non-verbal cues more accurately than men (Chamblee et al. 1993; Goos and Silverman 2002). According to research conducted by Myers-Levy, women are likely to prefer complex advertisements containing rich and detailed information on multiple features (whether verbal or visual information) and will encode more message claims as well as elaborate more extensively than men on specific claims (Myers-Levy 1989, Myers-Levy and Sternthal 1991). It seems that they also prefer advertisements focused on the product and its relationship to its product category, what Sanjay Putrevu, who conducted the research, calls ‘category oriented ads’. According to Putrevu (2004):

> 'Advertisers should present category-oriented messages to a female audience and attribute-oriented messages to a male audience. Specifically, ads targeting men should emphasize only those features that are unique to the advertised brand and highlight its differential advantage. In contrast, ads targeting women should focus on features that are common to the product category and highlight how the advertised brand fits in (or compares) with other brands belonging to the category.'
>
> (ibid. 60)

Other researchers have observed that advertisements in magazines aimed at men are more wordy and complex than corresponding advertisements in magazines aimed at women (Whissell and McCall 1997), suggesting that advertising agencies have some way to go in applying these findings.

Competition

It seems that attitudes to competition differ as well. According to Putrevu (2004):

> 'There is strong and unequivocal evidence that men and women exhibit sharply varying reactions to identical print advertisements. Specifically, women show superior affect and purchase intent toward advertisements that are verbal, harmonious, complex and category-oriented whereas men exhibit superior affect and purchase intent toward advertisements that are comparative, simple and attribute-oriented.'
>
> (ibid. 59)

The implications for an advertising agency are equally strong. As he says:

> '... this research suggests that men and women are likely to respond more favourably to messages that are in tune with their respective gender-role expectations and information-processing styles ... men show a preference for advertising messages that feature competition and engage in brand comparisons, whereas women favour messages that emphasize harmony and show importance to self as well as others. Also, perhaps due to differing levels of brain lateralization, women have a greater affinity for purely verbal information, whereas men benefit from visual reinforcement of verbal material. Furthermore, men prefer simple ads that focus on one or a few key attributes, whereas women prefer complex ads that contain rich verbal and visual information. Thus, advertisers would do well to create gender-specific ad campaigns that feature differing levels of hard versus soft sell, as well as differing levels (and types) of verbal and visual information.'
>
> (ibid. 60)

The reference to 'verbal' information leads us on nicely to looking at the interactive effect of gender on language. What does the research reveal about this?

Language

Although men and women technically speak the same language, some scholars have described differences in the way that men and women use language. This is a controversial area, with new research playing down differences in the way men and women use language (Cameron 2007a). Deborah Cameron, for example, Rupert Murdoch Professor of Language and Communication at Oxford University, has highlighted research findings that offers little support for the notion of sex differences in the way men and women use language. A case in point is a study by Janet Hyde collating the results of several studies (a so-called 'meta-analysis') showing either no differences or only small gender differences where conversational interruption, talkativeness, self-disclosure and assertive and affiliative speech are concerned. Cameron also reports the views of linguist Jack Chambers who has suggested that the degree of non-overlap in the abilities of male and female speakers in any given population is only about 0.25 per cent (Cameron, 2007b). In the same way, Melissa Hines, Professor of Psychology at Cambridge University, in her book *Brain Gender* (2004), describes gender differences in 'verbal fluency' as smaller, in relative and absolute terms, than sex differences in visual 3-D rotation tasks (see Chapter 8 for more details of her results).

We can see from this that those who speak of differences in the way that men and women use language appear to be on less robust ground than those who speak of differences in the visual field. To put the reader completely in the picture, however, and in order to counter-balance the somewhat negative reporting of linguistic differences found in Cameron and others, I report here and in the next pages on some of the earlier research on gender and language. This does not claim to be a critical discussion of the research literature but rather an introduction to some of the earlier research on the topic. Much of this discussion is taken, in fact, from a useful summary of this earlier research by Jaffe et al. and reading this summary, the reader will readily appreciate how far the debate has moved in the space of a few decades.

Use of Qualifying Words

Some of this earlier research takes the view that women use more qualifying words than men, making use of emotionally intensive adverbs such as 'so,' 'terribly,' 'awfully,' and 'quite' (Lakoff 1975), and using adjectives and adverbs that 'connote triviality or unimportance' such as 'sweet,' 'precious,' and 'darling' (Eakins and Eakins 1978). These suggestions of greater expressiveness in women's language provide echos to the finding (Soskin and John 1963) that wives produce significantly more expressive such as 'Ouch!' or 'Darn!' as compared with the husbands' greater use of directive and informative statements.

A related finding from the earlier research is that women tend to speak in a more tentative way than men, using more tag questions, and more questions in general (Coates 1993; Holmes 1988). Explanations for these observations seem to vary. According to Holmes (1988), the use of such language patterns indicates greater politeness and lower assertiveness by females than males, while Lakoff (1975) viewed such language patterns as a sign of 'insecurity' or 'approval seeking'. Fishman (1980), for his part, explained such patterns in terms of 'skilful strategies' to engage men in talk.

Harmony and Competitiveness

Another difference highlighted in the earlier literature concerns a purportedly greater emphasis on cooperative language on the part of women than on the part of men. This view was popularized by Deborah Tannen, Professor of Linguistics at Georgetown University and author of numerous popular and serious works on gender and language. Her book *You Just Don't Understand – Women and Men in Conversation* appeared in 1990, and one of the recurring themes is that women's talk is 'interdependent' and 'cooperative,' while male conversational patterns express 'independence' and assertions of vertically hierarchical power. This characterization of women's language as geared to harmony and men's to competition characterizes much of this earlier literature on language and gender.

We mention Tannen's work on this topic in the 1990s, but similar conclusions can be found in research conducted before and after Tannen's work hit the bestseller lists. Earlier research included work that had investigated male and female communication behaviour in mock-jury deliberations, finding that females gave significantly more positive reactions than males, and males used more aggressive language (Strodtbeck and Mann 1956). In a similar way, a discourse analysis of a CMC bulletin board contrasted the features that women tended to use, namely 'attenuated assertions, apologies, questions, personal orientation and support' with those used by men, namely 'strong assertions, self-promotion, rhetorical questions, authoritative orientation, challenges and humor' (Herring 1993). In line with these findings are those showing women asking more questions (Fishman 1978, 1983), making more apologies (Eubanks 1975), providing equal time to all groups, allowing them to express their thoughts and feelings (Geary 1998) and raising issues which are not reduced to theories and abstractions as they are when the object of male concern (Aries 1976; Steinem 1991; Swacker 1975).

One theory is that the women's style of discourse helps to develop and maintain intimate and reciprocal relationships with other girls and women (Geary 1998, 262) and that, by contrast, men's use of language helps them to assert social dominance (Geary 1998) and independence. The thinking is that men can achieve these objectives by exhibiting knowledge and skill, and holding centre stage through verbal performance such as story telling, joking, or imparting information (Wittig 1992) or interruptions (Geary 1998).

It is not just the style of discourse that these earlier researchers have thought could vary by gender, but choice of theme as well. In this way, several researchers have found that females are more likely to adjust to a male interlocutor, asking questions and introducing numerous 'male-specific topics' until males end up accepting a conversation (Aries 1976, 1987; Coates 1993; Spender 1980): By contrast, researcher Gloria Steinem found that subjects introduced by males in mixed groups were far more likely to 'succeed' than subjects introduced by women (Steinem 1991). It was observed that once males speak on a topic, they assume the mantle of experts and this behaviour has been interpreted as illustrative of the use of language for competitive rather than for relational purposes.

Social Status, Language, and Interruptions

Given the differences thrown up by some research, it is not surprising to see researchers speak of gender-specific conversational strategies (Lakoff 1975; Stern 1994; Cameron et al. 1992) with women described as less likely than men to exercise the 'powerful' style thought by some to be the hallmark of masculine discourse. The vexed question of why men should exercise this style has intrigued academics and one scholar has suggested that the masculine pattern is rooted in the biblical convention that obliged a wife to address her husband as a slave would a master or a subject a king (Daly 1991, 159).

One focus in linguistics research has been on the number of interruptions used by men and women and there is no shortage of research in this topic. West, working with Zimmerman (Zimmerman and West 1975) and then with Fenstermaker (West and Fenstermaker 1993) investigated mixed-gender conversations, taping 31 conversations in public places such as libraries, coffee shops and drug stores, of these 31 conversations, 11 were mixed-gender conversations, 10 male-only and 10 female-only conversations, and the findings indicated significant differences in terms of the use of overlaps and interruptions in same-gender and mixed-gender pairs. A word on definitions. Overlaps were defined as an act of anticipating the end of an interlocutor's sentence spoken by an interlocutor while articulating it with a topic-related response. An interruption, on the other hand, was considered as a violation of turn-taking rules with clear topical disarticulation is flagrant.

The results? These showed that all the overlaps were occasioned by male speakers and that 96 per cent of the interruptions resulted from men interrupting women. Interestingly, it has been observed that men rarely interrupt each other but use interruptions primarily when speaking to women, even when these are of high status (West 1984). Similarly, women are reported as using fewer overlaps with men than women since men tend to perceive overlaps as interruptions (Steinem 1991). Incidentally, West's study focused on male and female doctors' interactions with patients and it has been observed that whereas male physicians (as a group) initiated 67 per cent of all interruptions relative to their patients, female physicians (as a group) initiated only 32 per cent of interruptions relative to their patients (West 1984).

Amount of Talk

What of the relative loquaciousness of men and women? According to David Geary, Professor of Psychology at the University of Missouri in Columbia and author of a hefty tome *Male, Female: The Evolution of Human Sex Differences* (published by the American Psychological Association), studies have shown that women outperform the average man in 'the ease and speed of articulating complex words, the ability to generate strings of words, the speed of generating individual words from long-term memory ... the skill at discriminating basic language sounds ... [and] the length and quality of utterances' (Geary 1998, 263).

Reading this, the thrust of what Professor Geary is saying seems clear enough although the available research does not all concur with these views. In one study, for example, males and females were asked to describe three pictures and it transpired that males spoke for an average of 13 minutes per picture as against women's average of 3.17 minutes (Swacker 1975). In the same way, research by Steinem (1991) showed that men could talk more than women and that talkativeness was not an exclusive female trait. Similarly, the findings from a study of mock-jury deliberations, found that men were involved in significantly more speech acts than women (Strodtbeck and Mann's investigation 1956) and a later study found that women's messages were quite short (Kaplan and Farrell 1994).

Opinions have been offered to explain perceptions of men's or women's greater loquaciousness and have suggested that men's greater talkativeness in public, may be a feature of the competitive behaviour generated by these settings. In the context of private settings, it has been noted that women may focus on topics construed as trivial and unimportant and this has led Coates (1993) to suggest that if men's topics (sports, politics and cars) are construed as 'serious' and topics such as child-bearing and personal relationships as 'trivial', then we should not be surprised if men respond with silence, since this may be a way of denying conversation topics which do not interest them (Aries 1976, 1987; Spender 1980b).

Use of the Vernacular

Another area in which early research has spoken of difference is in the tone of the language used. Several studies have, in this regard, suggested that males tend to use a more vernacular style than females (Cheshire 1982; Coates 1993; Milroy 1980).

Practical Lessons

We have seen the extent to which there is a lack of unanimity amongst researchers as to the extent to which there are sex differences in language usage. Some speak in favour of differences in the way men and women use language and more recently, scholars are finding reasons to argue against this view.

Marketers find themselves caught in the epicentre of a raging academic debate, without any way of resolving the differences of opinion. Do men and women use language similarly or differently? We have noted the recent moves to play down differences in language usage, but other research has presented evidence for difference. Underlining many of these differences are suggestions as to men's greater individualism and women's greater collectivism with the latter encouraging women to use rapport talk (this facilitates connections and intimacy), polite language and questions (these help to avoid individualistic assertions or assertions of status). By contrast, men's putative greater independence would favour discourse that establishes status and independence (Tannen 1990; Stewart and Logan 1998), leading men to dominate mixed-gender interaction (Coates 1993) and to control topics of conversation, interrupting women and using vernacular language where necessary.

An article by Robin Croft, Clive Boddy and Corinne Pentucci (Croft et al. 2007) contains tables summarizing some of the much-discussed differences in men's and women's styles of communication and we reproduce them here in Tables 5.1 and 5.2 (those elements discussed in the overview here are shown with an asterisk). The reader can perhaps form their own view and in the light of the evidence presented here, and of their own experience, decide the position they wish to adopt.

Conclusions and Practical Lessons

If the reader supports the notion of difference, what then? The homogeneity principle holds that men and women will prefer objects and people that hold up a mirror to themselves and this implies that the language used in design and advertising should mirror that of the potential purchaser. According to Michelle Miller, it is not just words but business activities that stand to be affected:

> 'Men tend to concentrate on left-brain activities such as doing research, analysing and comparing products, choosing a brand and rationalising the decision. In contrast, a woman will do the same left-brain research but her decision will involve a lot more right-brain activity – gathering opinions, thinking about who she knows who's already bought something similar, visualising herself using the product and drawing on emotional memory and experience. Her experience of a business in general – everything from how easy it is to find, how pleasant it is to deal with – will affect whether she decides to shop with them.'
>
> (Miller and Buchanan 2008, 43–4)

Her conclusions may be based on anecdote, but the importance of connecting with customers, whether through concepts or language, cannot be emphasized too strongly.

Table 5.1 Gendered differences in conversational styles (from Croft et al. 2007)

	Male–male dialogues	Female–female dialogues
Content	Broad categories: products and services in general. Detail unimportant. Strategic	Specific product names, brands, retailers, locations, service providers. Day-to-day matters
Personal contributions		Discussion of opinions and observations *
Process of discussion	Ordered and logical: restricted, narrow, focused, linear	Undisciplined: constantly going off at tangents, iterative, fragmented, confused, chaotic, disordered
Body language	Limited eye contact. Restrained	Eye contact essential. Animated
Conversational styles	Monologues, turn taking, interruptions taboo *	Dialogues, discussion, argument, interruptions encouraged *
Verbal style	Limited, strained, unnatural *	Uninhibited, extensive, rich, natural, enjoyable, spontaneous *

Table 5.2 Gendered differences in conversational styles: middle class respondents (Croft et al. 2007)

	Male–male dialogues	Female–female dialogues
Conversational strategy	Authoritarian *	Communication *
	Established hierarchy *	Development of knowledge, understanding and opinions *

Final Words

We have surveyed a range of research literature on the evidence for different attitudes on the part of men and women. Just the surface of the evidence available has been examined, and readers are urged to explore beyond the confines of the material in this chapter. Suffice to say that there is a body of opinion, dating back decades, that points to differences in the way men and women use language and designers and marketers are counselled to frame their work so that the language used is appropriate to the end-user.

PART III

Applied Background

Chapter 6
Graphic, Product Design and Gender: Production and Preference Aesthetics

In Chapter 3 we saw that a variety of forms of graphic expression are consistent with each other, and that drawings and paintings reflect the personalities and gender of their originators. Since design is a form of graphic expression, one would expect that designs, like drawings and paintings, would also reflect the personalities and sex of their creators.

Strangely enough, when I started to delve into this and search for earlier literature on this topic, I could find almost no research examining whether a person's gender influenced the designs they produced and liked. This gap surprised me since if a person's gender were to play a part in influencing their designs and design preferences, there would be massive repercussions for the world of commercial design. Think about it. If men and women produce different kinds of design (as the previous chapter on drawings and paintings might lead one to expect given the consistency of all graphic expression) and if their preferences are in line with their productions (following the 'like attracts like' principle we saw prevail in experiments on artistic preference) then the business of determining how design appeal can be maximized for groups of men and women becomes more complex than has hitherto been realized. A new science based on understanding men's and women's design *production* and *preference* aesthetics looms into view, one we could loosely label the study of 'design psychology'.

The importance of responding to this new challenge cannot be underestimated. Design is the 'central feature of culture and everyday life in many parts of the world' (Buchanan 1995, xii), 'replac[ing] nature as the dominant presence in human experience' (ibid.). The 'pervasive[ness] of design in the contemporary world' (Buchanan 1995, xiii) makes it imperative for us to establish the foundations of this new science. Graphic and product design will be the focus of this chapter and web design that of the next, and after focusing on design *production* aesthetics we will turn to design preference aesthetics.

Comparing Male and Female Designs

Back in the 1990s there was precious little research on gender and design. This chapter describes the research I conducted over a fifteen year period to fill the gap. Since there so little research, it made sense to begin by getting an 'inside' view, looking at the opinions of those working in the field of design and related disciplines. To sound out the views of people working in the field of study is standard procedure in the social sciences, so you often find new avenues of research beginning with a series of interviews. The hope is that these will indicate some of the main issues, and it was in this spirit that I embarked on unstructured interviews with a series of people who were directly or indirectly connected with design (Moss 1999).

Interviews

The interviewees came, in roughly equal proportions, from the following four groups:

1. design practitioners;
2. design educators/administrators;
3. design students;
4. market research practitioners.

In selecting interviewees, the 'snowballing' technique was employed – a tool in which you allow one person to lead you on to another, and which is frequently employed for the purpose of selecting an illustrative sample of the kind needed here (Coolican 2004). As soon as I had the names of 40 people I called a halt to the snowballing process, since the object was not to find a sample that was statistically representative of the wider population, but to find one that would illustrate the views held by people in and around the areas of design and marketing. In the end, interviews were held with 14 designers, 10 educators, 2 market researchers, 3 administrators and 11 students. Two-thirds of the sample were female, but this is pretty much par for the course in psychology since the majority of psychology experiments are conducted using Psychology students and two-thirds of these are female.

Most of the interviews I conducted were carried out face-to-face (only two people were interviewed over the telephone) and interviewees were simply asked whether they thought that the designs of males and females differed or not After asking this question, the interviewers (myself) intervened as little as possible and only briefed the interviewee on the reasons for the research after the interview was completed. It should be noted that several respondents also commented on whether they thought that male and female design preferences differed and we will summarize these points later.

So what do these 40 people think?

Are male and female designs different?

All 40 interviewees were asked whether they considered that male and female designs differed and a massive 73 per cent spoke of differences. Only one respondent considered that there were no differences while another 25 per cent (ten people) were undecided. Amongst those who spoke of differences, there were certain recurring themes and these are shown below.

In a few cases, comments were of a non-specific nature. For example, an experienced designer in her early 40s, a graduate of Ravensbourne College and the Royal College of Art, remarked that 'if you give the same brief to a group of men and women, they will always come up with something different'. Wherever possible, I have quoted respondents comments verbatim and have identified each respondent by a number in brackets.

Quality of surfaces Two people associated hard surfaces with male designs. For men, 'noble steel is OK' (15). A mature student commented that men's work is more 'precise and hard-edged' than female work (31). By contrast, three people associated soft surfaces with female designs, with one saying that 'females like to work with soft materials and for this reason perhaps are drawn to certain crafts such as sewing, knitting, quilting and weaving' (16) and another saying that 'the work of males is strong and solid whereas that of females is delicate' (35). A third thought that female work was 'softer and more sensual' than male work (31).

Functionality/technical orientation Seven people associated greater concern with functionality with male design, with one head of Department of Art saying that boys had a more 'linear and technical' approach than girls (22). A teacher of Product Design at a UK university thought that males were interested in task-based objects, that is, objects that had an objective or a machine quality such as a motor car. The teacher volunteered that: 'Males are interested in the way something functions and will emphasize the motion in something whereas females will react to the experience of the object. They will seem to be aware of the experience of the object rather than the implications of it and it's their reactions that will count with them' (18).

A university lecturer in Product Design echoed these thoughts, citing the way a mixed group of men and women had responded to a project to create a hat from natural materials. According to her, the men had been concerned principally with 'the functionality of the hat, ensuring that it stayed on the head and did not fall down, the girls while the women were concerned more with the look of the hat and whether it was pretty and decorative' (17).

In a similar way, a mature student described men as drawn to subjects with a 'mechanical basis' (31) while a female designer described male designers as 'techno-orientated' and 'gadget-orientated', a characteristic which she said might lead a male designer to put a special dial on a female doll's motorbike (4). Another female designer expressed the view that males were more interested in function and technology than styling and that these male concerns had informed the Modernist and Bauhaus movements. She thought that Le Corbusier, with his belief in the house as a machine, was a typical male designer (10) and that design education in the 1990s reflected the male preference for function over styling (10). Her own experience at Ravensbourne College had taught her that students were encouraged to be more concerned about function than styling, with styling seen as the poor end of product design. 'If you started to play with shape, you were made to feel guilty about it – at Art College styling is a bad word'. She thought that women were losing out since they were more interested in styling than men and that were a course to concentrate on styling, it would attract more women than are currently drawn to product design courses.

Regarding the prevalence of male standards in design, a female design historian agreed that the current boundaries of design education and design excellence reflected the masculine underpinning of the modernist movement. According to this historian, the masculine element was apparent in the way the movement rejected everything identifiable with the feminine, whether is was allowing form to follow function, extolling work produced by machines or rejecting hand-crafted work such as quilt making, macramé and embroidery. In her opinion, this kind of hand-crafted activity is more naturally the province of women and does not attract the kind of public recognition that masculine forms do (15). Interestingly, a garden designer (14), although working in a different field, thought that men were more interested in machinery than women.

Size Four people mentioned differences in the way men and women use size with one designer (10) saying that men were more interested in 'huge schemes' than women. Another thought that male designs were more bulky than those produced by women (8) while a third commented that 'men like welding with big bits of steel' (15). A mature student commented that 'men tend to go for larger, more aggressive looking pieces' (31).

Colours No fewer than eight people spoke of differences in the way that men and women used colour. One female graphic designer (6), for example, spoke of the way that the male designers in the design consultancy in which she worked would often 'borrow' her sense of colour, saying that 'They often get this wrong and I step in to help'.

A head of a Foundation course, moreover, suggested that females accept colour for its own sake in a way that males do not (23), while a lecturer on Fine Art took the view that women are more interested in colour than men (24). In terms of specifics, one market researcher commented that women 'are not put off by light colours' (25) while a graphic designer (11) referred to the fact that females avoid the use of obvious primaries, using for example burnt orange rather than just plain orange. Women were also perceived to use more pastel shades (11 and 33) and thin washes (16), and to be generally more adventurous with colour (21).

The professionals were not alone in noticing these differences. One male student said that unlike women, he would never use bright pink (40), while a mature student observed that women favoured the use of yellow, red, orange and pink. If they used green, there would be a richness to it, blue would have a hue like petrol blue and overall women's colours would be vibrant and warm looking. By contrast, the colours men used tended to be green, blue and grey, with the green having a sharp or harsh appearance and the blue often navy. There would be a lot more white in male than female work (31).

Detail A total of five people commented on differences in the way that men and women used detail. One designer thought that female work was softer and more sensitive to details and materials than male work (9), while a teacher of graphic design commented that 'females are better at detail than males' (20). Another designer said that 'women are more likely to be interested in detail' than men (10) and a garden designer commented that women were more likely than man to break up a border with a variety of plants while men were more likely to prefer large swathes of a single colour (14).

Men's lack of interest in detail was thought to have far-reaching effects. According to a design historian, the Modernist tradition underpinning design teaching rejected everything identifiable with the feminine such as decoration and display (15), while a student commented that 'girls ... are more concerned with neatness and detail ... than males' (37). The difference between men's and women's relative interests in detail could have implications for the way designs are assessed.

Three dimensionality and clarity Two people mentioned this, with one taking the view that three-dimensionality was not a quality readily associated with women. This designer spoke of her own experience of designing and how she personally tended to draw things in two dimensions, adding only afterwards the shadows that would produce the illusion of three-dimensionality (11). The second person to raise the topic of dimensionality was the head of Department of Art at a large secondary comprehensive school and she mentioned that, boys tended to use tight outlines, a neat rather than blobby application of colour and a meticulous and precise way of presenting things (22). All of this was, in her opinion, less true of the type of work produced by girls.

Straight lines, verticality and rounded shapes Ten people referred to the shape and quality of the lines that males and females drew. One, a head of design at a London consultancy who had taught Graphic Design and Typography at Kingston University, noticed that boys 'liked drawing lines, even on brochures and other things when they were not needed' (5). Another designer commented that 'the male designer uses more straight lines than the female one' (6) while a third remarked on the direction of lines in male designs as aggressive (8). Interestingly, a male student commented that he was more interested in geometric forms and lines than flowers or colours (40).

An interesting comment came from a female teacher of product design who had asked a group of Foundation course students to construct a hat from natural materials . She had found that 'the boys' hats were all highly constructed, all made with twigs and therefore more angular than those of the girls while the girls' were made with leaves, flowers, moss and berries and were more organic in shape' (17).

An echo of these ideas came from a male teacher of Fashion Design who distinguished between shapes favoured by men and women. As he saw it, 'Coco Chanel was talking about ease of movement while male designers were putting women in square cages with tailored clothes. Christian Dior is an example with his "New Look" based on straight shapes and his so-called "A-line" – a concept characterized by wasp waists and a skirt that went out from the waist – forming the basis to his designs. The emphasis on the A-line and straight lines made corsets popular and the trend was followed by Balenciaga who, like Dior, also favoured straight lines, this time based on the letter H with the design known as "the sack". Paco Rabanne put women into metal and wood and Andre Correge into leather – the shapes of his designs were so plain that the female lost her shape completely' (21).

Not dissimilar to these ideas were those of a head of Department of Art at a comprehensive secondary school who described a project in which a class drew trees in Russell Square (London). She recalled how a male pupil gave the tree the shape of the Post Office Tower while another (female) gave it a more spread-out structure (22).

This was not an isolated comment since three designers commented on the fact that rounded shapes were more likely to come from the pen of females. 'The round is a more female than male shape' said one designer who commented on the extensive use she made of circles (16). Another designer said that she used a lot of circles in her illustrations (11) while a mature student commented on the way that female work tends to be softer and more sensual than male work, with sinuous lines. Men's work, on the other hand, tends to be more precise and hard-edged (31).

Subject matter Differences in the use of subject matter were identified by six subjects. One graphic designer (ex-College teacher) commented that she personally hated drawing males but that males she had taught were happy to do this. She also thought that men were more likely than women to use caricature and that women tended to use humour in more subtle ways (11). A second designer (16) commented on the way that women used flowers in their designs while a woman working in advertising commented on the fact that judges of advertising awards (largely men) tended to award prizes to advertisements concerned with sports, beer and cars (12) possibly because this is what they liked best. Other differences highlighted included women's preference for the organic (for example, leaves and shells) as against men's preference for the mechanical (31) and man made environment, for example, buildings (40). In the same vein, a head of a Foundation course thought that males were more interested than women in the mechanical aspects of things (23), while a student commented that girls tended to paint more fruit than boys.

She said that the boy had chosen pickled animals as a subject – not a choice the girls would have made (38).

As well as commenting on the appearance of male- and female-produced designs, interviewees occasionally remarked on the way that men and women went creating designs. We subsequently saw that there were enough comments to warrant a section on its own so these comments are noted in the next section.

Are male and female design processes different?

As many as 16 people volunteered the notion that men and women approach the design task in different ways and their comments are grouped together below.

Intuitive response Four people commented on the idea that women may work more intuitively than men. One of these, a designer, said of his jewellery designer wife that, when considering a process, 'she doesn't think about it – she just does it' (1). This view was echoed by a head of a Foundation course who thought that girls were more intuitive than boys, while boys tended to want to analyse things (23) and there are points in common with the thinking of a teacher of product design who expressed the view that 'females tend to work things out experientially whereas males tend to want to work things out systematically' (18). We find a similar idea voiced by a former design director:

> 'male designers are more formal in their approach whereas female designers have a lightness of approach. Women are more intuitive and can jump quickly into what is required' (27).

Practical and focused on the brief and the customer Thirteen people commented on men and women's relative focus on the brief and the customer. One designer suggested that women were more practical than men (3) while an interior designer suggested that female interior designers had a more practical, less abstract understanding of space than their male counterparts and that while a male designer would design an interior scheme from a simple floor plan, would tended to prefer to visit the location (13). According to a project administrator, women were more likely to think about the needs of the users (29) and one senior design administrator expected female designers to have a greater awareness of the needs of their customers than male designers. He considered, for example, that men would design a kitchen to suit their own logic while women would design it with an eye to the needs of the user (28) came from a male teacher of fashion design who thought that male designers had more adventurous ideas than female designers (21) while two other designers thought that male designers were more likely to go outside a brief than females, and more likely to want to 'do their own thing – they'll not want to do what is required of them but will feel that what they do is right. Females are more aware of answering the problem and focusing' (7 and 29). This view was echoed by another designer who considered that women were more customer-focused than males and that while a woman's attention would be divided equally between the design and the effect it had on the client (8), men would be focused on perfecting an image. A further designer thought that females thought through issues more than males did (9) while another designer considered that men tended to express their ideas as if they were set in concrete, with more relativistic, less final, realizing that their solution was one of a number of possibilities. 'Females came across as less confident and more honest and males cannot see the strength in that' (9)

This links with the views of a designer/teacher at a UK university who commented that:

> 'boys will bluster ahead and not seek any advice. Girls are more tentative and need more reassurance than males although they have the ability to concentrate and dissociate themselves from a subject' (19).

Discussion

As we have seen, no fewer than 40 people were interviewed and of these, 29 (73 per cent) considered that there were indeed differences between the designs produced by males and females. Only one thought that there were no differences while a further 10 (25 per cent of the sample) either had no views or were undecided. Moreover, in the course of the interviews, 29 people (73 per cent) commented on differences in the way that males and females approached design tasks, and as we have seen, many of the differences were thought to impact on the finished design (Moss 1999).

A summary of these differences is provided in Table 6.1, with the number of people identifying specific differences shown in brackets and an asterisk pointing to a parallel with one of the earlier studies examined in Chapter 4.

The reader will in fact notice a large number of asterisks and one of the more interesting points to emerge from the interviews is the extent to which the interviewees' views reflect the findings of the earlier studies investigated in Chapter 4. Table 6.2 shows the studies backing up the asterisked comments.

What can we conclude from this? Almost three quarters of the interviewees argued for differences between the designs of males and females and athough it is not possible to generalize from this small and unrepresentative sample, it is striking that such a large proportion consider there to be differences between male and female designs. Interviewees also commented on differences between men's and women's preferences, and these comments are reported later on in this chapter.

In order to take this study further and gather quantitative data on whether male and female designs do indeed differ, a series of experiments was conducted and this is described in the next section.

Table 6.1 Interviewees' views as to differences between male and female designs

	Attributes of male artifacts (the number of interviewees making comment referred to in brackets)	**Attributes of female artifacts (the number of interviewees making comment referred to in brackets)**
Differences between male and female designs	**Form and colour:** Hard surfaces (2) Large size (4) Straight lines and verticality (6)* Functional and technical orientation (7) Three-dimensionality and clarity (2) Male use of colour is different from females' (8) Subject matter: Draw males (1)* Draw caricatures (1)* Interested in sports, beer and cars (1)* Interested in inanimate subjects (1)* Interested in dead matter (1)*	**Form and colour:** Soft surfaces (3) Smaller pieces (3) Round, organic and fluent shapes (3)* Aesthetic and non-functional orientation (3)* Less emphasis on three-dimensionality and clarity of line (2)* Interest in detail (5) Pastel colours (2) Subject matter: Draw females (1)* Use humour in a more subtle way (1)* Interested in plant life, flowers and fruit (3)*
Differences between male and female design processes	Logical approach (4) Less focused on brief and customer than females (5) More confident than females (3)	Intuitive approach (5) More practical (1) More focused on the brief and the customer than males (7) Less confident than males (3)
Differences between male and female preferences	Like larger objects (1) Like aggressive lines (1) Like things for their functional attributes (1) Like gadgetry (2)	Like smaller objects (1) Like pattern and colour (2) Like things for their aesthetic attributes (1)

Quantitative Empirical Work

As we noted above, it is fairly standard practice in social sciences to begin a new project with interviews in order to establish preliminary views on the topic. In the case of gender and design, the first interviews revealed widespread support for the view that males and females produced designs that differed in terms of colour, shape and subject matter. This provided the confidence to move to a second,

Table 6.2 Interviewees' perception as to features that distinguish male from female designs and the studies which agree on these points

Interviewees' perception of male design characteristics and the studies which agree on these points	Interviewees' perception of female design characteristics and the studies which agree on these points
Straight lines and verticality: cf (i) Alschuler and Hattwick and (ii) Fisher	Round, organic and fluid shapes: cf (i) Alschuler and Hattwick (ii) Fisher (iii) Erikson (iv) Lippard (v) Majewski and (vi) Chicago
Three-dimensionality and clarity: (i) Kerschensteiner (ii) McCarty and (iii) Lippard	Less emphasis on three-dimensionality and clarity: (i) Kerschensteiner (ii) McCarty and (iii) Lippard
Draw males: (i) Hurlock (ii) Majewski	Draw females: (i) Gesell (ii) Hurlock, Lark-Horovitz and (iii) Majewski
Draw caricatures: (i) Hurlock	Different form of humour: (i) Hurlock
Interested in cars: (i) Franck and Rosen and (ii) Lark-Horovitz	Interested in plant life and flowers: (i) Ballard and (ii) Franck and Rosen
Interested in inanimate/dead subjects: (i) McNiff	

quantitative phase which would attempt to discover, through detailed analysis of male and female designs, whether these differences were supported by empirical research. Obviously, some carefully devised tests were called for (Moss 1995).

The first methodological questions related to whether the focus should be on the designs of children, adults or both and, as we say earlier, it is normal in work on gender differences to make inferences about adult behaviour from evidence relating to children as well as adults. For example, sex difference research in the 1970s by Corinne Hutt (1972) of the Department of Psychology at Reading University regularly tracked childhood behaviours through to adulthood and the authors of a classic book on sex differences, Eleanor Maccoby (one time Chair of Psychology at Stanford University) and fellow academic Carol Jacklin (1974) do the same. For example, writing about aggressive behaviour, they conclude that males appear as the more aggressive sex right across the age spectrum and John Archer and Barbara Lloyd (2002) follow a similar approach in their work on sex differences.

In terms of understanding the thread linking childhood and adult behaviour, Doreen Kimura (1992), Professor at Simon Fraser University in Western Canada writes that:

> 'The bulk of the evidence suggests ... that the effect of sex hormones on brain organization occur so early in life that from the start the environment is acting on differently wired brains in girls and boys.'
>
> (ibid. 81)

Since it appears to be the norm in studies of sex difference to focus on children's as well as adult's behaviour, it makes sense in any new study of sex differences to explore the subject in relation to children as well as adults. In the context of designs, this means comparing the designs of boys and girls as well as those of men and women.

Another important issue concerns the level at which results would be deemed to be statistically significant with the level of $p<0.05$ taken as the yardstick by which differences or relationships are counted as significant or not and the level at which results qualify for publication. As a consequence, results at the $p<0.1$ level will not be taken as significant while those at the $p<0.01$ level will be taken as highly significant. and the level that results should reach according to Hugh Coolican, Principal Lecturer in Psychology at Coventry University, 'if we are about to challenge a well-established theory or research finding by publishing results which contradict it (Coolican 2004, 249–250). In his words, this level of significance 'gives researchers greater confidence in rejecting the null hypothesis' (ibid. 250).

With the methodological discussions out of the way, the next step was to find suitable samples of design so that the male work could be compared with the female.

Sampling and Comparison of the Adult Work

In terms of collecting suitable samples for analysis, these need to be produced by Foundation course students (that is, students in the pre-degree year when they are sampling different disciplines), to be produced by equal proportions of men and women, and to emerge from a single project brief. Eventually, after searching for a while for suitable samples, there was a shortlist of two samples of adult work, each of the 12 designs contained six produced by men and six by women. The first sample was from a Graphics project to design a luxury chocolate box, and the second from a Product Design project to design a tomb and once they were photographed it was time to compare them.

Comparing them involved rating them against different criteria, and the first task involved eliciting the criteria according to which the designs should be rated. Of course, another option was to impose the criteria myself since there have been some classic experiments in which the researcher has created the criteria themselves, but this approach runs the risk of using criteria that reflect the biases of the researcher. In order to eliminate this danger and ensure that the designs were rated against valid criteria, third parties were involved in the identification of the criteria and a method based on the 'repertory grid exercise' of Dr George Kelly (1955) was used to elicit the criteria. Readers not interested in the methodological details may like to fast-forward to the results on the next page.

A word about the creator of the repertory grid exercise. Dr George Kelly was a psychologist practising in America during the 1930s depression and after counselling a large number of people from the poor farming area of Kansas, he realized that what really made a difference to his clients was having an explanation for their difficulties. As Dr George Boeree puts it:

> 'What mattered was that the "chaos" of their lives developed some order. And he discovered that, while just about any order and understanding that came from an authority was accepted gladly, order and understanding that came out of their own lives, their own culture, was even better. Out of these insights, Kelly developed his theory and philosophy which he called "constructive alternativism". The essential idea here is that while there is only one true reality, reality is always experienced from one or another perspective, or alternative construction. I have a construction, you have one, and a person on the other side of the planet has one.'
>
> (Boeree)

In the course of offering feedback to clients, Dr Kelly created a system for mapping the 'constructs' people use in their daily lives and this typically involved asking people to think of three people or objects and consider the way in which two of these differed from the third. If, for example, he asked Joan to think of three people, and she described the feature that distinguished person A from persons B and C as being the fact that they have high status, one could infer that Joan actively uses status as a construct. While if she highlighted wealth as a distinguishing feature, then one could fairly assume that financial status was a construct that she applied to different situations.

The system that Kelly developed for formalizing the collection of constructs across a number of people is one known as the 'repertory grid', a useful method for teasing out the features or constructs that people apply to distinguish people or objects. It is therefore also an appropriate method with which to tease out the constructs that people use to distinguish one design from another and, as such, could subsequently be used in rating exercises to compare the features in the male and female designs.

In the tried and tested manner, I used Psychology students to elicit the constructs and aimed to recruit 14 students, since this was the standard number used in other repertory grid experiments. The students were told quite simply that this was a study to determine the features that played a part in people's design preferences, and each was asked to volunteer an hour and a half of their time. All had completed at least one year of an undergraduate Psychology degree course, with some postgraduate students amongst them, and there was an even spread of men and women.

There has been some discussion on the effect on experiments of using Psychology students and Hugh Coolican (2004, 35) quotes research showing that 75 per cent of British and American psychological research studies are conducted on students, and that the usage is at least 50 per cent in the UK. In the experiments discussed here, the Psychology students were used to identify the features that distinguished one design from another, and then, at a later stage, to rate the designs against these features. Since psychology students are frequently engaged in experiments and need, themselves, to attract other students to take part as subjects, they are likely to be more willing to participate than students for whom conducting experiments is not the norm and moreover, since these are objective exercises, requiring no special expertise, the Psychology students are not only likely to be up to the task, but likely to carry out the required tasks with greater efficiency than other groups, given their greater experience in taking part in experiments. They would certainly have the advantage over design students of looking less critically than they might at a set of designs.

In the repertory grid exercise, the volunteers looked at predetermined sets of three designs and noted ways in which two of the designs looked similar but thereby different from the third. The criteria or 'constructs' that they volunteered in the course of doing this were then recorded and it is worth noting that the sets of designs shown to the students were such that every design was used on an equal number of occasions. Once all the answers were obtained, it was possible to ascertain the nine or ten features (or 'constructs') that occurred with the greatest regularity and construct rating scales around these with descriptions of the qualities which typified designs at the extremes (see Table 6.3).

Comparision of the male and female designs

The volunteers rated all the designs against each of the nine constructs, producing an objective evaluation of the features contained in the designs. When a statistical analysis was performed on the ratings (for the technically minded, the technique used was the repeated-measures analysis of variance), the results showed highly significant differences between the ratings ascribed to the male and female-produced designs ($F = 54.45$, dfs = 8,112, $p = <0.00$). The profiles of mean results across each of the nine constructs are plotted on the graph in Figure 6.1.

What we can see in the graph is the profile of the male and female designs and this shows how the female designs are judged to be more colourful, rounded and less technical than those of the males. What is more, these differences between the male and female work are in statistical terms highly significant (being at the $p = <0.001$ level), meaning that the differences are extremely unlikely to have occurred by chance alone (Moss 1995).

Table 6.3 The rating scales used

The nine rating scales used	The quality denoted by a score of 7	The quality denoted by a score of 1
1	Bright and colourful; preponderance of one or more bright colours	Dark and not colourful
2	Linear that is, predominance of straight lines or angles or geometrical shapes	Not linear that is, predominance of round, circular, lines
3	Technical that is, with technical complexity and technical detail	Not technical that is, without technical complexity and technical detail
4	Representative that is, representational and not abstract	Not representative that is, not representational and abstract
5	Futuristic that is, looks like something from the future	Not futuristic that is, looks like something that already exists
6	Appealing that is, whether the beholder liked it on first showing	Not appealing
7	Professional that is, whether the work looks that of a professional	Not professional that is, not looking like the work of a professional
8	Functional that is, whether the design fulfils its brief	Not functional that is, whether the design fails to fulfil its brief
9	Interesting that is, the design looks interesting	Not interesting that is, the design does not look interesting

Analysis of subject matter

A separate set of design samples was selected in order to study the subject matter chosen by male and female design students and just as in the earlier experiment, the students were at Foundation level, in other words studying at pre-degree level. Students had been asked to design a logo for one of three notional companies, the first of which was a theatrical agency named 'Top Banana', the second, a restaurant known as the 'Huntsman Restaurant' and the third, a sole trader design company. These themes had inspired the students to produce a total of 28 designs (both completed and partially completed) were available for analysis, 17 designed by male students and 11 by females and the distribution of the three company themes amongst the male and female students is shown in Table 6.4.

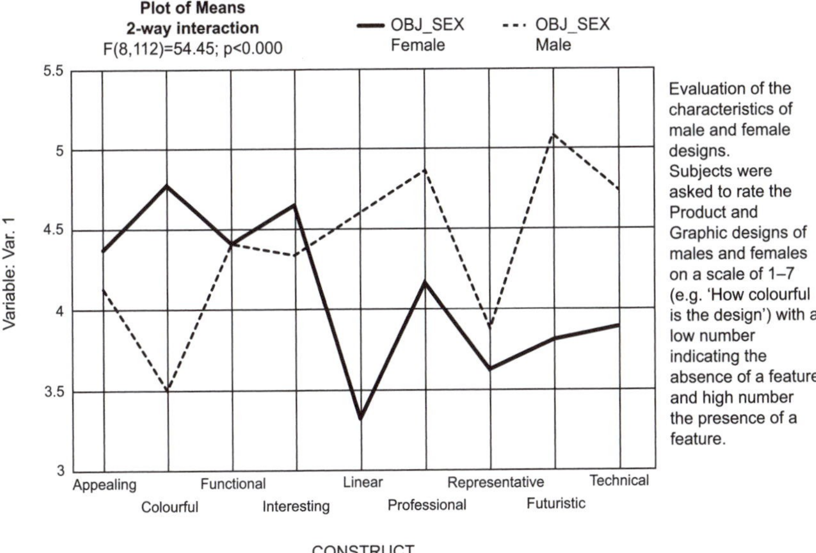

Figure 6.1 Ratings of the characteristics of male and female designs

Table 6.4 Logo themes selected by students

Subject matter used	**Male designs (N=17)** **No. as % of M designs**		**Female designs (N=11)** **No. as % of F designs**	
Own company	7	41	3	27
Top Banana	3	18	7	64
Huntsman Restaurant	7	41	1	9

Looking at the themes used by the male and female students, the greater use of the 'Top Banana' theme by women is noticeable, as is also the greater use of the 'Huntsman Restaurant' theme by men. In fact, conducting a statistical test (the chi-square test for two independent samples) confirmed that the selection of themes by males and females differed significantly (at the p = <0.05 level chi-square = 6.2, df = 2) suggesting that a person's sex is a powerful factor in thematic choices (Moss 1995).

Moreover, the fact that women were more drawn to depicting plant life and men to depicting violence may be seen as corroborating some of the earlier findings on boys' and girls' drawings. In particular, these findings echo McNiff's (1982) findings regarding male and female inverse preferences for themes of plant life and violence and they also parallel Ballard (1912) and Franck and Rosen's (1949) findings as to females' greater preference for themes related to plant life and fruit.

Graphic design: business cards

In the course of examining student work and comparing male and female versions of the same object, I regularly set aside time to attend graduates' design shows. These are cornucopia of design creativity with everything from graphic, product and furniture design to textiles, illustration and ceramics. At one of these shows, I picked up all the student business cards available and afterwards set about comparing the male and female cards. After all, the students had all been facing the same pressures, were all at the same stages in their design careers and all looking to attract clients. So, this sample was tantamount to a design project on a big scale.

When I returned to my office, I counted up the cards and found I had a total of 227, 144 by females and 83 by males and all produced by design students who had specialized in either graphic, product, furniture or textile design. A print shop had said that the standard size for business cards was 85–90mm × 50–55mm and that the standard colour was white. So an important research question was whether there was any noticeable difference in the extent to which the male- and female-produced cards used the standard size and colour. It is worth noting that since there was nothing subjective about the process, I conducted all the measurements myself and did them twice in order to guarantee their accuracy.

What emerged was very interesting indeed. After obtaining the crude scores, a statistical test (the chi-square test) revealed significant differences (at the $p < 0.01$ level), with men more likely than women to adopt the standard sizes and more likely to adopt the standard colour, namely white.

On further inspection, it was apparent that some cards had been produced using the standard length (85–90mm) but not the standard height (50–55mm), a tendency which served to emphasize the square character of the card rather than its rectangularity. The females were more likely than the males to do this, and also more likely to produce round-shaped cards. Performing a chi-square test on this and the other three factors (use of standard size, white card, non-standard dimensions) produced a significant result of $p < 0.001$. In statistical terms, this result was highly significant, showing that the differences between the male- and female-produced cards were most unlikely to have been the effect of chance.

The findings, which I wrote up later in a journal article co-authored by Andrew Colman, Professor of Psychology at Leicester University (Moss and Colman 2001), show that when female designers make business cards they are more likely than their male counterparts to choose colours other than white and are more likely to choose larger sizes, and sizes which are squarer in shape. Interestingly, the female preference for a non-white colour is paralleled by interviewees' comments about females' greater adventurousness with colour (interviewees 3, 24 and 40), while the use of non-standard sizes may be paralleled by the female tendency discussed by some interviewees, to put aesthetics above practical considerations and form above function (see comments of interviewees 13, 14, 17 and 18).

Children's designs

It was now time to turn to children's designs (Moss 1996b). Although there had been a number of studies comparing the *drawings* and *paintings* of children, none had actually compared the *designs* that they produced and so it was fortuitous that I came across a sample of children's designs when visiting a national food exhibition in Birmingham. The New World Cookers stand had a cooker unlike any I had ever seen before, painted in a large number of colours. I asked a few questions and discovered that a national colouring competition had produced a winner whose design had been translated into a life-size cooker.

The competition had been open to children up to the age of 11 and was run in a total of 11 local newspapers, producing 397 entries and I wrote to New World Cookers to ask whether it might be possible to look at the entries since the sample would provide an opportunity to discover whether there were similarities or differences in the way that boys and girls coloured in the outline of a cooker. The company, fortunately, allowed access to as many entries as I wanted and in order to reduce the experiment to manageable proportions, I sought information on the number of entries received by region and where each region was concerned sought information on the number of entries received by sex.

The figures revealed regional disparities in the number of entries received from boys and girls so I asked for the entries from the three newspapers with the smallest number of disparities. These were the entries from the *Tonbridge Wells Courier*, the *Bucks Advertiser* and the *St Albans Herald* and between them, there were no fewer than 204 entries, 90 from boys and 114 from girls.

The children had been asked to colour in a cooker whose shape was given, so the only area in which the children had freedom to express themselves was with regard to colour. Looking at the cooker, it became apparent that there were six ways in which colour could be applied:

1. The square shape at the bottom of the oven could be coloured in with a single colour or coloured in using more than one colour.
2. The handle of the cooker could be coloured in with the same colour as the surround or coloured in with a different colour.
3. The switches could be coloured in with a single colour or coloured in using more than one colour.
4. The 'New World' logo could be coloured in with a single colour or coloured in using more than one colour.
5. The switches at the bottom of the cooker could be coloured in with the same colour as the surround or coloured in with a different colour from the surround.

6. A few or a great number of separate colouring pens/pencils could be used per cooker.

The analysis as to the way in which colour was used was an entirely objective process so I performed it myself twice, in fact in order to be sure that there were no errors in my assessments. After a couple of hours, the results were ready and sorted by age. You can see the distribution of designs by age in Table 6.5 with a comparison of the way the cookers were coloured in by the boys and girls in Table 6.6. The features contained in the 204 entries are shown in Table 6.6 and the analysis in Table 6.6 shows that the girls are less likely than the boys to emphasize the square shape surrounding the oven and, at the same time, more likely to use separate colours for the switches, as well as separate colours for the handle and surround. These differences are significant at the $p = < 0.03$ level, a level indicative of statistical significance. In terms of the overall number of colours used per picture, there were, by contrast, no differences between the boys' and the girls' use of colours and nor were there significant differences in the extent to which more than one colour was used for the logo or for colouring the switch at the bottom of the cooker.

These findings show that three of the five elements investigated produce statistically significant differences in the way boys and girls use colour and if the design sample I had chanced upon is representative of that of other children of this age group, then this experiment may point to the fact that the design style of boys and girls differs from an early age.

Of course, willingness to accept this conclusion depends on accepting that the differences revealed by the analysis reveal the intuitive responses of boys and girls. This is not something that is universally accepted. After presenting my results at a sociology conference, several people sought to explain the results with reference to the notion that girls are taught to colour in a different way from boys. My response was that one could not comment categorically on whether girls were taught a different colouring-in technique from boys, but it was doubtful if this was the case (I have known many children and they were not taught colouring techniques at school). When later, I overheard someone in the corridor asking 'Who allowed *her* into the conference?' I was reminded of the fact that, explaining gender differences through anything other than societal influences is heresy in certain settings.

Table 6.5 The number of submissions by age and sex

	Age 4	**Age 5**	**Age 6**	**Age 7**	**Age 8**	**Age 9**	**Age 10**	**Age 11**	**Age 12**
Female	8	27	28	16	14	14	8	1	–
Male	12	25	14	11	12	9	4	11	–

Table 6.6 Number and percentage of boys and girls using certain features in the colouration of cookers

Feature	Male no	Male %	Female no	Female %	Significance (using a chi-square test)
Square shape at bottom coloured with a single colour	46	51	40	37	Chi-square = 5.30 df = 1 p = <0.03*
Handle coloured in a different colour from surround	30	33	62	54	Chi-square = 9.00 df = 1 p = <0.01**
Knobs coloured in using separate colours	36	40	64	56	Chi-square = 5.24 df = 1 p = <0.03*
'New World' logo coloured in more than one colour	10	11	23	20	Chi-square = 3.05 df = 1 p = <0.12 (not significant)
Switches at the bottom of the cooker coloured in differently from the surround	39	43	51	45	Chi-square = 0.04 df = 1 p = <0.95 (Not significant)
Average number of separate colours used per cooker		6.2 colours per cooker		6.2 colours per cooker	No difference

*p <0.05 **p <0.01

Moreover, willingness to accept that the sample offers insights into the different colouring habits of boys and girls relies on accepting the representative nature of the sample and, although the sample came from a national colouring competition and consisted of large numbers, some might still cast doubt on the representativeness of the sample.

The question of local newspaper readership is clearly an important one and a lengthy conversation with a researcher in the marketing department of a large regional newspaper group revealed that a variety of local newspaper titles are distributed free to as many as 50 per cent of households across the region and since the region is home to people from a variety of socio-economic backgrounds, the papers are distributed to a range of socio-economic groups. This shows that, in this large region and probably others too, the papers are far from the exclusive preserve any particular socio-economic groups.

Market research data aside, one might question whether it is likely that socio-economic factors such as class would explain the differences in the way boys and girls colour in cookers, particularly as the earlier research comparing the drawings and paintings of males and females produces results which are pretty consistent with the results of this cookers study. For example, the boys' tendency to emphasize the square shape of the cooker door finds an echo in the tendency, for males to paint straight and angular shapes (several researchers including Alschuler and Hattwick (1969), Fisher (1979), Franck and Rosen (1949), as well as myself in other research have made this observation). Likewise, the girls' tendency to use more than one colour for the switches, and to use a different colour for the handle from that used in the surrounding area, mirrors the tendency noted by Alschuler and Hattwick (1969) as well as myself (working singly and with Dr Rod Gunn) for girls to have a more intense use of colour than boys.

Both sets of findings, moreover, are in line with differences referred to spontaneously by the interviewees we encountered earlier in this chapter. Thus the girls' tendency to colour the switches in different colours is paralleled by interviewees' comments concerning females' greater adventurousness with colour (respondent 21), different use of colour (6, 21, 23 and 26) and greater interest in detail (see interviews 9 and 12, for example).

Conclusions and Practical Lessons: Male and Female Design Production Aesthetics

We have surveyed a range of designs produced by adults and children and across four separate samples have found statistically significant differences in use of colour, shape and theme between the male and female designs, with chi-square significance test results in the order of $p = <0.01$ or $p = <0.001$. Interestingly, these differences are in line with differences highlighted in earlier research on drawings and paintings as well as with the findings from interviews conducted with people working in related fields. Where use of thematic material is concerned, it was found that there were also differences in students' choice of thematic material.

We can see that there is a great deal of research to back up the notion of differences between the designs of males and females and this raises important questions about the selection of designers and whether the 'male production aesthetic' can best be produced by men, and the 'female production aesthetic' by women. Are the skills of designing like a man or woman teachable, or are they fixed and unchanging? We do not have answers to these questions yet but we hope that some of the data presented here will encourage others to conduct investigations that will help answer these questions.

So much for the type of designs that men and women produce. Let us move on now to consider the type of designs that they are likely to prefer as observers.

We saw earlier that people are drawn to drawings and paintings produced by people with similar personalities to their own, so could there be a similar effect for gender? in other words, are men likely to prefer the sort of designs that men produce (that is, displaying the male production aesthetic) and are women likely to prefer the type of designs that women produce (that is, displaying the female production aesthetic)? We will turn to these questions in the next section.

Design Preferences: The Impact of Gender

What do people like in a design or piece of advertising? How is this influenced by gender? In this section, we will also ask whether people are similar in their aesthetic choices and if they are not, whether there are variables that can help us predict people's likely responses. To kick off, we will return to the interviewees we met in the last chapter.

Interviews

In the course of interviewing the 40 people connected with design or marketing and in response to the question as to whether male and female designs are different, seven respondents commented on differences between male and female design preferences. Their views are outlined below and, as before, individual interviewees are referred to by number.

Choice of work One interviewee (39) talked about the time she had selected paintings for an exhibition, and how, reflecting on the process, she realized that 90 per cent of the works she had preferred (and therefore selected for the exhibition) were produced by women. She emphasized that she had only realized that she was drawn to works by other women after completing the selection process.

Hard vs. soft surfaces One person commented that men seemed to prefer strong, sturdy packs to soft, round shapes (25) while girls seemed to like soft, delicate surfaces (26). An expert on children's preferences found that the men's preferences applied to boys as well with both liking objects which are sturdy and robust (26).

Functionality and machine aesthetic One designer commented that men tended to like 'machine-looking' objects since they tended to be more techno- and gadget-orientated than women (4 and 5). A similar comment was made by an interior designer highlighted the fact that 'a man will define his preferences in relation to the functionality of a solution whereas women will be more likely to define them in relation to aesthetic considerations' (13). Others expressed similar views, with a teacher of design saying that 'males tend to like task-based objects, in other words objects with a machine quality, for example a motor car' (18).

Colour According to one designer, women are more drawn to colour than men (3), an opinion corroborated by artists and critics over centuries, according to a Fine Art historian (24). A similar view was voiced by a market research expert who said that men feel happiest when responding to 'strong, deep, dark colours' (25) and women are not put off by light colours. According to this respondent, women are likely to respond favourably to (warm) pastel shades (25 and 26) while a market researcher, a specialist in children's preferences, said that girls had 'a very strong preference for pink. By contrast, boys liked vivid colours and black' (26).

Detail One designer commented on women's preference for pattern, another on women's preference for 'pattern, texture, embellishments and mixing prints' (3), while the market research expert specializing in children's preferences found that girls 'had a strong preference for frills' (26). Where garden design was concerned, a female garden designer commented on the fact that in her experience women gardeners tended to like prefer introducing variety into the design of borders, while men tended to prefer using single blocks of colour (14). Where other design was concerned, men tended 'not to like fuss or clutter' (4) and, as one market researcher remarked, 'males respond more enthusiastically (than women) to strong, bold, clean, direct lines' (25).

Straight lines vs. circular shapes Two people commented on women's preference for soft, feminine, hemispherical-shaped lines rather than straighter forms (25) and one expert in children's preferences said that she thought boys preferred 'angular, hard lines' (26).

Subject matter Where subject matter was concerned, one interviewee thought that products related to sports, beer and cars had particular appeal for men (12).

A summary of these differences regarding men's and women's preferences are provided in Table 6.7.

Although relatively few interviewees commented on male and female design preferences, those that did revealed something rather interesting. For example, if the comments they made on preferences are compared with those they made on male and female designs you will notice a correlation between the productions and preferences attributed to males and those attributed to females. This correlation suggests that people's preferences follow a 'like attracts like' tendency, rather than an 'opposites attract' one, just as we found to be the case when looking at preferences for drawings and paintings. Of course, only experimental work can establish with any certainty whether there are particular patterns to people's preferences so details of new empirical work follows.

Table 6.7 Interviewees' views as to differences between male and female designs

Male preferences	Female preferences
Hard surfaces Machine aesthetic Functional objects	Soft surfaces
Dark colours	Bright colours
Clear surfaces	Light, pastel colours
Straight, angular lines	Surfaces with pattern or detail
Sports, beer and cars	Rounded lines

Experiments on Design Preferences

This section looks at men's and women's reactions to the designs of adults and children across a series of three experiments, referred to here as 'preference tests'. As noted earlier, there had been very little research on this topic and so much of what follows describes experiments I conducted between 1995–2009.

Experiment 1: charting design preferences

The first experiment (Moss 1995) set out to chart men's and women's reactions to design samples produced by male and female design students and was in two phases. The first phase involved the selection of design stimuli and testing as to whether these were of a homogenous standard; and the second phase involved using the samples as stimuli in preference tests. Details of both these phases follows and if it is the results that you are primarily interested in. then you can fast forward to p. 126 and avoid the details of these two phases.

Phase 1: selecting and testing the design samples for quality Three samples of design work were chosen as the basis for preference tests, with each sample consisting of 12 designs, six by men and six by women (all photographed). The samples used were all the work of Foundation course students, and two of the samples had been used in the earlier experiment in which the designs were rated against constructs emerging from the repertory grid exercise. If you have read about this experiment, you will remember that this rating exercise demonstrated that the samples of male- and female-produced designs differed in statistically significant ways, and although a similar analysis had not been carried out on the third sample (a sample of packaging designs), a cursory glance revealed that the male and female designs differed in similar ways to the other two samples. For example, the male designs in this third sample contained more straight lines and angles than the female ones, contained more standard typography and also showed greater three-dimensionality than the female designs.

Before using the samples in tests of people's preferences, it was important to establish whether the male and female designs in each of the three samples were of similar quality. If they were not, then people's preferences could relate to the quality of the designs rather than to features within them. If, on the other hand, the designs were all of similar quality, then an expression of interest in a particular design would relate to something other than to differences in the quality of the designs.

How to establish the relative quality of the different designs? Two lecturers in an Art and Design Faculty were asked to rate each of the designs on a scale of one to ten, with the key criterion being how well the student had interpreted the design brief. A score of one indicated that the brief was 'inadequately interpreted' while a score of ten indicated that it was 'as well interpreted as could be expected'. The collated scores achieved for the male and female designs were then compared in order to compare the quality of the two samples. The results were as follows:

1. Sample of graphic designs.
   The mean of the ratings of the two judges for the male designs was 6.6, while that for the female designs was 7.4 and a one-way Manova (with the two dependent variables being the ratings from the two raters and the between-groups factor being sex) revealed that the main effect for sex was not significant (Wilks-Lambda = 0.658, df = 2,9, p = 0.152). This shows that the mean quality rating of the male designs was not significantly different from that of the female ones.

2. Sample of product designs
   The mean of the ratings of the two judges for the male designs was 6.5 and the mean of their ratings for the female designs was 5.33. A one-way Manova was carried out (with the two dependent variables being the ratings from the two raters and the between-groups factor being sex) and the result showed that there was no main effect for sex (Wilks-Lambda = 0.587, df = 2,9, p = 0.091) indicating, once again, that the mean quality rating for the male designs was not significantly different from that of the female designs.

3. Sample of packaging designs
   The mean of the ratings of the two judges for the male designs was 6.5 and the mean of their ratings for the female designs was 5.83. A one-way Manova was carried out (with the two dependent variables being the ratings from the two raters and the between-groups factor being sex) and the result showed that there was no main effect for sex (Wilks-Lambda = 0.937, df = 2,9, p = 0.745) indicating that the mean quality rating for the male designs was not significantly different from that for the female designs.

We can see that the results show that the quality of the male- and female-produced designs was similar across the three samples and it follows that any preferences that people express for one design over another is likely to relate to factors inherent in the design rather than factors relating to its quality.

In terms of the subjects used for the preference tests, these consisted of both students and staff in the library and Psychology Department of a British university. Interestingly, the library users spanned a range of academic disciplines, age groups and nationalities so that the samples could not be said to be made up of UK nationals alone. The number of subjects (referred to here as 'judges') used in the preference tests was as follows:

- Graphic designs preference tests: 39 male and 35 female judges.
- Product designs preference tests: 39 male and 35 female judges.
- Packaging designs preference tests: 28 male and 28 female judges.

Phase 2: conducting preference tests The tests were carried out in three stages. In the first, the 12 graphic design samples were laid out on a table in a preset order (this order ensured that the male and female designs were intermingled) and the subjects were asked to look at these and identify their three preferred designs. The number three was chosen on the basis that, if both male- and female-produced designs were selected, there would be a majority of either male- or female-produced designs. A note was taken of the three designs selected and then the whole exercise was repeated for the other two samples of design (the product and packaging samples).

A brief word on how the results were classified. Judges were classed as showing 'same-sex preference' if two or more of the designs they chose were by designers of their own sex and showing 'opposite-sex preference' if two or more of the designs they chose were by designers of the opposite sex. In the statistical analysis that was subsequently carried out, data were tested against the Null Hypothesis that judges are equally likely to show same-sex preference or opposite-sex preference using the chi-squared one-sample test.

Results Taking the preferences of all the judges together (39 male and 35 female judges of graphic and product designs, and 28 male and 28 female judges of packaging designs), the preferences are shown in Table 6.8.

As you can see, the tendency for judges to show an 'own sex preference' across all three samples of designs, that is, to prefer designs produced by people of their own gender is significant at the 0.001 level, a level that in statistical terms, is highly significant. In terms of reactions to individual samples, those relating to the product design and packaging samples are statistically significant but not those relating to graphic design. This may have something to do with the fact that the graphic design sample, unlike the other two, was not homogenous in its subject matter since the students who produced these designs had a choice of three themes on which to base a logo.

Table 6.9 presents the results of subjects' reactions to the product design samples.

Table 6.8 Male and female reactions to all three samples

Same-sex preference		Opposite sex preference		Total number of selection episodes (i.e. selection of 3 out of 12 designs)
Observed	**Expected under Null Hypothesis**	**Observed**	**Expected under Null Hypothesis**	
128	102	76	102	204

Chi-square = 13.25 with one degree of freedom, p <0.001 that is, the Null Hypothesis can be rejected with 99.9 per cent confidence

Table 6.9 Male and female preferences for the product design samples

Same-sex preference		Opposite sex preference		Total number of selection episodes (i.e. selection of 3 out of 12 designs
Observed	**Expected under Null Hypothesis**	**Observed**	**Expected under Null Hypothesis**	
50	37	24	37	74

Chi-square = 9.13 with one degree of freedom, p <0.01

Table 6.10 Male and female preferences for the packaging samples

Same-sex preference		Opposite sex preference		Total number of selection episodes (i.e. selection of 3 out of 12 designs)
Observed	**Expected under Null Hypothesis**	**Observed**	**Expected under Null Hypothesis**	
37	28	19	28	56

Chi-square = 5.78 with one degree of freedom, p <0.05

The results of people's preferences for the packaging designs are shown in Table 6.10.

As we saw earlier, the preferences for the graphic designs (showing logos representing a number of companies) did not show significant tendencies to own-sex preference and this result may reflect the fact that this sample of designs did not display a common theme and this may have confused the judges and made if difficult for them to make a clear choice.

Discussion If you look at the aggregated results for the preference tests across the three design samples, you can see that there is a greater tendency (significant at the p <0.001 level) for preferences to reflect an own-sex preference, in other words, for people to prefer designs produced by people of their own gender, using the production aesthetic associated with that gender. Interestingly, this finding that preferences follow a 'like attracts like' pattern is in line with earlier findings regarding the link between personality and artistic preferences. I therefore decided it was important therefore to run a separate test in order to establish whether similar results would occur with a different sample. This second test is described in the next section.

Experiment 2: Christmas cards

It was approaching Christmas and it seemed appropriate to compare people's reactions to cards produced by men and women (Moss and Colman 2001). As you can imagine, the pool of cards from which to select stimuli was large, so I narrowed down my selection criteria to the following factors:

1. the cards should use the same/similar themes;
2. the name of the artist/designer should be provided/visible through the packaging so that the gender of the painter/designer could be identified;
3. equal numbers of male- and female-produced cards should be selected.

In the end, four cards were selected which satisfied these three criteria with the common theme being Christmas vegetation (three showed a Christmas tree, while the fourth showed an outdoor snow-filled scene). The four cards selected were shown to various groups including librarians in a local reference library, assistants in shops (for example, newsagents and dry cleaners), acquaintances (including their children) and people attending a charity function. The respondents were asked to indicate which of the four cards they preferred, and the preferences of the male and female subjects are shown in Table 6.11.

The results indicate a tendency, once again, for subjects to prefer a design produced by someone of their own sex, and a chi-square performed on the results shows that the results are significantly different at the 0.001 level. This is an extremely high level of significance and suggests (with a 99.9 per cent certainty) that there are significant differences in the reactions of male and female subjects.

Table 6.11 The number of male and female subjects expressing a preference for cards originated by people of their own or opposite sex

	Respondent preferences	
	Female respondents	**Male respondents**
Female-designed	24	7
Male-designed	11	23

There are, of course, questions as to the representativeness of this sample and the extent to which the results can be generalized to a wider population. Relevant to this question is the fact that people in the sample embraced a number of nationalities (English/Scottish, Indian, Turkish, Algerian, German, Italian and American), ages (children and adults) and occupations (shopkeepers, librarians, lawyers, psychologists, business consultants, secretaries, entrepreneurs). The heterogenous nature of this sample makes it considerably more representative of the wider urban population than the many student-only samples used in a large proportion of psychology experiments. There are therefore strong grounds for thinking that this experiment with Christmas cards, like the other preference tests discussed earlier, points to a tendency on the part of men and women, boys and girls, to prefer designs produced by people of their own gender. To this extent, we have further evidence here of what we might term a 'self-selecting' tendency.

Experiment 3: commercial designs

In order to further compare male and female design preferences, I teamed up with marketing specialist Dr Gabor Horvath, to create a design questionnaire (Moss et al. 2007b). It can be difficult to discover the design history of products and whether a single person or team is responsible for a particular piece of graphic or product design, but over a number of years of chasing up the design histories of different items, I had built up a bank of designs which had each been produced by a single designer. Gabor and I selected paired items where the two items in the pair were rated as similar in terms of quality and function but differed only insofar as one was designed by a man and one by a woman. The items in our final shortlist included postcards, chairs, pillow cases, food packaging, drink cans, Christmas cards (two from the previous experiment) and Underground station designs. We set these out in a questionnaire and asked male and female respondents to rate these on a scale of one to ten in terms of their preference for the item.

Naturally, respondents were not told that gender was the focus of this research and that preferences were being examined in relation to the gender of both the respondent and the designer. From a methodological point of view, this would have been unwise since it would have detracted from the neutrality of respondents. Instead, respondents were advised that this was an experiment exploring people's design preferences and that they would be asked their views on a wide range of products. They would be asked, in particular, to indicate which of a series of paired objects they preferred and to score both on a scale of 0–10 (where 0 = 'I hate it' and 10 = 'I like it very much'). They were also asked to indicate what they liked/disliked about each item a new quantitative element to the questions. The respondent group included managers, web developers and creative designers (eight males and four females).

Results Figures 6.2 to 6.7, produced by Dr Gabor Horvath, show the percentages of male and female respondents preferring the product designed by men (column noted as 'male designer') or women (column noted as 'female designer') designers and as you can see, many of the results reveal a preference on the part of respondents for designs originated by people of their own gender. As far as the men are concerned, this is the case with three out of six products (chairs, pillowcases and Christmas cards) while women's preference for own sex-produced items is more consistent with women preferring the female-produced items in five out of six cases. There was only one instance (the case of the children's chairs) where women showed an equal liking for the male- and female-produced items while men had a greater balance of opposite sex designs.

The aggregate responses of the men and women are illustrated in Figure 6.8 and this shows quite clearly that a higher proportion of women (75 per cent) have a greater preference for own-sex produced items than men (60 per cent).

The fact that women are more strongly drawn to female-produced items than men to male-produced items is reinforced by the scores that the men and women allocated to the various items (see Figure 6.9). As you can see, although both men and women assign higher scores to own-sex designs compared to opposite-sex designs, men interestingly ascribe higher scores to female-designed products than the women do to male-designed products and this is further evidence of the fact that, given a choice, men have greater tolerance of the female design aesthetic than women do of the equivalent male aesthetic.

We shall see, when looking at web design in the next chapter, that preference tests conducted with a sample of just under seventy people produced very similar results so although we cannot make claims as to the representativeness of the sample used here, the fact that the results correlate with the preferences of a larger, more representative sample makes the results more worthy of attention. In fact, the two sets of results together have potentially massive implications (as we shall see in Chapter 9) for the world of marketing and design, since notions of 'good design' are frequently anchored in what is, in reality, the male production aesthetic. This male production aesthetic is the default aesthetic across a whole raft of products, on the assumption perhaps that it has mass appeal for men as well as women.

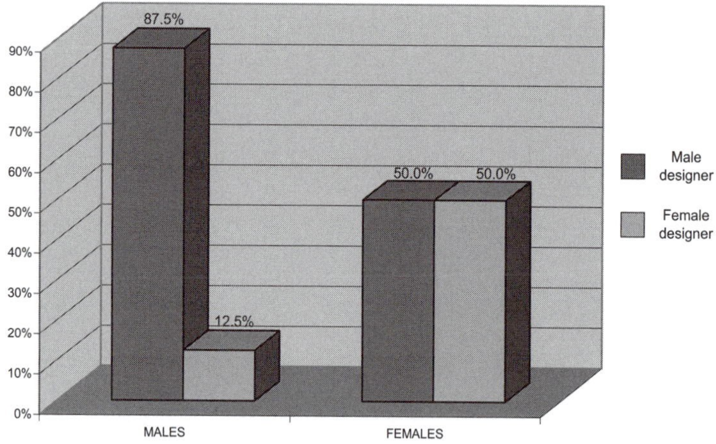

Figure 6.2 Respondents' preferences as between male- and female-designed children's chairs

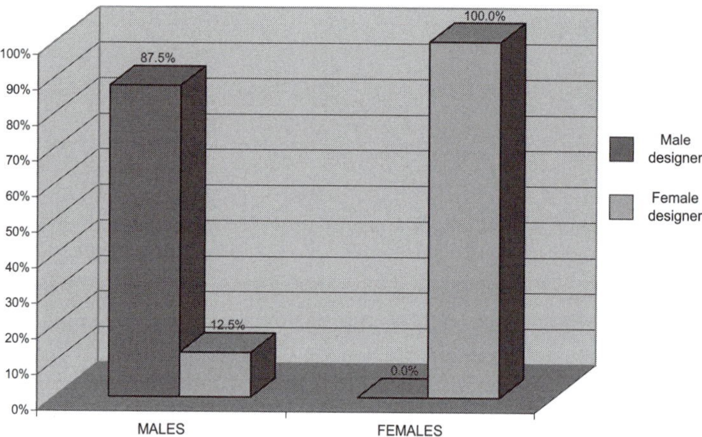

Figure 6.3 Respondents' preferences as between male- and female-designed pillow cases

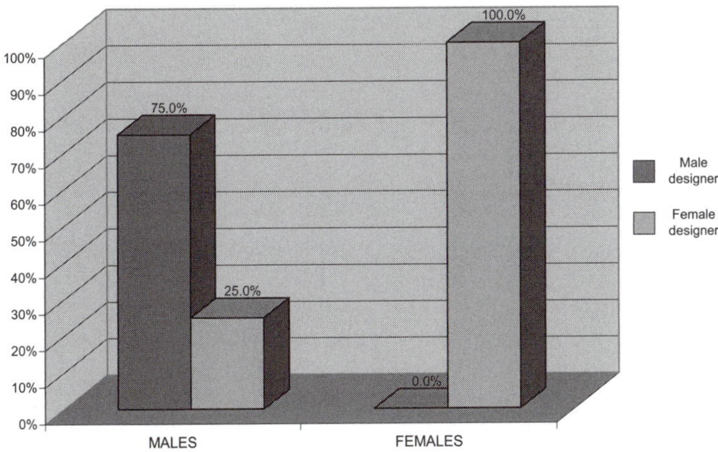

Figure 6.4 Respondents' preferences as between male- and female-designed Christmas cards

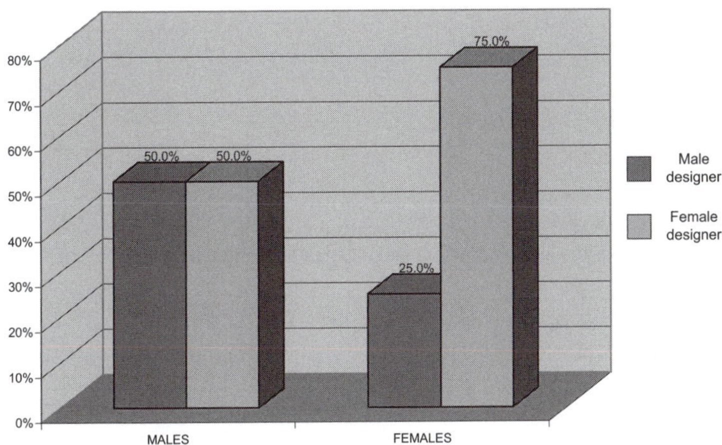

Figure 6.5 Respondents' preferences as between male- and female-designed drink cans

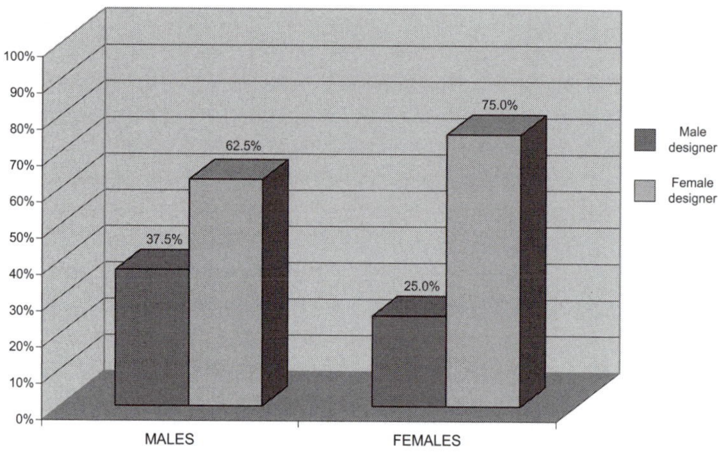

Figure 6.6 Respondents' preferences as between male- and female-designed food packaging

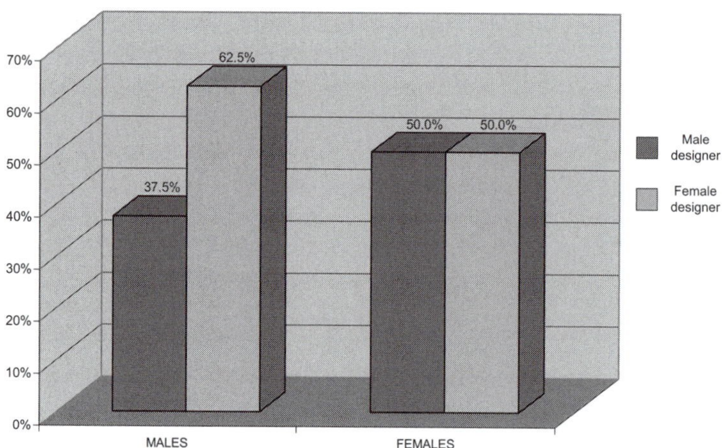

Figure 6.7 Respondents' preferences as between male- and female-designed Underground station designs

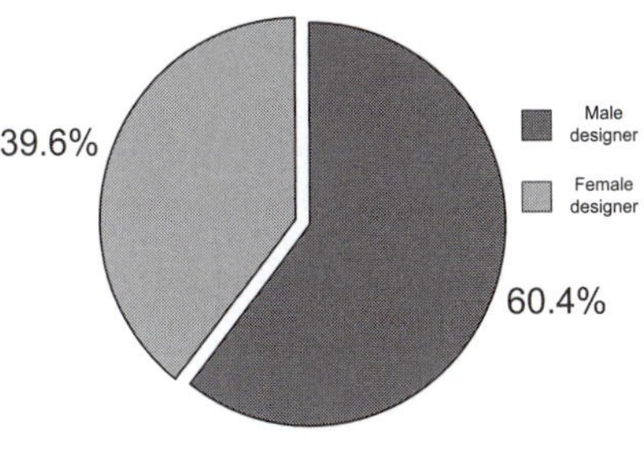

Male respondents

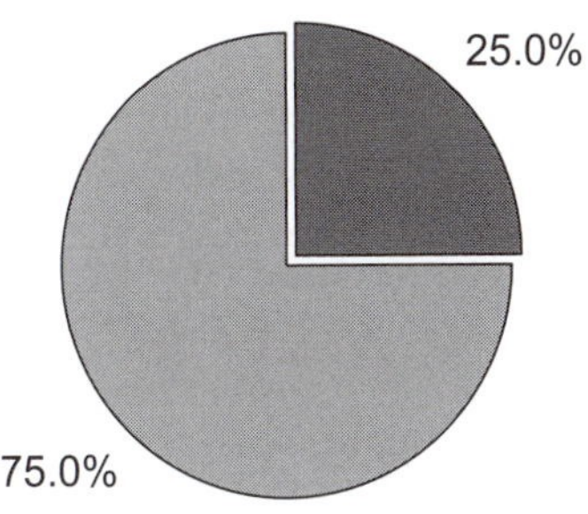

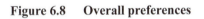

Female respondents

Figure 6.8 Overall preferences

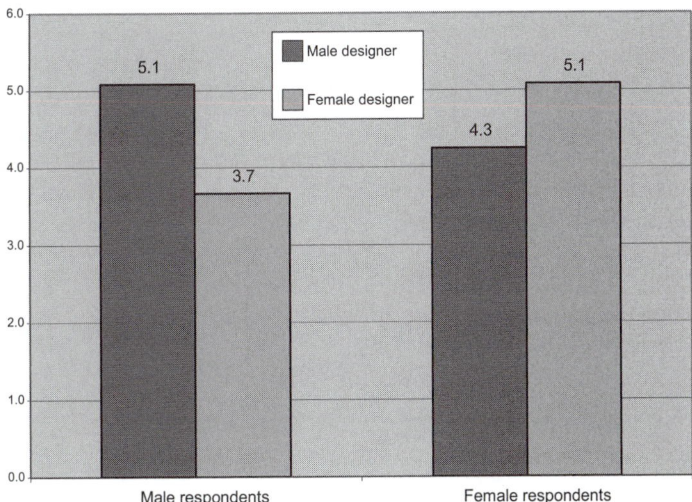

Figure 6.9 Average scores

What the results of these preference tests reveals for the first time, however, is that it might actually make more sense to use the female production aesthetic as the default aesthetic, not only because it is preferred by women (an important consideration given the significance of women as consumers and decision-makers) but because men have a marginally greater preference for it than women have for the male aesthetic.

Before moving away from this experiment it is important to point out that, after collecting people's quantitative responses, we asked respondents *why* they preferred one item over another and Table 6.12 summarizes the factors that were highlighted by the men and the women.

As we can see, the women tended to express a preference for products with detail, bright colours, nice patterns and unconventional (childlike) typography. We can see that women tend not to like the elements that typify the male-produced items (for example, absence of detail, absence of colour, and conventionality) while the male respondents appear to like the bright colours and patterns found in the female-produced designs. Interestingly, these results seem to corroborate what we said earlier concerning men and women's asymmetric preferences for own-sex designs.

Table 6.12 Summary of constructs used by men and women

	Male respondents	**Female respondents**
What I like about those products (designed by men)	Simple Neutral colour Bold Strong Not busy Traditional	Colour (when it was red) Modern looking Nothing (!)
What I dislike about these (male-designed) products	Bit dark Cheap looking Colour (when it was red)	Lack of colour Too plain, no pattern Dated Convential
What I like about those products (designed by women)	Bright, fresh Fun Clean lines Naïve	Colourfulness Detail Rounded shapes Childlike typography
What I dislike about these (female-designed) products	Too childish Too busy Irregular writing	Bit too bright Bit busy

Experiment 4: pub visuals

Finally, we will look at one last study in which I have been involved with marketing academics at Glamorgan University (Moss et al., 2009). One of the academics, Marketing lecturer Scott Parfitt, conducted interviews with University students about what they liked and disliked about nightclubs and bars and together with Senior Lecturer in Marketing Heather Skinner, we set about gathering the points arising from the interviews into a questionnaire. This was then administered to all 98 members of a class with a clear instruction that there was no obligation to complete it. The choice of students as a respondent base was not accidental, but a function of the fact that 90 per cent of respondents were aged between 18 and 25 (n = 54), and this age range mimicked the market for clubs and nightclubs. As a Mintel market research study reports:

> 'A key market segment targeted by mainstream nightclubs is that of 18–24 year olds, fairly evenly divided between men and women with students accounting for one third of this market.
>
> Age is the most significant factor affecting attendance – clubbing dwindles significantly once respondents reach 25.'
>
> (Mintel 2006)

The sample of students constituted a non-random sample in the sense that a particular class of student was chosen but one that could nevertheless be taken as representative of the industry's main target group. In the end, 60 responses were obtained, giving a response rate of 61 per cent and the gender distribution showed that 40 per cent of respondents (n = 24) were male and 60 per cent (n = 36) female. In terms of nationality, over 78 per cent of respondents (n = 47) were from the UK, 15 per cent (n = 9) were from other EU countries, and almost 7 per cent (n = 4) defined their ethnicity as Asian, black or of mixed race. As we might have expected given the market research data on pubs and clubs, 80 per cent of survey respondents were frequent visitors to mainstream city centre pubs, clubs and bars, visiting such venues at least once a week.

One of the respondent tasks was to rate factors that had been identified at the interview stage as prompting a first or second visit. One of these factors was the impact of the external décor and the relative importance of this item to men and women is shown in Table 6.13.

As you can see from the summary of all the data (see Table 6.14), men's decisions are influenced primarily by the gender of the clientele, the location of the dance floor (arguably an extension of this point since a dance floor located close by will permit easier views of the clientele!) and the comfort of the seating area. For men, the quality of the exterior décor is of subsidiary influence. As you can see from Table 6.15, the gender of clientele that most men are searching for is female.

Table 6.13 The salience of the exterior décor of a club for men and women

Factor	% of women giving this as a prompt for a first or second visit		% of men giving this as a prompt for a first or second visit	
	First Visit	Return Visit	First Visit	Return Visit
Exterior décor	65	9	38	5

Table 6.14 The influence of various factors in prompting a first or second visit

Factor	% of women giving this as a first or second choice		% of men giving this as a first or second choice	
	First Visit	Return Visit	First Visit	Return Visit
Exterior Cues				
Exterior décor	65	9	38	5
Level of security	12	9	12	5
Interior Cues				
Gender of clientele	15	15	33	36
Customers' level of sobriety	3	12	0	4
Spatial Layout and Functionality				
Comfortable seating area	20	23	25	18
Cleanliness of toilet facilities	9	17	4	14
Location of dance floor	3	12	25	42

Table 6.15 The gender of the clientele that men and women hope to find in a bar

Type of clientele preferred	By women (%)	By men (%)
Largely female clientele	13	43
Largely male clientele	7	8
Mixed clientele	80	53

As a consequence, our study concluded that:

> 'Since a prime motivator for male customers for a first and subsequent visit is the presence of females, paying more attention to the needs of female customers is likely to attract male as well as female customers.'

What we were saying, in other words, was that if pubs and clubs satisfied the female customer (by providing her with the servicescape she required), then ultimately the male customer would be satisfied too.

Stereotypical Images

The final question here concerns the extent to which men and women will tolerate traditional and non-traditional images of themselves. What does the literature tell us?

Fortunately, there have been several pieces of work examining this specific question in relation to advertising, an area which images of men and women have been heavily gender-typed, with stereotypical images of independent, active, assertive, work-oriented men and dependent, passive, domestic women. Although some changes in the direction of more equal representation of men and women in advertising have occurred over the past 20 years, the general consensus of opinion is that women are typically displayed in stereotypical roles in advertising (Lundstrom and Sciglimpaglia 1977). Gilly (1988) supports this view in research extending empirical work beyond the confines of North America and the UK to Australia and Mexico and more recently, research by Kacen and Nelson (2002), corroborates these earlier findings and, interestingly, reports that very little appears to have changed in the preceding 15 years.

The nature of these traditional portrayals? Men are more likely than women to be portrayed in career activities and outdoors (Bretl and Cantor 1988), and more likely to be purchasing weighty or expensive items such as automobiles or financial services (Klassen et al. 1993). On the other hand, women, when depicted as buyers, are shown purchasing relatively inexpensive items such as cosmetics and cleaning products and when women are shown as experts on an advertised product (most often when endorsing women's products on television), the advertisements are typically backed by an authoritative male voiceover that provides men with the final word in these commercials (Lovdal 1989).

These, then, are tradition portrayals and Maria Morrison and David Shaffer of the Psychology Department of Georgia University decided to test the impact of less traditional portrayals of products (2003) on 246 American undergraduates whose gender role attitudes had been rated as 'traditional' or 'non-traditional'. The principal finding was that male and female participants with traditional gender-role expectations expressed more favourable product evaluations and stronger purchase intentions towards products displayed in traditional advertisements (that is, those showing men endorsing traditionally 'masculine' products or women endorsing traditionally 'feminine' products) than products displayed in non-traditional advertisements. Moreover, traditional participants reported traditional advertisements to be more effective than non-traditional participants did and there was a statistically significant tendency for respondents to favour advertising based on traditional roles, or products with typically masculine or feminine. It was also found (although not to a statistically significant level) that non-traditional participants responded more favourably to non-traditional than traditional advertisements and that they offered significantly lower evaluations of products endorsed by traditional advertisements than participants with traditional gender-role orientations, and also showed lower purchase intentions.

The authors consider that the results offer support for the so-called 'gender-role congruence model' of advertising effectiveness and that the only unanticipated outcome is that non-traditional advertisements appear to produce no more favourable product evaluations and purchase intentions from non-traditional participants than they do from traditional participants. These results led the authors to conclude that, since those with traditional gender-role orientations constitute a clear majority of the respondent sample (59 per cent), and an even larger share of the wider public, the marketing approach most effective for the greatest numbers of prospective consumers would be based on advertisements with stereotyped images and role portrayals. This leads the authors to conclude that:

> 'The results of this experiment suggest that the strategy of continuing to produce advertisements that portray gender-stereotyped images is still well-founded.'
>
> (Morrison and Shaffer 2003, 273)

They go on to conclude that:

> 'Since non-traditional participants in the first experiment displayed a slight preference (in terms of their product evaluations and purchase intentions) for non-traditional advertisements, and were much less favourable in their evaluation of products endorsed by traditional advertisements than traditional participants … a continuing reliance on traditional advertisements may not be the most effective way to appeal to a substantial minority of the consuming public.'
>
> (ibid. 273)

So much for findings regarding traditional and non-traditional gender role portrayals. In a separate experiment investigating people's reactions to advertisements featuring men and women in occupational and non-occupational settings (conducted by Ulrich Orth of the College of Business at Oregon State University and Denisa Holancova of the Department of Marketing and Trade at Mendel University in the Czech Republic in 2004), it was found that both men and women respond most favourably to exclusive portrayals of their own gender. When you read these results, you may have a sense of déjà vu since we saw earlier how people tend to depict other people of the same gender (see Chapter 3). Orth and Holancova's study has parallels with research by the car manufacturer, Toyota (Wilkie 1994) showing that recall of vehicles was higher among women when the drivers depicted were women rather than men.

The fact that both these studies found people responding positively to depictions of their own sex, and preferring representations of people of their own gender, shows that a mirroring is taking place between male and female *production* and *preference* aesthetics. This mirroring is in line with the tendency we saw earlier for people to prefer designs displaying the production aesthetic associated with their own gender.

Conclusions and Practical Lessons: Design Preferences

We have received evidence here of the extent to which the graphic and product design preferences of men and women differ with the main features underpinning respondents' choices being:

- shapes (a greater tendency for females than males to prefer round shapes);
- colours (a tendency for females to prefer colourfulness);
- use of detail (a tendency for females to prefer detail);
- typography (a tendency for women to prefer less conventional and less regular typography than men);
- gender of person shown (a tendency for each sex to prefer to see representations of people of their own gender);
- originality (a tendency for men to prefer more conventional advertisements than women); and,
- traditional nature of the depiction of men and women (a tendency for traditional respondents to respond more favourably to traditional depictions than non-traditional ones).

If these results are representative of wider opinion, then they are enormously important. As we shall see in the next chapter, many of the results are not dissimilar to those obtained in preference tests using websites, and the parallels and strength of the findings across design disciplines underlines the importance of ensuring that organizations target customers using the aesthetic that is appropriate to that gender. This may be particularly important in markets dominated by a particular gender.

Chapter 7
Web Design

Computers now have a massive impact on people, influencing where people work, the layout of offices, what people do while working and the demand and rewards for people with different skill sets. We have now arrived at the point where most people would agree on the profound impact of computers on modern economies, the labour market, the education system and society as a whole.

Towards the end of September 2007, a YouGov survey commissioned by Zurich Insurance found that almost a third of full-time employees are now resisting the delights of the office to spend some time each month working at home. According to this survey, these 'ad hoc home workers' clock up an average of almost 16 hours working at home each month, roughly half a day a week and the poll responses from more than 1,000 adults working full-time predicts an increase in the proportion of time working from home (Ward 2007). The fact that even those who do not officially work at home are checking emails or reading documents at home shows what is fuelling the change in working patterns – access to the Internet.

This survey shows the potential of the Internet to touch our working lives but of course it is not just our working lives that are affected. Since 1998, Internet use has grown at a rate of 20 per cent per year (Van Iwaarden et al. 2004) and it is estimated that the Internet user population will grow from 1.08 billion people worldwide in 2005 to 1.8 billion in 2010 (Clickz Stats 2007). In marketing terms, the network does more than just add another selling channel, for 'it is estimated to produce 10 times as many units [sold] with one-tenth of the advertising budget' (Potter 1994). It also eases customer retention (Van Iwaarden et al. 2004) and facilitates flexible response (IITA 1994), an advantage with shrinking product life cycles. These factors together have worked to 'transform the way business is conducted' (Grover and Saeed 2004).

Recent research reveals both men and women to be active participants in this revolution both at home and in the workplace. From the UK, research shows that similar proportions of men and women are using the web (Jupiter Communications 2004) with women accounting for about 51 per cent of the total online adult population, while European usage reveals female usage of the web to be an average of 38 per cent (ibid.). Data on the proportion of new users who are male and female, and the frequency of usage is also available from the US, and one study (Katz et al. 2001) shows that women constituted the majority of new Internet users during 1997–2000. Meanwhile, a separate study (Ono and Zavodny 2003) showed that by 2000, the online gender gap in the US had disappeared and that women were significantly more likely to use the Internet than men.

In terms of time spent online, figures from the UK produced by the communications regulator Ofcom show that women aged 25–49 are spending more time on the Internet than men with this tendency particularly pronounced in the 25–34 age group where women contribute 55 per cent of the time spent online. This demonstrates that the medium once thought of as dominated by 'solitary, glass-wearing male nerds' (Sabbagh and Blakely 2007) is increasingly used by women. As we shall see in the next section, e-design has an important role to play in attracting visitors, so a vital question concerns the extent to which web design reflects the male and female presence now becoming a fact of life.

The Importance of e-design

The website serves a variety of functions ranging from informing, persuading and reminding users (Anderson and Rubin 1986) to sustaining traffic, in other words attracting the casual surfer to linger (Schenkman and Jonsson 2000) and revisit the site (Joergensen and Blythe 2003). The competition for the user's attention, as well as the shift to consumer-controlled interaction (Wedande et al. 2001), makes this a challenging task.

The search for the factors that will influence websites' usefulness, enjoyment, ease-of-use (Van der Heijden 2003) and satisfaction (Van Iwaarden et al. 2004), has led Human Computer Interaction (HCI) researchers to attempt to understand the elements (technical, visual and content) in web design that are valued (Schenkman and Jonsson 2000) as well as those that produce a deficit between expectations and experience. Although there are many definitions of HCI (Preece 2002; Schneiderma, 2003; Dix et al. 2004), the one fairly extensively used (Hewett et al. 1996) is of a discipline concerned with the design, evaluation and implementation of interactive computing systems for human use, and the study of major phenomena surrounding them.

The search for these factors is a prize worth fighting for. As we saw earlier in Chapter 2, retailing research is driven by the notion that the physical form of a product is an important element in its design (Bloch 1995) and that it creates certain effects in buyers (Kotler 1973–74). Importantly, it has been found that products perceived as pleasurable are not only preferred (Yahomoto and Lambert 1994) but, when liked, are given greater attention (Maughan et al. 2007). Moreover, products perceived as pleasurable are used more frequently than those not perceived as pleasurable (Jordan 1998), leading to enhanced purchasing (Groppel 1993; Donovan et al. 1994).

While the values and identities of products and retailing environments have been extensively studied (Schroeder and Borgerson 1998), a relatively unexplored area concerns online preferences in relation to the non-interpretive elements of e-navigation such as, content, form and colours. Joergensen and Blythe (2003) comment that there are 'no principles of good www design ... set in stone' while a recent study refers to the relative 'paucity of research' on web design (Lavie and Tractinsky 2004). The absence of research on people's reactions to different aspects of web design represents a significant gap and if we needed further proof of this, it comes from a study by Van Iwaarden (2004) which lists computer graphics as one of the ten factors with the greatest deficit amongst Internet users in the US and Netherlands. Obviously, we need to understand something about web design aesthetics before we can even begin to think of fixing the problem.

Web Design Aesthetics

We saw earlier in Chapter 2 that discussions of aesthetics tend to be anchored in either the universalist paradigm (Kant 1978) which assumes aesthetic preferences to be universal, or in the interactive paradigm, which assumes aesthetic preferences to vary between individuals. The same holds true for discussions of web design aesthetics, with the majority of such studies being anchored in the universalist paradigm (Schenkman and Jonsson 2000; Van der Heijden 2003; Lavie and Tractinsky 2004). The focus on a universalist approach means that relatively little work has been conducted within the interactionist paradigm which tends to view aesthetic judgements as a function of individual perception (Porteous 1996). This interactionist work postdates 2000 and, as you will see in the next section, it includes several studies I have conducted myself.

The interactionist paradigm

As we saw, the so-called interactionist perspective allows for the possibility that preferences may vary between observers and it links with the 'empathy principle' according to which aesthetic value is not inherent in objects, but is the product of empathy between object, perceiver and artist (Crozier and Greenhalgh 1992). Before I started to conduct investigations, five studies had made initial forays into the topic of web design.

The first two studies are described in an article which purports to examine the influence of gender on the design of web pages (Miller and Arnold 2000). The first of these two centres on a comparison of web pages originated by men and women, and its conclusion is that men's pages are shorter than women's and that female-produced pages make greater reference to the reader than do male-produced pages. However, beyond stating that an opportunistic sample of pages from a non-institutional setting was used, no details are supplied regarding the study's methodology, a potentially major weakness in the study. No details are supplied, for example, of the number of web pages used by gender, the method of selection used, the method of rating used, the method of calculating difference or quantification of differences. The difficulties resulting from just one of these problems – the absence of a method of rating is apparent when one considers that the term 'pages' used in the conclusion is nowhere defined and could refer to either an individual page or to a number of linked pages. The second study reported by these authors appears similarly flawed with 'opportunistic and haphazard' (author's words) sampling of social science colleagues' home pages and no information on the number of sites consulted. Moreover, rating methods are not explained and remain at the level of concepts such as 'fluffy feminine' and 'macho technical'. As a result, the authors' conclusion that 'gender differences ... intrude in cyberspace' cannot be relied upon.

The absence of a robust methodology reduces, similarly, the value of a third study that purported to demonstrate higher evaluations for opposite-gender credibility evaluations than same-gender credibility evaluations (Flanagin and Metzger 2003). Unfortunately, the conclusions of this study are rooted in respondents' evaluations of a sample of just one male- and one female-produced website, and the methodological limitations of just using a single website as a focus for comments are compounded by the fact that the gender of the web designer was revealed to respondents. Both these limitations (that is, the small sample size and the revelation of the web designer's gender) mean that the conclusions cannot be relied upon and given any validity. Moreover, other similar reports, for example those suggesting women's preference for simple and relevant navigation (Leong 1997; Oser 2003), are similarly flawed in the sense that details of the studies in question are not provided.

A more recent study conducted in the interactionist paradigm (Moss et al. 2006b) appears to avoid the methodological shortfalls of these earlier studies and before describing it, it is useful to highlight earlier research that underlines the importance of the visual element. This earlier research emphasized the centrality of non-price mechanisms of differentiation (Gupta 1995) and also emphasized the fact that the perceived visual attractiveness and content of the website (Coldsborough 2000) can influence perceptions as to the site's usefulness, enjoyment, ease-of-use (Van der Heijden 2003) and satisfactions (Van Iwaarden et al. 2004). Relevant factors were thought to relate to technical and navigation issues (such as speed of loading), content (Joergensen and Blythe 2003) as well as visual form (Schenkman and Jonsson 2000; Lavie and Tractinsky 2004). Given the importance of these last three elements, this more recent study (Moss et al. 2006b) analysed the appearance of three elements – navigation, content (language) and visuals – in 60 websites produced by equal numbers of men and women attending a British university. Overall, 23 factors were rated, and statistically significant differences across the male- and female-produced websites emerged on 13 out of the 23 factors rated. The 23 factors were spread across the three elements of navigation, language and visual content.

Where navigation is concerned, the 60 websites were rated on features highlighted in earlier work on gendered preferences (Leong 1997; Oser 2003) and included the number of links on the home page, the number of subjects covered and their consistency, the use of a site map and a contents page. Where language is concerned, the features used derived from research illustrating gendered differences in use of language (Tannen 1990), with men allegedly evincing a more competitive style than women. To test some of the findings from linguistics, the use of formal and expert language, self-promotion, welcome message, exposition of own achievements, the amount of self-denigration and avoidance of grammatical abbreviations (all allegedly male features) were measured in the websites.

With regard to visual features, many of the factors rated derived from research exploring the gendering of design (Moss 1995; 1999) with two main sets of rating characteristics used: thematic content, and non-thematic content. On the first, the literature discusses six features (Moss 1995; 1999) that distinguish male from female designs and these were translated into features against which the websites could be rated. These included the style of photos (formal or informal snapshots), gender of images used (with tendency to feature own gender), use of inanimate vs. animate themes, self-propelling vs. stationary objects, serious vs. light-hearted themes and the use of Institution's crest vs. own logo. With regard to non-thematic content, a number of features were measured, namely the relative use of straight or rounded lines, regular or irregular typography, a small or large number and range of colours in the typeface or the background. The extent to which design elements looked three-dimensional or two-dimensional and the type of typeface colours used were also measured.

The results of the study showed that in terms of the 23 different factors against which websites were rated, 13 of these produced evidence of statistically significant differences between the male- and female-designed websites (Moss et al. 2006b). These factors included the number of separate subject areas covered, the character of the language (men favouring formal and expert language, self-promotion, infrequent use of abbreviations), the character of the images used (men favouring use of a company logo, images of men and formal images), visual elements (men favouring the use of straight as opposed to rounded lines, and a conventional horizontal layout) and the character of the typography (men favouring formal typography and a smaller or greater number of typeface colours). These differences were sufficiently numerous and significant to be suggestive of a masculine/feminine web design *production aesthetic* continuum and these were new and exciting findings.

Another piece of research in which I was involved (Moss and Gunn 2009) examined the parallal topic of the web design *preference aesthetics* of men and women and found that what men liked in the way of web design was significantly different from what women liked. The results are based on the preferences of 64 students (38 male and 26 female) and are shown in Table 7.1..

In terms of overall preferences, these results show a remarkably strong and consistent tendency (statistically significant at the high level of 0.01) for men and women to prefer websites displaying the production aesthetic of their own gender and in doing this, they mirror the results of earlier research in the field of product and graphic design (Moss 1996a; 1999; Moss and Colman 2001; Moss and Gunn 2007). In terms of preferences for different elements of web design, the results show that women prefer *all* aspects of web pages which have strong female elements, while men are not as strongly drawn to male sites with strong male elements. Moreover, the results show that men have no strong preferences between shapes with a male or female gender coefficient and that they tend to prefer the pictures that females place in their websites to those appearing in male-produced sites (Moss and Gunn 2009).

As we can see, these experiments into web production and preference aesthetics have shown the extent to which web production aesthetics differ by gender, and the extent to which men and women may prefer the production aesthetic associated with their own gender. Given the importance of the Internet, one of the crunch questions is the extent to which web design sofware can deliver both male and female production aesthetics.

Some answers are to hand. Dr Gabor Horvath (Horvath et al. 2007) of Glamorgan University, rated a large number of randomly selected free web designer software programs in order to ascertain whether, and to what extent, the templates they provided were capable of delivering the full spectrum of the web aesthetic design continuum, from the masculine through to the feminine. The research method consisted of rating the templates (the researchers examined 3,682 templates in total) of these website builder programs against a number of different criteria based upon the earlier research of Moss et al. (2006b).

The results showed that the majority of web designer software programs offer templates that are rooted in the male production aesthetic and therefore do not readily offer the means of creating sites that exemplify the full aesthetic range. This makes it difficult to develop sites displaying the female production aesthetic and, as such, present practical difficulties in the way of delivering sites that mirror women's aesthetic preferences. To do this demands the availability of software that offers templates rooted in the female production aesthetic and currently these are not widely or freely available.

Table 7.1 Preference test results: the significance levels show the extent to which each gender prefers websites (or elements of the websites) produced using the production aesthetic of their own gender

	Male preferences	**Female preferences**
Overall preference for website	0.01	0.01
Language	0.01	0.01
Pictures	Prefer the female prod aesthetic	0.01
Shapes	No sig preference	0.01
Layout	0.01	0.01
Typography colours	0.01	0.01

Conclusions and Practical Lessons

We have seen that the websites that women produce look very different from those produced by men and that the main differences cover 13 features, ranging from the number of colours to the shapes used on the screen. We also saw a statistically strong tendency for each gender to prefer the output of its own gender. These findings, repeated over several experiments, suggest that for optimum results, websites should mimic the web preferences of the target market.

Is this happening at the moment? By and large, male target markets are presented with websites bearing the male production aesthetic, but female target markets are presented with sites that web designers think women will like. In reality, these fall short of providing the elements that appeal to females even though web designers may make concessions to appeal to female taste (for example, by using pink or mauve). The problem is that they do not always balance the use of colour with all the other many features that need to be attended to such as shapes of lines, number of colours, style of typography, type of images and use of language and the free software currently available does not help matters since, as we have seen, it is not geared to delivery of the female web production aesthetic.

Clearly, there is scope for dramatic change in the way websites are presented to female markets. However, a study of the demographics of the web design and IT industries shows us industries that are strongly male-dominated and it remains to be seen whether this will stand in the way of delivering the female production aesthetic. Two questions arise:

- Whether men can be taught to produce websites displaying the features of the female production aesthetic?
- Whether more women be brought onboard in the web design and IT industries?

Given the male bias in current web design software, as well as the high proportion of male web designs, the first question is a pressing one. Only new research will give us the answers.

Chapter 8
Accounting for the Differences

'Sex affects absolutely every aspect of our lives' says neuroscientist Dr Karen Berkley from Florida State University (Melton 2006, 10). 'The difference between the sexes is a continuing interplay between our physiological and hormonal processes and what is happening around us as we move through the lifespan. It's a continuous back and forth between physiology and sociocultural issues.'

These thoughts appeared in the newsletter of the Wellcome Institute in an article, entitled 'Sex Differences: Mars and Venus in the Lab'. The author, Lisa Melton wrote about how, for a long time, it was ideologically fashionable to insist that aside from the obvious physical differences, differences between the sexes were minimal.

Living testimony to this comes from Oxford biologist David Taylor who recalls the hostility his lectures on sex differences triggered in the early 1970s (ibid.). Talk of a landscape that is hostile to discussion of sex differences puts one in mind of the 'socialist-feminist' perspective expressed in Helen Haste's book on cultural feminism, *The Sexual Metaphor* (1994). Helen Haste is Professor of Psychology at Bath University that 'beliefs about sex difference served the needs of a patriarchal society, and are largely illusory distortions.

Over in America, it seems that things were not much different. Dr Anne Fausto-Sterling, Professor of Biology and Women's Studies at Brown University, in her article 'The Five Sexes: Why Male and Female Are Not Enough' (1993) writes that Western culture is defying nature by maintaining a 'two-party sexual system'. 'Biologically speaking', she says, 'there are many gradations running from female to male; and depending on how one calls the shots, one can argue that along the spectrum lie at least five sexes – and perhaps even more' (ibid. 21). A similar message is found in her book *Myths of Gender* (1992) which attacks a number of studies purporting to shows evidence of fixed biological differences between the sexes. A few years later, the American academic Leslie Brody, based in the Psychology Department of Boston University and writing about men's and women's emotions in her book *Gender, Emotion and the Family* (1999), describing the dangers of conducting research into sex differences:

> 'The research on the biology of gender differences is only in its infancy, and there is some debate among feminists about whether or not it is worthwhile to pursue, given the abuses to which it can be put.'
>
> (ibid. 103)

In contrast to these views, Lisa Melton, writing in 2006 speaks of a greater respectability for efforts to probe differences. These efforts have included work concluded in the 1990s as well as more recent work. A case in point is a book by Melissa Hines, Professor of Psychology at Cambridge University. Entitled *Brain Gender* (2004), her book investigates sex differences in human beings, and has compared the strength of differences across different measures. As you can see from her graph (reproduced in Figure 8.1), after height differences, 3-D rotations, the one visuo-spatial skill in her list, surpasses all the other cognitive sex differences listed. This is important for us since 3-D rotations are firmly within the spectrum of visuo-spatial skills and therefore relevant to our discussion of design and marketing.

Her conclusions are not isolated. Doreen Kimura, in an article for *Scientific American* on sex differences (1992), wrote that of all the cognitive sex differences, only visuo-spatial differences consistently display effect sizes (that is differences between the scores typically obtained by men and women) of more than 0.7, a difference she describes as being a medium to large effect size. Kimura now retired, holds a visiting professorship at Simon Fraser University in Canada, and her thoughts are echoed in work by Diane Halpern, Professor of Psychology at Claremont McKenna College and President in 2004 of the American Psychological Association. Professor Halpern has taken the view that variations in the visuo-spatial abilities of males and females are amongst the most robust and persistent of all the cognitive sex differences (Halpern 2000) and this finding appears to be widely supported. Moreover, it is not simply in relation to other cognitive abilities that visual-spatial skills score highly but in an absolute sense too as is apparant from an article (Voyer et al, 1995) summarising the evidence of 286 studies on visuo-spatial differences. Voyer's landmark article concludes 'that sex differences in spatial abilities favouring males are highly significant' and strongly suggest

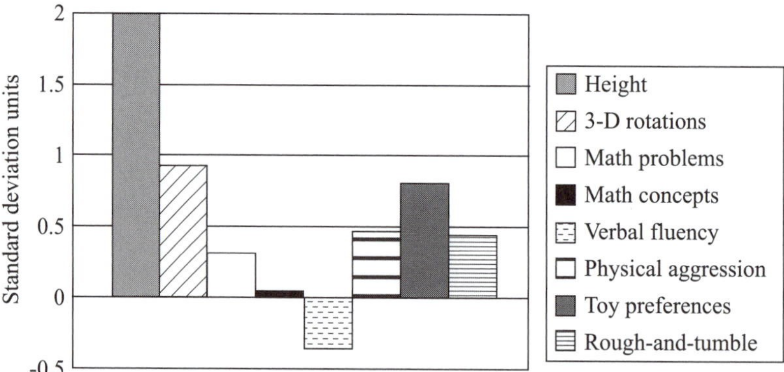

Figure 8.1 Magnitude of some well-known sex differences in human behaviour compared to the magnitude of the sex difference in height (Hines 2004)

that sex differences in spatial abilities do exist' (ibid. 253–4). The authors go on to quantify the size of the male advantage by saying that 'on average, males outperform females by about 0.6 standard deviation units in mental rotation and 0.4 standard deviation units in spatial perception' (ibid. 257).

This is an exciting time for the study of sex differences and biology and evolution theory may now be accorded a more important role than was the case 'in the last several decades' when, 'the dominant perspective has been that gender is socially constructed, and that gender differentiation is best understood as a product of socialization' (Maccoby 1998, 3). The legacy of evolution theory is apparent in Maccoby's reference to 'the adaptive characteristics of the human species are thought to have evolved during the long period of time during which fairly small bands of humans roamed the savannas, hunting game and gathering wild cereals and fruits' (ibid. 91).

On the biological side, many of the influences on the male and female brain are brought to light in the *Female Brain* (2006) by Dr Louann Brizendine, Director of the UCSF Women's Mood and Hormone Clinic at the Langley Porter Institute in San Francisco. Dr Brizendine claims that for a long time scientific research was based primarily on a study of men but that increasingly science is revealing the biological factors that shape the perceptions of men as well as women.

In a world of ever-increasing competition, it is important that designers and marketers gain an understanding of how their own way of seeing may be distinct and different from other people's. Then, much like an actor getting under the skin of the character they are playing, if they notice a difference between the customer's and their own way of seeing, they can 'borrow' the customer's spectacles and try to imagine the world as seen through their lenses. The information on biology and perception is helping with this.

The information that science is bringing us, may upset cherished beliefs, but the prize – increased customer satisfaction – makes it invaluable. So in the rest of this chapter we will present a summary of the science or sex difference and then go on to consider the implications for design and marketing. The discussion that follows will be divided into two sections, with the first concerned with a wide variety of visual skills from mental rotation, spatial perception and spatial visualization (skills commonly referred to as 'visuo-spatial' skills) to colour vision and field independence. In the second section, our main concern will be with levels of aggression, empathy and specialized processing. Our focus, in our discussion of these two areas will be the differences between the visual-spatial abilities of men and women and then the proximate and ultimate causes of these differences. In doing this, I will draw heavily on an article I wrote with Dr Colin Hamilton, Senior Lecturer in Cognitive Psychology at Northumbria University and author of a book on sex differences and cognition, as well as with Dr Nick Neave, Reader in Psychology at Northumbria University (Moss et al. 2007a).

A note about studies on cognitive sex differences. When psychologists consider the strength of sex differences they normally analyse and evaluate the results of earlier studies. One such study, described by Janet Hyde (2005) as a 'watershed', was Maccoby and Jacklin's book *The Psychology of Sex Difference* (1974). This book reviewed more than 2,000 studies of gender differences and concluded that sex differences were well established in four areas, two of which were visuo-spatial abilities and aggression. Shortly after this important work appeared, the statistical method of 'meta-analysis' was developed.

In meta-analyses, the comparison of studies usually produces an 'effect size' which measures the magnitude of an effect. Janet Hyde, Professor of Psychology and Women's Studies at the University of Wisconsin-Madison, suggests (2005) that effect sizes between 0.1 and 0.35 should be considered small, those between 0.36–0.65 should be considered in the moderate range, and 0.66–1.00 in the large range. Professor Hyde's interpretation is followed in the results that are reported in the next section.

Sex Differences in Visuo-spatial and Language Abilities

The areas on which earlier research has focused are:

(A) Mental rotation and spatial perception.
(B) Targeting accuracy.
(C) Colour blindness, colour recognition and colour preferences.
(D) Daylight vision.
(E) Attention and location memory.
(F) Field independence.

(A) Mental rotation and spatial perception

As noted earlier, when psychologists report on visuo-spatial skills they normally refer to just three types of ability, namely mental rotation skills, spatial perception and spatial visualization. *Mental rotation skills* measures the ability to imagine the appearance of three-dimensional objects rotated in space, while *spatial perception* is commonly understood as referring to the ability to determine spatial relations despite distracting information. The third skill, *spatial visualization*, is one commonly described as the ability to manipulate complex spatial information.

With regard to sex differences in these areas, two significant studies have been conducted. The first, by Linn and Petersen (1985), concluded that sex differences in spatial perception and mental rotation were robust and this study was followed up by a further meta-analysis which claimed to provide 'a nearly exhaustive review of the published literature on sex-related differences in spatial abilities up to 1993' (Voyer et al. 1995, 252). The conclusion of Voyer's study was that 'sex differences are clearly established in some areas of spatial abilities' (ibid. 265). So confident, in fact, were the authors of their findings that they anticipated that their study would 'close the debate concerning the existence of sex differences in spatial abilities' (ibid. 265).

Even Janet Hyde, the proponent of the gender similarities hypothesis (this downplays the statistical evidence for most cognitive sex differences) was convinced of the robust nature of differences in the field of mental rotation and spatial perception. She writes that these routinely demonstrate effect sizes of 0.7 and 0.4 respectively, levels indicating a large and medium effect (Hyde 2005).

A word on the skills normally considered in the 'visuo-spatial' category. Where *mental rotation* is concerned, differences in this ability are thought to emerge early in life, with a number of studies finding evidence of sex differences in pre-school and primary age children (Levine et al. 1999b; Petersen and Crockett 1985; Kerns and Berenbaum 1991). The early appearance of these differences is interesting and makes it unlikely that they are occasioned exclusively by the learning of gender-related norms and expectations. In terms of the size of the sex difference, by the time men reach the ages of 15 and 20, around four-fifths are better able to generate and manipulate three-dimensional images mentally than the average female while between the age of 20 and 35, about six out of seven men outperform the average woman (Geary 1998). Meta-analyses conducted on mental-rotation skills have shown mean effect sizes of 0.73 (Linn and Peterson 1985) and 0.56 (Voyer et al. 1995).

Interestingly, in relation to our later discussion of the evolving origins of these differences (with evolutionary pressures on men and women being the spur to developing skills suited to a gendered division of labour), superior rotational skills are thought to be linked to the generation of maps for novel environments, skills in which men are thought to have the edge (Holding and Holding 1989). Skills such as these would be relevant to those assuming the role of hunter, especially if they were roaming over large distances.

In terms of *spatial perception* (commonly understood as the ability to determine spatial relations despite distracting information), tests in this category have produced mean effect sizes of 0.44 (Linn and Peterson 1985; Voyer et al. 1995) favouring men. In terms of *spatial visualization* (the ability to manipulate complex spatial information when several stages are needed to produce the correct solution), meta-analysis has not yielded evidence of consistent sex differences (Voyer et al. 1995).

(B) Targeting accuracy

Since throwing accuracy has been found to correlate with superior manipulation of three-dimensional images, it is not surprising to find that research has found males to be more accurate in guiding or intercepting projectiles than females. In one experiment (Smith and McPhee 1987), a group of males and females carried out a coincidence timing test in which subjects had to press a key when a moving target was coincident with a stationary line and the girls turned out to be less accurate than the boys. Another related ability is dynamic visual acuity in which there is relative motion between the observer and the stimulus being viewed and this again shows an advantage in favour of men.

(C) Colour blindness, colour recognition and colour preferences

Another crucial way in which men's and women's visual skills differ is in the area of colour vision. It is a rich field since it is well established that a larger proportion of males (anything from 8 per cent to 14 per cent) than females (0.8–1 per cent) suffer from colour blindness, a disorder in which individuals have a partial or total inability to detect certain wavelengths of the visual spectrum. This condition was first documented by John Dalton in 1978, when he described his own defective colour vision and consequently, colour blindness is also known as Daltonism.

The most common problem in colour-blind people involves the inability to distinguish red and green with the most frequent defect involving the green receptors and the second most common defect involving the red receptors. In terms of distinguishing berries from foliage and distinguishing ripe (that is, not green) from unripe fruit, colour blindness would have posed major problems although when it comes to hunting it would have conferred distinct advantages since colour blindness renders visible hues that are indistinguishable to colour-normal persons. In this way, colour-blind people can see through camouflage and also have improved night-time vision. This assists hunting in low levels of light (BBC h2g2 website).

Interestingly, the levels of colour blindness in men are not constant across the world, but fluctuate in accordance with the duration of twilight, with the shorter duration of twilight at the equator leading to lower levels of colour-blindness and the longer periods of twilight at higher latitudes leading to a lower incidence of colour blindness. Could this explain, I wondered, why the colours of the Oslo Underground struck me, with my female eyes, as so strange? Perhaps the designers, if male, were colour blind?

In contrast to men, a tiny proportion (about half a per cent) of the female population suffers from colour blindnesss and the rest have either normal trichromacy with three functioning colour pigments (red, green and blue) or, as research in the last ten years has revealed, four colour pigments with the additional fourth cone lying smack between the standard red and green cones. A researcher in this field, Dr Neitz, is of the view that only women have the potential for tetrachromacy since the genes for the pigments in green and red cones lie on the X chromosome, and only women have two X chromosomes. The significance of women's two chromosomes lie in the fact that it offers the opportunity for one type of red cone to be activated on one X chromosome and another type of red cone on the other one and similarly with green cones (Roth 2006). In terms of the proportion who have four colour pigments, this has been estimated at 3–50 per cent of women (Neitz et al. 1998; Jameson et al. 2001) which in a population the size of the UK (58.8 million people according to the census in 2001) would correspond to between 96,000 and 15.1 million women. Importantly, although there may be no tetrachromat men, it is thought that 8 per cent of men may have similarly heightened visual skills (Jameson et al. 2001) which in a population the size of the UK, would correspond with a little over 2 million males.

The researchers behind these bombshell revelations about the existence of tetrachromat women are academics at American Universities. Dr Jan Neitz is a renowned colour vision researcher at the Medical College of Wisconsin, while Dr Kimberley Jameson and her two co-authors, Susan Highnote and Linda Wasserman, are at the University of San Diego in California. In the article by Dr Jameson and her colleagues, the authors write in their concluding remarks that four photo-pigment female individuals may constitute between 15 and 50 per cent of the female population (Jameson et al. 2001). So their estimates of the proportion of women who are tetrachromat are higher than those of Dr Neitz who estimated their numbers at 2–3 per cent (Roth 2006).

This is explosive stuff. Bees may also be tetrachromat to help distinguish the colour of flowers, but no other mammals are and an additional colour pigment adds spectacularly to the range of colours perceived. In the case of humans, it would boost the colour vision from the several million perceived by a trichromat to the hundreds of millions perceived by a tetrachromat. In fact, these differences in colour blindness and colour pigments are not the only differences in the way that men and women envision colour. A large team (Cowan et al. 2000) found that men and women used different techniques for processing colours and had different cortical responses to the stimulation of blue and red light wavelengths. This was consistent with an older study (Mollon 1986) that found women to be more sensitive than men to the long-wave spectrum of light that detects red. It was consistent also with the finding that when looking at a field of uniform brightness, women held the perception of red significantly longer than green (McGuiness 1976), and that during the after-image study, all the female subjects (but only 50 per cent of the males) reported seeing red.

Importantly, two recent studies have confirmed women's love-affair with pink and lilac. The first, by Dr Yazhu Ling et al. in 2004, showed how women single out lilac-pink colours from a range of equally light (that is, bright) colours. The second, by Professor Anya Hurlbert and Dr Ling, both at the University of Newcastle upon Tyne, tested the colour preferences of 208 volunteers. The study was published in 2007 in the journal *Current Biology* and the volunteers aged 20–26 were asked to

Table 8.1 The relationship between number of colour pigments and shades perceived

Number of pigments	Number of shades that would be discerned with a given number of colour pigments
1	200
2	10,000
3	Several million
4	Hundreds of millions

viewed about 750 different pairs of colours spanning the entire rainbow, and in each case had to indicate which of the two shades they preferred by clicking with a computer mouse. While most of the participants were British white Caucasians, a sub-group of 37 were recent immigrants to the UK from mainland China, with almost equal numbers of men and women. The idea of testing the two groups was to separate out whether culture or biology might influence gender preferences for colour. The results made the media headlines since, the male favourite was a pale blue while the female favourite was a lilac shade of pink.

Hurlbert expressed surprise at these findings: 'Although we expected to find sex differences, we were suprised at how robust they were, given the simplicity of our test' (Macrae 2007). She added that although some might think women's preference for shades of pink was a feature of living in cultures where pink represented girlishness and femininity, the Chinese women in her study who grew up without commercial toys such as Barbie, showed an even greater liking for pinkish hues than their British counterparts. So Hurlbert believes that women's attraction towards pinkish colours is innate rather than learned.

Pink is an example of a 'bright' colour, a quantity relating to the quantity or intensity of light and not surprisingly, according to the author of *The Colour Handbook*, women have a preference for brighter colours than men of the same age (Danger 1987). Interestingly, women have been found to have a significant memory advantage for the purple-pink range of colours (Pérez-Carpinell et al. 1998) and the origin of this has been attributed to the relative prominence of male and female colour mechanisms (Bonnardel and Herrero 2006). The existence of perceptual mechanisms responsible for the relative importance of pink across genders could account for women's memory advantage in the absence of evidence of a verbal strategy. Maybe, these differences are factors in the discrepancy we observed in the extent to which boys and girls used up the pink crayons in the experiments conducted in Japan by Iijima (2001).

In terms of other colour preferences, a review of colour studies by Eysenck (1941) noted a significant gender difference to be the fact that yellow is preferred to orange by women, and orange to yellow by men. Natalia Khouw states, 'this finding was reinforced later by Birren who found men preferred orange to yellow; while women placed orange at the bottom' (Khouw; Birren 1961).

If we put colour to one side for the moment, we can turn to some of the remaining differences psychologists have discussed in relation to men and women's visual faculties.

(D) Daylight vision

Diane McGuiness, in a chapter on perception, says that men have better day as well as night vision than women (1976).

(E) Attention and location memory

In experiments using ecologically valid stimuli (real plants in complex naturalistic arrays), women display superior object memory (Geary 1998; Neave et al. 2005).

(F) Field independence

Finally, there is some evidence that men may be more field independent than women, in other words more likely to perceive stimuli divorced from their surroundings (Halpern 2000). Women, conversely, may have less ability to detach themselves cognitively from their surroundings or to disembed hidden figures (Hall 1984).

Other Cognitive Differences

(A) Aggression vs. need for affiliation.

Earlier, we compared children's drawings and paintings, we saw how the drawings produced by the boys in McNiff's experiment displayed greater aggression than those produced by girls. Could cognitive sex differences be a factor in this? Intriguingly, greater aggression and assertiveness in men than women has been reported in empirical research across multiple settings and age groups, with males reported to be more violent than women (Kashani et al. 1999; Graves 2007) even in the presence of increasing levels of violence among females. In fact, even Professor Janet Hyde, originator of the 'gender similarities hypothesis' which holds men and women to be more alike than different on several psychological variables has found that, compared with women, men are more physically aggressive. In meta-analyses she conducted on sex differences in aggression she found effect sizes of 0.50 on aggression of all types, and 0.60 on physical aggression (Hyde 2005). These findings are not dissimilar to the conclusions from a meta-analytical study conducted a year earlier by Archer (2004). As you can see from Table 8.2, these show medium to large effect sizes in favour of men on a measure of direct and physical aggression and low effect sizes in favour of women on a measure of indirect aggression.

Where needs for affiliation are concerned, researchers studying personality traits have consistently found that women score higher on affiliation orientation than men. They also score higher on a concern for other people's feelings, on approval seeking behaviours, on creating nurturing relationships, for maintaining interpersonal harmony, being empathic and alterocentrist (Schultheiss and Brunstein 2001), and being gregarious and tenderminded (Feingold 1994). In fact, where this last characteristic is concerned, females scored higher than males on all scales of tendermindedness, with effect sizes ranging from 0.17 to an extremely large 1.67.

Table 8.2 The effect sizes of gender differences in levels of direct and physical aggression (positive results evidence men having a greater tendency to the characteristic in question; negative results evidence women having a greater tendency)

Effect sizes	Direct aggression	Physical aggression	Indirect aggression
Observations	0.49	0.53	-0.74
Peer reports (before removal of outliers)	0.57	0.84	-0.19
Peer reports (after removal of outliers)	0.63	0.80	
Teacher reports (before and after removal of outliers)	0.42–0.47	0.40–0.33	-0.13

Source: Archer, 2004.

Men, on the other hand, are noted has having a higher drive to assertiveness, independence and self-centredness (Maccoby and Jacklin 1974; Feingold 1994). Where assertiveness is concerned, Feingold's meta-analytical study revealed that males scored higher than women on all assertiveness scales, with the range of effect sizes varying (according to the scale) between 0.22 to 0.88.

(B) Specialized processing

There is an extensive literature suggesting that men are more specialized processors than women on account of the fact that their brains are more lateralized (Wager et al. 2003). The reader is encouraged to follow up on this fascinating area of research for details of the way differences in brain lateralization affect men and women's thinking.

Ultimate Causes of Differences: The Role of Society and Biology

We have explored a number of cognitive sex differences, whether in the visual or affective arenas, and the question as to the relative roles of biology or society in establishing these differences is something of a battleground amongst researchers. Some hold that these two work together and others that they work singly. We will review some of the evidence in relation to some of the differences we have discussed in this book.

Society influences biology

There is a view that the environment acts on humans to bring about changes in biology and this thinking lies behind Leslie Brody's view (1999) that certain aggressive or dominant behaviours (for example, winning a competition) can trigger a rise in testosterone levels. This shows that social processes, not just biology, can influence hormone levels and the interactive impact of biology and social factors led Stanford University Professor Emeritus of Psychology, Eleanor Maccoby, to suggest that environmental conditions can impact on behaviour directly and indirectly by altering biological processes (Carpenter 2000).

Eleanor Maccoby was speaking in 2000 in acceptance of a book award for her 1998 book *The Two Sexes: Growing Up Apart, Coming Together* and the ultimate examplar of the way society acts in concert with biology to bring about sex differences is the evolutionary view that human patterns of behaviour has worked on biology over millennia to produce the behaviour and attitudinal patterns we see today. This process is illustrated in Figure 8.2.

It was against the background of this type of thinking that I wrote an article with two British psychologists, Dr Colin Hamilton and Dr Nick Neave, Reader in Psychology at Northumbria University, arguing that a sexual division of labour in which men hunted and roamed long distances and women gathered fruit and nurtured young life was one that produced visual skills that were highly specialized on these tasks (Moss 2007a). This, in turn, produced sex differences in visual

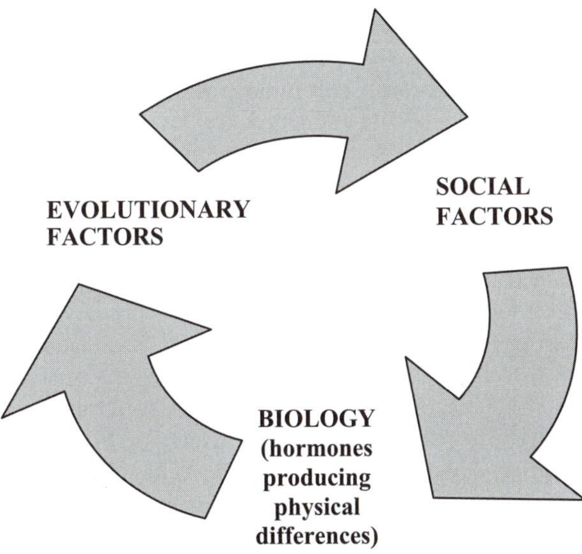

Figure 8.2 A model integrating social and biological factors in differences between male and female design aesthetics

abilities and preferences and these underlay the gender differences in design I had noticed. In presenting this argument we drew on the work of Professor Geary and other distinguished scholars who referred to evolutionary pressures as major factors in the development of visual-spatial sex differences.

It is appropriate to pause for a moment and imagine ourselves back in the Lower Palaeolithic period, the oldest part of the Stone Age. This period lasted for about two million years up to the end of the Pleistocene epoch, and was one in which men and women probably lived as hunter-gatherers. This way of life probably lasted until the last Ice Age and the ensuing arrival of human encampments, and according to an American professor and expert on sex differences, Professor David Geary (1992 and 1998), cognitive sex differences may be adaptive consequences of the hundreds of thousands of years during which men and women acted as hunters and gatherers respectively.

Since visual-spatial differences are the most robust of the cognitive sex differences and a primary focus of this book, we can ask how men's and women's visual activities would have developed in response to the division of labour then operating. A first step in doing this is to understand the tasks in which men and women were engaged, and then consider the spatial skills needed to fulfil these.

If we focus first on the roles that men adopted in the hunter/gatherer society, these are likely to have involved extensive travel, hunting prey (often at a distance), and defending territory from animals or hostile forces. What spatial abilities would these have required? According to American academic Irwin Silverman, Professor of Psychology at York University, the ability to navigate large areas, and locate and target prey against a dark-coloured and distant horizon (Silverman et al. 2000) would have been essential, as would also the ability to perceive stimuli independent of the environment in which it was situated. These skills would have required, respectively, excellent directional skills (to help with navigation), excellent three-dimensional skills (to help locate and target prey), colour-blindness (leading to better night time vision as well as to the capability of seeing past camouflage) and field independence (to help disassociate stimuli from the ambient environment). In fact, these are many of the skills in which men have a distinct advantage over women.

What of women? Evolutionary psychologists argue that in the division of labour that operated for thousands of years, one of women's primary tasks would have been to pick berries from bushes, a task no less vital than that of hunting. Some anthropologists also argue that while men were away in organized groups hunting, women were involved in creating and maintaining the social and material fabric of the environment (Briffault 1927; Reed 1954). According to these commentators, these tasks would have involved everything from building homes (serving as the architects), making pottery (acting as the designers) nurturing the young (serving as proxy teachers), maintaining everyday social relations (acting as the managers of the day) to picking berries. Where the visual domain is concerned, these tasks would have necessitated sensitivity to rounded shapes (in order to notice berries and bond with babies), object location memory (to remember food sources) and finely developed skills of colour vision (to provide increased opportunities to find fruit and leaves to eat, to provide sensitivity to changes in skin colour of children, to monitor changes in health and mood, and sensitivity to the moods of other people). In the emotional domain, this division of tasks would have necessitated empathic skills amongst women and aggressive skills amongst males.

The extent to which this picture of a women's extended responsibilities is correct could be open to debate, but one group of researchers (Regan et al. 2001) has established the link between many of women's visuo-spatial skills and the task of gathering. These scientists argue that colour vision evolved 35 million years ago to help with gathering, and that the ability to detect yellow fruit and edible red leaves against a backdrop of green foliage conferred an evolutionary advantage since it facilitated the identification of ripe, yellow fruit from a surround of green foliage, and also facilitated the identification of edible red leaves amongst unripe green foliage. In addition to these skills, visual acuity in the discernment of pink and red may also have conferred an evolutionary advantage insofar as it would have helped discriminate emotional states, socio-sexual signals and threat displays (Changini et al. 2006). More specifically, being finely attuned to colour may have helped women forage for plant food and undertake the caretaking of infants (Alexander 2003) and these skills would also have helped gauge the mood of adults, and whether it was safe to approach them (Tarr et al. 2001). Aside from colour, recent research reveals women to be quicker and more accurate at finding and identifying plants than men, with better object-location memory (Neave et al. 2005) so these skills would also have assisted in recalling the best places for berry-picking.

Crucially, research suggests that women were the main beneficiaries of these particular skills (Silverman and Eals 1992) and just as an understanding of the division of labour in prehistoric times can help with an understanding of visual-spatial differences, so too can a knowledge of gender differences boost our understanding of the division of labour that operated in this distant time. In this way, we can see women's strengths in object location, memory and colour would have helped with foraging for plant food, maintaining the fabric of society, managing people and caretaking of infants and their greater empathic skills, and their leaning towards the collective, would have assisted with this too. By contrast, the high incidence of colour blindness in men would have been a major advantage in hunting activities but not in gathering activities (due to the inability to distinguish red from green, and thereby select ripe fruit) and likewise, men's strengths in 3-D vision, field independence and their greater aggression (reflected in the themes they used in drawings) would have been an aid in hunting. Quite conceivably, however, men's greater individualism would not have assisted with maintaining the fabric of society, and maybe this was an area that was left to women.

If you now map the visual skills that increased men's and women's survival opportunities against the design features that we saw earlier characterized men's and women's visual preference (something I did in the article I co-authored with Dr Hamilton and Dr Neave on the impact of gender differences on male and female design, and which is summarized in Table 8.3) then you can see how male and female hunter and gatherer skills impact on male and female design skills. It is as though the male design preference for straight lines, darker colours, lack of detail, 3-D character and field independence come straight from the time when men were engaged primarily as hunters (when they needed to be able to use geometric cues such as distance and direction to navigate in unknown territory) and women's design preferences for rounded shapes, detail and bright colour are skills that complement the division of labour in which women acted as gatherers, nurturers of the young (needing responsiveness to rounded shapes, colours and close up 2-D vision) and homemakers (in a literal sense, making the homes). So in referring to the male design aesthetic, we might refer to the 'hunter style' of design and to the 'gatherer style' when referring to the female design aesthetic. This would apply both to the 'production aesthetic' and to the 'preference aesthetic'.

Visual aesthetics

Much of what was described in the earlier chapters concerning differences in the male and female visual aesthetic illustrates the consequences of the sex differences in the visuo-spatial abilities we have discussed in this chapter. Table 8.3 summarizes the impact of these visuo-spatial differences on men's and women's design production aesthetic but given our finding that preferences parallel production tendencies, one could expect the manifestations of visuo-spatial differences in the production aesthetic to be mirrored in the production aesthetic as well.

A word of caution. Much of the thinking presented above concerning the impact of evolution on visuo-spatial abilities emerges from the field known as 'evolutionary psychology', an area defined as 'the study of human behaviour and cognition by evolutionary theory'. Interestingly, a lecturer in Psychology at Sheffield Hallam University, Dr Rick O'Gorman, writes that the 'social sciences have been in large part resistant to acknowledging that at least some aspects of human behaviour and cognition are likely due not primarily to socialization processes, ill-defined as these are, but due instead to a result of the … evolutionary theory of *Homo sapiens'* (1999, 96). Instead, he writes, there is a favouring of a belief in the 'arbitrary reversibility of gender roles' (ibid. 96) and the notion that 'we can create any world we want simply by changing our socialization practices' (Daly and Wilson, quoted in ibid. 96).

Such a belief, Rick O'Gorman argues, assumes human cognitive abilities to be 'domain general' so that what is true of humans of one culture or gender is true of humans of another culture or gender. This assumption, he says, rests on a belief in what he calls a 'cognitive tabula rasa', a notion he refutes with evidence of 'domain-specific' cognitive processes. An example from the animal world is the disposition of cats to pounce on a piece of string dragged in front of them, a disposition not found amongst rabbits and the gender differences we have discussed in visual-spatial abilities would also be examples of 'domain specific' cognitive processes. In Dr O'Gorman's view, evolutionary theory offers a framework for the study of

Table 8.3 The way in which men and women's visual-spatial differences are reflected in design tendencies

Visuo-spatial ability	The features of the *male* production aesthetic in which this difference in visuo-spatial ability will manifest itself	The features of the *female* production aesthetic in which this difference in visuo-spatial ability will manifest itself
Men have better 3-D rotation skills than women	Preference for 3-D ability representations; because this skill arguably evolved in relation to hunting and spying prey at a distance against a distant horizon, there is a preference for straight lines, mimicking the distant horizon, over rounded shapes At a distance, colours look dark, and no detail is apparent so the evolved abilities for hunting would be associated also with fondness for darker colours and lack of detail	Preference for 2-D representations; because this skill arguably evolved in relation to gathering, and seeing berries close-up, there is a preference for rounded lines, mimicking the berries that were the object of attention Close-up, colours look lighter, and detail is apparent so the evolved abilities for gathering would be associated with a fondness for brighter colours and detail
Colour blindness, colour recognition and colour preferences	High proportion of men will be colour-blind and perceive colours differently from women; no tetrachromats in the male population and therefore less extreme sensitivity to colour; preference for blue over pink	Low proportion of women will be colour-blind and therefore will perceive colours differently from men; some there maybe a high proportion of tetrachromats in the female population and therefore some extreme sensitivity to colour; preference for pink over blue
Daylight vision	Superior night-time vision may mean that men require less night-time illumination than women	Inferior night-time vision may mean that women require more night-time illumination
Attention and location memory	Inferior object location memory may make it less attractive for men than women to have detail	Superior object location memory may make it more attractive to have detail
Field independence	A greater propensity to field independence may make men more tolerant of discordances in intersecting planes	A lesser propensity to field independence may make women less tolerant of discordances in intersecting planes

human behaviour and cognition that encompasses existing psychological research knowledge and embeds within a larger paradigm accounting for the behaviour of all forms of life.

Unfortunately, it would appear to be difficult to achieve a constructive dialogue between the holders of the 'domain general' and the 'domain specific' approaches. By way of example the references to evolutionary champions in Deborah Cameron's book *The Myth of Mars and Venus* published in 2007. As we say earlier, this book, plays down the role of sex differences in men's and women's use of language and in the course of it describes evolutionary champions as 'politically motivated critics' whose accounts are 'based not on facts, but on myths' and who, in respect of adversaries (that is, those who deny sex difference or argue for the primacy of socialization) 'just denounce them and those who advance them as reactionary and bigoted' (Cameron 2007b). If this is the reaction of evolutionists, then it would appear to characterize both sides of the debate!

It is important to be mindful of the fact that Deborah Cameron's subject is sex differences in language use, an area in which evidence for sex differences is much weaker than in the area of visuo-spatial abilities where differences are, as we have seen, the most robust of all the cognitive sex differences. While Cameron argues against sex differences in language use, other commentators, as we have seen, have argued strongly in their favour. If we accept that there may be sex differences in the use of language, then explanations could, like visual differences, reside in evolutionary theory (the more competitive style of men's language accompanied the hunter lifestyle, while the more empathic style of women accompanied their nurturing activities). The differences could also be explained as a result of the social pressures that men and women experience in the present day. We will expand on these present-day sociological influences in the next section.

Sociological Influences on Behaviour

Visual differences

In an article I wrote with Andrew Colman, Professor of Psychology at Leicester University (Moss and Colman 2001), we argued that the different cultural experiences of men and women could have a role alongside biology in explaining the differences between men's and women's visual preferences. We cited the fact that experimental evidence has established that, other things being equal, familiarity for objects of all kinds tends to lead to increased liking for them (Zajonc 1968), at least up to a very high level of familiarity (Colman et al. 1986). So even if the ultimate origin of differences is biological, some of the gender differences reported in this book could be influenced by familiarity effects.

We went on to argue that the reported male preference for linearity, technicality, three-dimensionality and functionality in design may also reflect the fact that these attributes are more characteristic of male than female toys and other cultural objects, and that this familiarity may lead to greater liking. Likewise, the greater female interest in colour may reflect the fact that female toys and other cultural objects are more often brightly coloured than their male counterparts, even if this difference in the colouring of toys is ultimately due to biological differences in colour vision. The fact that representations of human forms by both sexes tend to be biased towards same-sex representations could be similarly influenced by the fact that, other things being equal, people tend to choose that they know best. Using this logic, the phrase 'I know what I like' could often be translated as 'I like what I know'.

One of our conclusions was that the cultural explanation for these differences had to remain speculative and that it merely pushed the problem back a step. It still remained to be explained *why* toys and other cultural objects tended to be gender-typed in the way that they are. For example, the fact that men may have a greater tendency than women to value functionality over aesthetics may well be explained by their greater exposure to functional objects throughout the socialization process, but that does not explain very much because the male gender-typing of functionality remains unexplained (Moss and Colman 2001). The limitations of a sociological explanation are likewise apparent in the experiment in colour preferences conducted by Professor Hurlbert and Dr Ling of the University of Newcastle upon Tyne since the experiment showed that colour preferences along gender lines can occur even in cultures where toys are not gender-typed thereby removing the possibility of an immediate cultural explanation.

Language differences

There are many sociological explanations for the putative differences in the way that men and women use language, with many of them raised in an essay on the topic (Meunier n.d.).

Use of the vernacular If one assumes that vernacular forms are lacking in elegance when spoken by a woman, then females may be encouraged and rewarded for using 'elegant' language whereas boys may be allowed more flexibility and roughness in language use: 'Rough talk is discouraged in little girls more strongly than in little boys, in whom parents may often find it more amusing than shocking' (Lakoff 1975, 6). Dale Spender writes that what is usually perceived as compliance to societal forms on the part of females is, in essence, the result of 'a long social imprisonment', leaving men the use of the 'powerful language' of creation (Spender 1980a).

Assertiveness It has been argued that the language historically used by females stems from oppressive structures whereby women addressed men as their masters (Daly 1991a) and Cameron also points out to the origins of these linguistic practices in children's activities that shape various styles of speech: 'Boys tend to play in large groups organized hierarchically; thus they learn direct, confrontational speech. Girls play in small groups of "best friends", where they learn to maximize intimacy and minimize conflict' (Cameron 1992, 73).

Politeness, although positively valued today, was once a sign of humility and since females historically addressed their husband with reverence, this may explain why females are often found to be more polite in anthropological studies. However, since the relationship between language and gender is dependent on context (Meunier n.d.), the way politeness can be used in modern society has lost some of its historical function.

Biological Factors

Having examined societal factors, there remains to be discussed possible biological ones. Diane Halpern, Professor of Psychology at Claremont McKenna College, and President of the American Psychological Association, wrote of the changes that took place in her own thinking around the time she wrote her book on sex differences (Halpern 2000) moved her to downplay the importance of sociological factors. As she writes: 'At the time [I started writing this book], it seemed clear to me that any sex differences in thinking abilities were due to socialization practices, artifacts, and mistakes in the research. After reviewing a pile of journal articles that stood several feet high and numerous books and book chapters that dwarfed the stack of journal articles, I changed my mind' (Wikipedia: 'Sex Differences in Cognitive Abilities').

Some of this rethinking involved a shift in the importance given to biological factors. One of these is 'sex differences in the structure and functioning of the brain systems' which according to David Geary, Professor of Psychology at the University of Missouri 'support some spatial abilities' (Geary 1998, 293) and also support language used. As Geary has written 'it appears that many basic language skills are represented in both the left and the right hemispheres for many women but that these functions are largely represented in the left hemisphere for most men' (Geary 1998, 266). Moreover, according to Geary (1998, 267) 'the larger corpus callosum of women allows the language centers of the left and right hemispheres to communicate with each other'.

One factor creating these differences in brain structure may be hormones. According to doctor and psychiatrist Dr Louann Brizendine (2006), hormones play an important role in influencing behaviour and this is something she first noticed as a medical student at Yale. At that time she had asked about the gender of subjects in a particular experiment and the professor in charge stated quite simply that they never used females in these studies since 'their menstrual cycles would just mess up the data' (Newland 2006). It took several decades, according to Brizendine, for the medical scientific community to recognize that, medically, women were not just small men, and then to start to throw money into researching gender-specific medicine. Until then, the medical establishment had assumed that men and women's reactions were inter-changeable and that women did not have unique experiences, a way of thinking that made it difficult for patients suffering from PMT. 'When these patients tried to talk to their own doctors or psychiatrists about how their hormones were affecting their emotions, they would get the brushoff' (Tyre and Scelfo 2006). Brizendine now works as a gender-specific psychiatrist at the Langley Porter Institute in San Francisco, treating about 600 women a year and in her view, hormones can 'create a woman's reality' shaping 'women's desires, values and the very way she perceives reality' (Brizendine 2006, 3).

According to Brizendine, early oestrogen can stimulate not only the female brain circuits and centres for observation, but also communications, gut feelings, tending and caring. Her view is that 'genes and hormones create a reality in [women's] brains that tell them social connection is at the core of their being' and she explains that while hormones do not cause the behaviour they 'raise the likelihood that under certain circumstances a behaviour will occur' (Tannen 2006). She explains how up to the beginning of the eighth week of life, all brains start off as female ('female is nature's default gender setting') and that from that point onwards the male brain is shaped by testosterone, a hormone that shrinks the brain's communications faculties and limits the ability to empathize and spot emotion. Brizendine argues that the testosterone-formed boy brain does not look for social connection in the same way as the oestrogen-formed female brain, citing the fact that disorders that inhibit the perception of social nuance (so-called 'autism spectrum disorders' and Asperger's syndrome) are eight times more common in boys than girls. Moreover, the fact that these differences emerge early in life and across cultures, points, in her view, to the involvement of biological factors in the production of male and female behaviours.

This view appears to be shared by Stanford University Professor Emeritus of Psychology Eleanor Maccoby who, in her speech accepting the Eleanor Maccoby Book Award for her 1998 book, *The Two Sexes: Growing Up Apart, Coming Together*, she commented that:

> 'Developmentalists have placed too little emphasis on how biology interacts with environmental influences to guide children's gender development. … By and large, the daily routines of family life do not have much impact on the strong tendency of children to separate into same-sex groups, and probably not on the distinctive activities enacted by male and female groups.'
>
> (Carpenter 2000)

Maccoby went on to speak of research that underscores biology's role in shaping behaviour, referring to experiments with nonhuman primates in which testosterone administered to female foetuses late in gestation yields more typically masculine behaviour and ethological studies in which gender divergences are highlighted in animals as well as humans. This leads her to conclude that: 'The parallels are sufficiently strong, I believe, to give us some confidence that there is an evolved, genetic basis for several of the robust gender divergences that have been documented in human children' (ibid.).

There is no shortage of additional evidence. By the time boys become men, and peaking at age 21, they are producing ten times as much testosterone as women, a hormone that is associated with sex drive and aggression and that has been shown to decrease talking as well as interest in socializing (Rowe et al. 2004; Sanchez-Martin et al. 2000). This could be a factor in the greater aggression found in men in empirical research across multiple settings and age groups (Putrevu 2004) and one might similarly ask whether it could also be a factor in visual-spatial abilities

An answer is not hard to find. In *utero* and postnatal exposure to gonadal steroids (principally testosterone and estradiol) are associated with differential spatial ability in humans and some animal species (Moss et al. 2007a). There appears to be a nonlinear relationship (an inverted U shape) between steroids and spatial ability such that spatial ability appears maximal in the low–medium male-typical range and poorer under the female-typical situation of low levels (strangely, poorer spatial ability is also associated with high levels). In terms of the impact of androgen, it appears that exposure during foetal life promotes the sexually dimorphic development of the visual processing pathway, and visual biases for object movement or form/colour (Hampson 2000; Alexander 2003). The resulting differences between the visuo-spatial abilities of men and women are considered to be the most robust and persistent of all the cognitive sex differences (Halpern 2000).

These hormones may be at the root of some of the differences we have observed between men's and women's eyes and their vision. As we have seen, not only are there differences in the relative incidence of colour blindness and tetrachromatism in men and women, but men's eyes are also larger than women's, configuring them for a type of long-distance vision, arguably a factor in men's superiority in guiding or intercepting projectiles (Watson and Kimura 1991; Moss et al. 2007a). Furthermore, research has shown that on average men's eyes are set further apart (63mm) than females' (58mm) and since distance between the eyes correlates with improved stereoscopic vision and greater depth perception (by allowing the eyes to rotate at a wider angle), this greater distance between men's eyes may be a factor in their superior visual-spatial skills (Evereklioglu et al. 2002 and Ing et al. 2006).

The view that biology has a major influence on behaviour is widely, although not universally, held. Dr Helen Cronin, Visiting Fellow at the London School of Economics, believes that evolved differences in biology explain many of the differences observed between men and women. As she says in an article written in 2005:

> 'A wealth of evidence backs up this view of our evolutionary endowment, ranging from newborns (even at one day old, girls prefer a human face, boys a mechanical mobile) to pathology (females exposed to "male" hormones in the womb are typically "tomboyish" and surpass the female average in spatial skills – and vice versa for males) and children's play (boys' games are competitive, big on rules and establishing a

> winner, girls' are more cooperative and end in consensus). These and other predictable sex differences are robust across cultures, and throughout history.'
>
> (Cronin 2005)

Similiary, Simon Baron-Cohen, Professor in the Department of Psychiatry and Psychology at the University of Cambridge, argues for the role of biology, arguing that the female brain is more hard-wired for empathy than men (2003). He goes on to argue that the career outlets for people with the 'female brain' are restricted largely to nursing, counselling, social work, therapy, personnel and primary school teaching (1993, 20) and one might well add other jobs to the list, such as the job of manager since most research supports the notion that the best managers are those with 'transformational leadership' skills, a set of skills involving teamwork and empathic skills. In other words, a recognition of these skills in women, far from condemning them to low-paid jobs, should open doors. The fact that the possession of empathic skills may not be to the exclusion of logical skills but rather a rich addition to them, if this makes these skills relevant to a wide range of managerial, teaching and administrative positions. Moreover, some of the professions Baron-Cohen pinpoints as particularly suited to the 'male brain' (music and the law) would also lend themselves to those with empathic and logical skills.

Before leaving this round-up of those advocating a role for biology in behaviour we should mention Sandra Witelson, Professor of Psychiatry and Neuroscience at McMaster University, in Ontario Canada who believes, like others before her, that gender shapes the anatomy of male and female brains in separate but equal ways, beginning at birth. This leads her to state:

> 'What is astonishing to me is that it is so obvious that there are sex differences in the brain and these are likely to be translated into some cognitive differences because the brain helps us to think and feel and move and act.'
>
> (Witelson 2005)

She anticipates that many people will not want to accept this since 'there is a large segment of the population that wants to pretend this is not true' (ibid.).

The Lack of Consensus as to Causes

Talk of biological differences in cognitive behaviour will send shock waves through certain circles and indeed Simon Baron-Cohen, Director of the Autism Research Centre at Cambridge University, waited several years before writing his book on sex differences *The Essential Difference* (2006), feeling that it was too 'politically sensitive' to complete any earlier. The notion of biological origins to sex differences is in fact a long way from finding universal favour particularly as there is still no unanimity concerning the nature of sex differences. Helen Haste, for example, Professor of Psychology at the University of Bath, takes the view that

'... beliefs about sex difference served the needs of a patriarchal society, and were largely illusory distortions.' In her view:

> 'The duality of gender, maps on to the much deeper cultural metaphor of dualism which permeates Western thinking, and both reinforces it and is reinforced by it. To challenge distorting stereotypes of gender requires challenging the underlying cultural metaphor of dualism.'
>
> (Haste n.d.)

In a similar vein, Melissa Hines, Professor of Psychology at City University and author of *Brain Gender* (2004), also expresses concern about the risk of stereotyping. She argues that some of Brizendine's links have yet to be established and that some people will use the information 'to indicate that all our stereotyping of males and females are biologically innate' and will not take sufficient account of the fact that 'the brain is changeable; it changes all the time' (Midgley 2006). In fact, there does not appear to be the yawning chasm between viewpoints that these opinions suggest, since Dr Brizendine makes it clear that biology is just the starting point, with experience as a further factor shaping brains. So, although people often refer to the 'nature vs. nurture' debate as if we have to choose between these two factors. Eleanor Maccoby sanely suggested in her 1998 book *The Two Sexes: Growing Up Apart, Coming Together* that the explanation for sex differences lies in a combination of social and biological factors. As she puts it, 'Nature and nurture are jointly involved in everything human beings do' (ibid., 89).

It should be clear by now that the approach adopted in this book is to take a middle line between the sociocultural and the evolutionary psychological perspectives, largely because the research evidence points to influences from both sets of factors.

PART IV

Implications

Chapter 9
Implications for Graphic, Product, Web Design and Marketing

As we saw earlier, men and women both critical roles to play as consumers and decision-makers. In the US, women control over 50 per cent of the available wealth (Johnson and Learned, 2004, 8), spend more than two trillion dollars a year (ibid. vii) and account for 51 per cent of purchasing managers (ibid. 9). In the UK, they are responsible for greatly in excess of 50 per cent of purchases of grocery items, furniture, books, health and beauty products and new cars (Moss 1999). Men, by contrast, have a dominant role in the purchase of petrol, computers and large electrical goods. Yet, despite the major influence that men and women both have on purchasing, the issue of how products should best be framed for markets of men and women has to a great extent been overlooked. This book fills the gap by presenting much of the evidence currently available and it is hoped that this will offer new insights to design and marketing managers as well as stimulate new research.

Why does this matter? Customers remain at the heart of any organization (Mohanty 1999) and therefore companies need to keep abreast of changing customer requirements (Andriopoulos and Dawson 2009). As we have seen, the mirroring principle holds true that people are attracted to products that mirror their own self-concept and if a full appreciation of what attracts men and women is not currently available, then it is less likely that products will be offered that fully match their preferences. This would be a major failure. As Leslie de Chernatony, Professor of Brand Marketing at the Birmingham Business School says 'Many regards effective marketing as … a matching process where suppliers' value-added processes are structured in such a way to almost mirror buyers' needs' (1995). A failure to match customer preferences will mean that products are suboptimised and since design can add competitive advantage in situations of intense market conditions (Andriopoulos and Dawson 2009), profitability will be impacted too.

In this final chapter, we will explore some of the implications for organizations of the evidence for gendered aesthetics presented earlier. We will begin by looking at a sample of products and websites and, in each case, will look at the extent to which these appear to match the markets for which they are intended. Underpinning this discussion will be the conclusions discussed earlier concerning gendered design and marketing preferences (summarized in Table 9.1). In the rest of this chapter, we will examine the extent to which organizations are reflecting these differences in the marketing and design of their products, and discuss some of the obstacles to doing this.

Table 9.1 Summary of the visual and linguistic differences discussed in this book

	Male productions and preferences	**Female productions and preferences**
Visual elements	Straight lines and shapes	Rounded lines and shapes
	Use of few and darker colours	Use of many and brighter colours
	Regular typography	Irregular typography
	3-D images	2-D images
	Lack of detail	Detail
	Images of men	Images of women
	Moving objects	Stationary objects
Informational elements	Simple, factual information with just one or two features	More original information with multiple features
	Attribute oriented adverts	Category-oriented adverts
	Competitive situations within the advertisements	Equal preference for competitive, harmonious or self-competitive situations
	Depiction of large groups	Depiction of large or small groups
	Comparative advertising appeals	Harmonious relationships
	Stereotyped role portrayals except for a substantial minority of non-traditional consumers	Stereotyped role portrayals except for a substantial minority of non-traditional consumers
	Discourse is based on monologes and turn taking but not interruptions	Discourse is based on dialogues and argument with interruptions encouraged
	The verbal style used is limited and unspontaneous	The verbal style is uninhibited, rich, natural, enjoyable and spontaneous

Product and Web Design

The products I will discuss here are ones I have been involved with in the course of research or consultancy projects and I make no claims as to their representativeness. The same caveat will apply to the websites investigated later on in this chapter.

A word on the importance of products. Simon Marks, son of the founder of Marks and Spencer, would often talk about the three Ps as being crucial to success – Product, People and Property (Bevan 2007) and a successor, Rick Greenbury (Chairman from 1991 to 1999), the first man to take Marks and Spencer's annual sales over the £1 billion point, described how obsessed Lord Marks was with the product and getting this right. This obsession is echoed by other successful companies.

Mobile phone manufacturer Nokia is a textbook example. Frank Nuovo, Nokia's chief designer, has talked of the need for product designers to ensure that product appeal and functionality are tied to specific customer expectations (CE Designers 2005) and he may have been taking his cue from Jorma Ollila, the head of Nokia, who takes responsibility for focusing the company on consumers and giving them what they want. This approach is all the more remarkable since it occurred at a time when rivals like Motorola and Ericsson were concentrating on engineering products that were technological marvels. Olilla, meanwhile, encouraged his staff to focus on the role that mobiles played in people's lives and, under his direction, the company focused on making easy-to-use phones. This has been a winning strategy for Nokia and by 1998, it owned a quarter of the mobile phone market and, by 2000, it was making one in three mobile phones worldwide. By 2007, Nokia's share of the market in handsets had increased to 38 per cent, nearly three times that of its nearest rival, Motorola (Mobiz 2007).

Focusing on the Customer

How common is this obsession with understanding what the customer wants? A we saw earlier, there are many market segments and companies that are not focusing sufficiently on the needs and preferences of the end-user and many have a long way to go in translating what we now know about men and women's design preferences into products and marketing campaigns. To some extent, however, it appears that the failure to produce products that fully reflect customer preferences is rooted in a failure to focus on the demographics of the target market and fully register the gender balance of this market. To some extent, however, the failure to produce products that mirror customer preferences is due to ignorance regarding the relevant research findings. To give companies their due, this is not their fault since much of the research information has appeared only in specialist marketing journals and this is the first book to bring this information to the attention of a wider audience.

Of course, without a detailed understanding of the research findings regarding male and female design and advertising preferences, firms' attempts to tailor products around customers' needs and preferences will be of limited success. However, if organizations do make the effort to delineate the market and shape products around the needs of their customers, then they will be taking an important step towards satisfying the homogeneity or congruency principle which, as we have seen, lies at the heart of successful marketing.

The steps that firms need to follow are shown in Figure 9.1. As you can see, the first step involves identifying the target market and the demographics of the customers within this, while the second involved identifying *lifestyle* elements connected with the target market. The third and final stage involves identifying distinguishing features related to the *thematic* and cognitive *visual* preferences of the target market, with some of the main points that will come into play shown in Table 9.1.

As we shall see in the next sections exploring four relatively progressive market segments, some pioneering companies are embarking on the first phase of this process by identifying the target market. Some have even moved into phase two by identifying the lifestyle of this target market. However, although some companies have ventured into stage three, they rarely make use of more than one or two of the features that distinguish male and female preferences, and seldom take a comprehensive look at all the features that distinguish male and female productions and preferences (see Table 9.1).

It is to be hoped that, as knowledge concerning the aesthetic gender continuum becomes better known, companies will spend more time exploring the ways in which the features shown in Table 9.1 can be better exploited to provide customers with designs and advertisements that fully satisfy their visual and linguistic preferences. Some of the obstacles that prevent organizations from doing this will be discussed later in this chapter.

Meanwhile, we will look at four relatively progressive sectors which have all embarked on stage one of the process. Some have progressed to stage two and some have even started to consider a few of the stage three elements. The first of the sectors we will look at is the Small Electrical Products sector.

Phase 1	**Phase 2**	**Phase 3**
Indentifying the gender demographics of the target market	Identifying distinguishing features about the *lifestyle* of the target market	Identifying distinguishing features concerning the *thematic* and cognitive *visual* preferences of men and women as well as any differences in their linguistic preferences

Figure 9.1 Conceptual stages in achieving the homogeneity/congruity principle

Small Electrical Products Sector

The category of small electrical products covers products such as computers, cameras and personal digital assistants and women's share of this market amounts to 57 per cent of the $96 billion annual spend (Consumer Electronics Association 2003). This is a market, moreover, in which women buy these products largely for themselves and so tend not to act in 'provider mode' by buying these products for other people (Warner 2006, 93). For example, other studies have revealed that even where men are the primary *purchasers* of products, women can still have a signigficant influence on the purchase. An example is the fact that, according to Warner (2006), women influence 75 per cent of the purchases of high-tech goods such as DVDs, flat-screen televisions and complex stereo systems. This fact draws attention to the important role that women, play in purchasing decisions regarding electrical goods. Yet, despite this importance, a meagre 1 per cent of women surveyed by the Consumer Electronics Association (2003) thought that manufacturers had them in mind when creating products. This is a dismally low figure but the picture is not entirely bleak since some companies are noticing the demographics and taking appropriate action.

Bob Scaglione, for example, Sharp's Vice President of Marketing noticed that the female population was being ignored a bit (Wong 2004) and, as a result, made some changes. In 2002, its flat-panel TVs were redesigned with women in mind and the product line was renamed AQUOS to connote fluidity and a softer touch. It also changed its TV advertising policy by expanding its TV advertisements beyond sports and prime-time slots to Lifetime, the Food Network and The Learning Channel. By 2004, the company claimed to have more than 50 per cent of the market for LCD flat-panel TV screens and these design changes may have been an important factor. They were not the only electrical products company to be responding to the demographics, since Tri-City Electronics, a high-end audio-visual store in North Carolina, introduced a raft of measures to satisfy the female element of its customer base. It replaced the utilitarian atmosphere with a homlier layout, installed a children's area, and even offered tours of the store owner's home to show the products in a real-life setting. According to co-owner Sibyle Hager, 'Revenues have been climbing since' (Wong 2004). Another American electronics retailer, Circuit City, decided to carry an advert prominently featuring one of the sleek TVs in a kitchen and Epson, a leading maker of scanners and printers achieved success by identifying that there was a female-dominated scrapbooking market. If you think about these cases, then you will see that these are examples of companies making a more conscious effort to target end-users using what they know about consumers' lifestyle. So, Sharp connects its product with food while Circuit City makes an association with the kitchen, both areas or domains in which women are thought to have a strong focus.

This kind of targeting marks a modest departure from what other companies are doing insofar as the end-user has been clearly identified and the product developed or displayed in a way that matches what is known of the consumers' *lifestyle*. Other vital steps, as we saw in Figure 9.1, are to match what is known of the consumers' *thematic* and *visual* preferences for colour, shape, detail, 3-dimensionality and match with the environment. Occasionally, you see cases where companies have made adjustments in one of these areas and even if it is just the smallest of changes, it does at least mark a step forward.

A case in point is Sony's Liv line which includes CD players for the kitchen and shower radios. This product range was introduced under the direction of Ellen Glassman, a director of Sony, and was targeted specifically at women. As she says, 'The first question we ask is "who are we designing it for?"' and once the target market is determined, the designers can focus their attention on factors such as style, function and technology. The Liv product line was inspired by Ellen's philosophy that 'The smaller designs should fit better in a home – characteristics desired by consumers in general and women in particular' (Wong 2004) and this is a rare glimpse of a company shaping a product around the visual preferences of the end-user. In this case, it sounds very much as though Ellen Glassman has appreciated the importance of appealing to women's greater field dependence, as evidenced in a desire for products that blend in with their surroundings. The awareness may or may not have come from the modest amount of research evidence pointing towards this but conceptually it marks a big leap forward insofar as it provides an example of an organization mapping what it knows about the target market's *visual* preferences onto product development. As such, it marks a move to Stage Three of our three-stage model for achieving congruence and as such should be applauded. How many other household products are seeking to blend in with their surroundings?

Another product which shows some signs of venturing into Stage Three, is the kettle. This is the most used utensil in the UK household, picked up on average fifteen times a day and with a pattern of sales that has remained stable since a high proportion of kettle sales (one in five) are replacements. The UK market research data shows that most purchasers of kettles are female (Moss 1995) and this finding is consistent with data from the Family Expenditre Survey which shows that a significantly greater number of women than men buy small electrical goods (ibid.).

In terms of their design history, kettles have progressed from the old 'Copper Kettle', to the whistler and the immersed element kettle of 1907. From there they moved on to the automatic kettle that switched itself off when the water reached boiling point, the plastic kettle and the jug kettle in in the late 1970s. The final design innovations were the 'pistol grip' handle and the forward design which enabled the kettle to be used without lifting. The creation of the cordless kettle followed shortly after this in 1985 (Moss 1996a). These design landmarks are summarized in Table 9.2.

As you can see, the designers of all these landmark kettles were male and in the 1990s when I collected this information, the vast majority of designers at the companies producing kettles (Kenwood, Philips, Russsell Hobbs and Morphy Richards) were male. In fact, the Design Director at Morphy Richards described

Table 9.2 Kettles and their designers

Kettle	Designer
Immersed element kettle, 1907	Peter Behrens, AEG Electric
Automatic kettle, 'K1', 1954	Russell Hobbs
Kenwood kettle, 1950s	Kenneth Grange, Pentagram
'The Rainbow', 1973	Paul Moss, Hoover
The jug kettle, 1979	Max Byrd, Redring, and a male Consultant
'The Freeline', cordless kettle, 1985	Richard Seymour and Dick Powell, Tefal

Sources: (i) Cohen (1993) (ii) information from individual kettle manufacturers.

how in 1995 he had tried to recruit some female designers but how, in his view, the quality of the 'girls' work' was not really up to scratch.

What would a kettle designed by a woman look like? The dearth of female product designers makes it difficult to compare male and female-produced kettles and so in order to get a better idea of how male and female-produced kettles might compare, I asked three female designers to design an electric kettle. One of these actually went on to work as a designer for the Terence Conran's 'Habitat' chain of furniture stores and the sketch designs that they produced revealed a completely new look to kettles. Instead of bulbous, bulky objects in a single colour, we had compact shapes, closer in style to a rotund teapot, with the body of the kettle in a different colour to the spout and handle. Pink, bright yellow and turquoise were the dominant colours used and in some cases, the handle was decorated with polka dots and the spout with stripes.

These kettle designs were so different from the designs produced commercially that I embarked on an experiment. I set these designs alongside photographs of jug kettles dating from the 1990s – square-shaped objects with square shaped handles, in a bottle green or navy coloured plastic and asked 30 male and 30 female users of a university library to indicate which kettle they preferred. Of course, there were methodological weaknesses in this experiment since the images, although similar in size, were not similar in quality (some showed design sketches and some finished kettles. However, despite these weaknesses, the results (Moss 1996a) gave pause for though since they showed that 62 per cent of the females' choices were for kettles designed by females, while 52 per cent of the men's selections were for male-designed kettles. Once again, the results pointed to a 'self-selecting' tendency in people's preferences and, since the majority of purchasers of kettles are female, the results suggest that kettle manufacturers might do well to add elements of the female production aesthetic to the kettles they produce.

Have kettle designs changed since the 1990s? A roundup of contemporary kettles reveals that they are still bulky in shape and fashioned in only chrome, stainless steel or white. Most of these are bulbous, penguin-shaped objects with bulky black handles, and very different from the designs produced by the three female designers. Seeing the contrast makes it apparent that there is potential for redesigning kettles to appeal more to the cognitive preferences of the female consumer, the major purchaser of this item. Kettle manufacturers turned to coloured kettles in 1987, a consequence either of a growing realization of the importance of colour to women, or perhaps as a result of fashion. Whatever the reason, the concern to improve on an element in the overall design – colour – must be seen as positive and as an example of a move into Stage Three of the three steps to Congruity. One could still have concerns about the appropriateness of the colours chosen and the fact that, on it own, this colour is not sufficient to give the kettles a female look even if the colours were appropriate, we would still be left with a shape and lack of detailing that seems more characteristic of the male than female production aesthetic. All these other features would need to be considered and changed if a kettle fully reflecting the female production were to be produced.

Sportswear

We saw earlier how the market leader, Nike, had given relatively little attention to the question of marketing and developing goods for women. One of the results was that in 2001, only 20 per cent of its sales revenue was from sales to women and, according to the author of *The Power of the Purse* (Warner 2002), for 'much of history' the company was 'about men'. One has to acknowledge the irony in the fact that a firm whose name bears testimony to a *female* goddess, the goddess of victory, overlooked its female market. However, to give the company its due, it did finally awake to the full marketing potential of its name.

Initiatives to attract the female purchaser, include the creation of 'Nike goddess' stores (designed according to a new set of principles with light blue and white colours predominating, and the music softer and less harsh than in the average Niketown) and new products advertised in ways that cease to treat athletes as heroes. This new way of thinking is spelt out by Janelle Fisher, the women's marketing manager for Nike, when she comments that 'No woman thinks that she'll be able to run like Marion Jones because she wears shoes that are named after her' (Warner 2002).

The DIY Industry

The DIY industry has witnessed similar drives to move away from the traditionally masculine marketing of its products. In the US, according to Barbara Kavovit, producer of a line of stylish, affordable tools, 'the home improvement industry is a quarter of a trillion dollar industry and a quarter of it (or about $5 billion) are purchases made by women' (Puente 2004). By way of example, the 'Home Depot' company which until recently used to market its power tools and drywall to men, is now aggressively pursuing women. One of the ways it does this is through classes that teach women how to do home repairs and it is also pursuing entertainment partnerships with home improvement TV shows that are widely watched by women.

In the UK, 80 per cent of buying decisions in the home are made by women and this has inspired the DIY store, B&Q, to take remedial action. The company's director of organization development, Nathan Clements, said that the company's brand was evolving to reflect its growing female customer base and that its 320 stores needed to reflect the broader talent pool. This way of thinking has produced a concern to address the gender balance in 'opinion-forming' functions, including store, regional and general managers, and a concern to recruit more women into senior roles. As Clements said:

> 'Practically, this means working with our suppliers to ensure that when we get a shortlist, that is reflective and balanced from a gender point of view' (Phillips 2008).

The rebrand also meant more DFY ('done for you') products as opposed to the more 'blokey' DIY, Clements added (Phillips 2008).

All these moves are signs that the company has recognized the importance of the large female element in the target market. These steps signal the fact that the organization has passed Stage One of the three-stage process to congruity, and is embarking on Stages Two and Three of the process and modifying products around the needs and wants of the end-user.

The Car Industry

What are the demographics of those who purchase new cars? A Conde Nast report estimated that in 1996, women made up 60 per cent of car sales in the UK. In France, Vincent Dupray of the Automotive department at TNS Sofres estimated that women had a strong role in car purchases: 'One motorist in two in France is female and women account for one-third of the new vehicle market' (*Peugeot Citroen Magazine* 2008). Women also make up 40 per cent of the main users of a vehicle in France.

The growing importance of male as well as female car users and buyers has prompted Ford and Land Rover to organize regular meetings of engineers and pollsters in a bid to encourage them to dream up female-friendly features. These attempts to respond to the demographic patterns of the target market mark a presence at Stage One of the three-stage process and this initial step is to be applauded. Unfortunately, the demographics of the car design industry remain resolutely male with the vast majority of car designers being men. It is difficult to see how this could change in a hurry since one of the entry points for designers, the prestigious MA in car design at the Royal College of Art, is one in which, according to the course leader, David Ahmad, 'a women would have to brave the boys-and-toys world if wanted to succeed' (Allen 2004). The odds are all against it and even an eminent female designer, Jane Priestman, who used to advise car manufacturer, Jaguar cars, said that she was 'only ever allowed to offer advice on the *inside* trim of the car'.

Apparent signs of change can be misleading. In 2000, for example, Anne Asensio was appointed Director of design for medium-sized cars at Renault and then moved to General Motors in 2000 as head of GM's brand studios' designers, in charge of Cadillac, Chevrolet, Buick, Pontiac, Oldsmobile and GMC. However, at the time she left GM, she was Executive Director of Interior Design, a field traditionally the domain of women. According to an article in *AutoObserver* (2007), she told the *Automotive News Europe* Congress in Prague in 2007 that if the motor industry did not involve more women in its product decisions, it risked becoming irrelevant, 'The industry doesn't need cars designed for women but by women', she told the gathering as reported by the sponsoring publication.

One of the consequences of the failure to afford women the opportunity to make a greater contribution to car design may be to make it difficult for the car industry to progress beyond stage 2 of the three-stage process. Unfortunately, this would be to miss out on valuable opportunities to respond to perceived differences in what men and women like in cars. As Valerie Nicolas, Colours and Materials Designer at Citroen's styling centre says: 'Women do not have the same expectations as men. They are more receptive to criteria such as safety – particularly for chidren – economy, respect for the environment, easy maintenance, compact dimensions, convenience and easy handling. And, of course, women are highly sensitive to styling, often more so than to power and performance'.

We have looked at a number of product sectors which are taking steps along the three-stage process to matching customer expectations. These have been in the area of product design (cars and small electrical products), advertising and promotion (DIY) and retailing design (sportswear). An area that we have not highlighted as moving along the three-steps model is that of web design and in the next section we will consider the role that websites can play in achieving greater customer satisfaction.

Websites

Internet marketing is the process of growing and promoting an organization using online media (Tribble Advertising Agency 2008) and its importance is such that leading marketing experts predict that by 2010, the majority of consumers will use the web to inform their choice of purchase, with a third using it to carry out a proportion of their purchasing online (Holland 2008). This prediction makes it likely that by 2010 web sales will account for between 15 and 20 per cent of total retail sales (ibid.). One of the factors feeding the attractions of the world wide web as a marketing tool is the impressive growth in Internet usage worldwide with men and women active participants in this revolution. In the US, equal proportions of men and women use the web and men are ahead of women only in respect of the frequency with which they use the web (Bimber 2000).

Factors that influence Internet usage are said to include socioeconomic status, interest in computers and social networking (Ono and Zavodny 2003) and 'sites that are responsive to user needs' is seen as 'critical for all site designers and managers' (Palmer 2002, 1). In terms of responsiveness, relevant factors are thought to include technical factors such as speed of loading, content (Joergensen and Blythe 2003) as well as design, form (Schenkman and Jonsson 2000; Palmer 2002; Lavie and Tractinsky 2004) and graphics (Chau et al. 2000). The importance of graphics also emerges from study which highlighted the potential of ten factors to cause dissatisfaction amongst users in the US and Netherlands, with one of these being graphics (van Iwaarden et al. 2004). The critical impact that design can have on user experience leads Human Computer Interaction (HCI) specialists to attempt to understand the elements (visual and content) in web design that are valued and those that currently produce a deficit between expectations and experience.

The concentrated effort to understand the elements that will satisfy the customer should not come as a surprise. The business advantages of factoring in customer preferences to products, a practice widely favoured now in the American automotive industry (Irwin and Flass 2003), is widely acknowledged in the practitioner marketing literature. In the case of the positive online experience, this is credited with having a more significant role in customer retention (Aaker 1991; De Chernatony and McDonald 1992; Kapferer 1992) than traditional attributes such as product selection and price (Ibeh et al. 2005). As we saw earlier, my own studies of web design preferences have charted the extent to which people's preferences can vary in line with their gender. As we saw, the most detailed findings emerged from a study in which male and female students rated to websites produced by a further sample of male and female students. A total of 38 male and 26 female students were involved in the rating and the male and female-produced sites that they were rating were selected as being typical of their gender (Moss and Gunn 2009).

The results? These showed a highly significant tendency on the part of men and women to ascribe higher ratings to sites exemplifying the production aesthetic typical of their own gender than to those exemplifying the production aesthetic of the other sex. These results (Moss and Gunn 2005, 2008 and 2009) are statistically highly significant and exemplify the tendency not only for consumer preferences to be differentiated along gender lines (Till and Priluck 2001) but for preferences to follow a mirroring process such that the male production aesthetic is preferred by males (with the exception of images produced within the female production aesthetic) and the female production aesthetic by females. This conclusion supports the development of websites that match the aesthetic preferences of their target market. In fact, the weight of the available evidence suggests that this is a preferable strategy to that of displaying male or female androgyny, an option discussed by Zahedi et al. (2006).

To what extent are companies providing websites that match customer preferences? We will take a look at websites targeting different markets, whether those with equal proportions of men and women, or those with a predominance of either men or women. In the first case (websites targeting markets consisting of equal proportions of men and women) one might expect the websites to show elements of both the male and female web design production aesthetics while, in the case of markets focused on a single gender, one might expect the website to utilize the web design production aesthetic associated with the target gender. This proposition is illustrated in Figure 9.2.

In order to analyse the extent to which this matching or mirroring principle is currently applied, colleagues and I analysed the web aesthetic used in a number of industries. The first of these was higher education, with a target market of roughly equal numbers of men and women (Moss and Gunn 2005) while the two other industries were the Angling and Beauty industries with predominantly male and female markets respectively (Moss et al. 2007c). The research was focused on establishing whether these industries' websites matched the preferences of their target markets. If they did, then one would expect that the websites from the Angling industry, with a predominantly male market, would display features from the male production aesthetic while the websites from the Beauty industry, with a predominantly female market, would contain features draw on largely from the female production aesthetic. By contrast, in a sector such as higher education targeting equal proportions of men and women, one would expect that the websites would contain a mixture of features from the male and female production aesthetics.

A brief word on the markets in these three industries. If we consider the Angling industry, studies in the UK of randomly selected anglers have found them to consist predominantly of men (from 78–98 per cent) (Levine et al. 1999a; Kyle et al. 2004: Hammitt et al. 2004) and this is in line with US research on the Angling industry which reveals 98.9 per cent of anglers to be male. It is in line, also, with

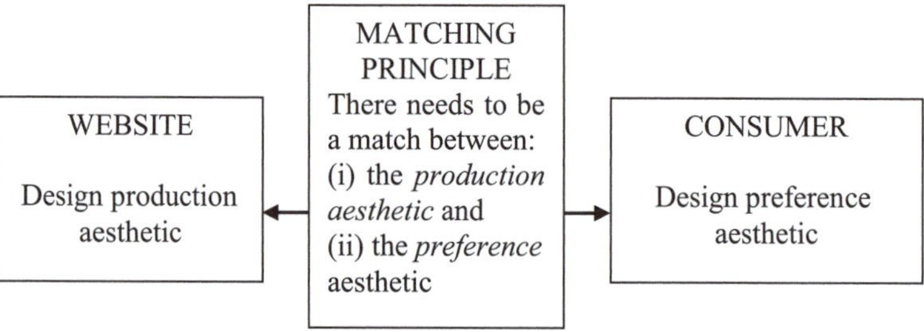

Figure 9.2 The match needed between the design production and preference aesthetic of consumers

UK Government-sponsored research which reveals that 80 per cent of anglers in the UK are men (Environment Agency 2001).

The Beauty industry, by contrast, is focused largely on a female market with market research indicating that women are twice as likely as men to have had health and beauty treatment over the past year and being more willing to spend money on it than men (Mintel 2005) this kind of treatment (ibid.). Further analysis of participation rates shows that women are three times as likely as men to have sun tanning, eight times as likely to have eyelashes/eyebrows tinted or shaped, and ten times as likely to have hair-removal treatment. Moreover, manicure and pedicure treatments are almost completely dominated by female consumers. Overall, the majority of men in the UK have never had health and beauty treatments.

The market for higher education, by contrast, attracts roughly equal numbers of male and female undergraduates and the figures in Table 9.3 shows the percentage of men and women in the student population over a number of years.

These three sectors were chosen since they had clear and distinct markets and the study set out to establish the nature of the aesthetic used in a random sample of websites. To this end, thirty websites were randomly selected and analysed from each of the three industries and rated against the elements that had emerged as significantly different in male and female-produced websites (Moss and Gunn 2006). From this it would be possible to produce a 'gender production coefficient' for the sites and, by comparing this with men's and women's preferences, it was possible to establish the extent to which there was an aesthetic match between the websites of a given sector and its target market.

The results showed an aesthetic match in the case of the Angling industry websites since these displayed a predominantly male production aesthetic (with an overall male gender coefficient of 0.66) in a market made up largely of men (Moss et al. 2007c). However, such a close match between production and preference aesthetics was not found in either the Beauty or higher education sectors (Moss and Gunn 2005; Moss et al. 2007c) since these industries' websites employed a predominantly male design aesthetic (with gender coefficients of 0.68 and 0.72 respectively) all the while targeting markets consisting largely of women (the case of the beauty websites) or an equal proportion of men and women (the case of higher education in the UK).

Table 9.3 UK HEIs, full-time undergraduate students by gender 1995–2003 (HESA online statistics)

	1995/96	1996/97	1998/99	1999/00	2000/01	2001/02	2002/03
Female	50%	53%	52%	53%	53%	53%	53%
Male	50%	47%	48%	47%	47%	47%	47%

The fact that a predominantly male production aesthetic is employed in industry websites targeting a medium to high proportion of female customers, suggests that these websites are unlikely to be optimized for their target market. It suggests also that a greater use of the female production aesthetic would produce a better match between website aesthetic and customer preference.

Others have reached similar conclusions in relation to other industry websites. For example, Michelle Miller commented in April 2007 on the American Airlines *Women Travelers Connected* webpage, a page devoted to female travellers this webpage features travel tips, lifestyle travel packages and business ideas around the idea of being 'connected' and it was very 'left-brain' in orientation and design, with all kinds of boxes, sharp corners and tiny type. In terms of her own reaction, she notes how 'the design leaves me cold ... my first impression when visiting the page was "Wow … good idea, but it certainly doesn't speak to me"' and concludes that, 'if you're going to give women something to hang their hat on, it has to have substance … You have to go deeper – understand a female consumer's needs from within, and learn the language she speaks' (Miller 2007).

Unfortunately, from what we have seen here and earlier on in this book, there are areas of design, including web design, that are not informed by the research we have discussed in male and female design aesthetics. As a consequence, there are likely to be many areas of design and marketing that have a limited grasp of the 'language she speaks' and, consequently, several areas which would have difficulty producing designs or advertising copy that mirrors the preferences of a female target market.

Implications for Organizations

Leslie de Chernatony, Professor of Brand Marketing at Birmingham University has, as we have seen, described effective marketing as following a matching process whereby suppliers processes mirror buyers' needs. He has focused on the demands of service brands and in this area has suggested that similar perceptions are needed between teams and their consumers (1995). As a result, he said that the functional and emotional values of services brands are highly dependent on the staff who deliver the brand promise (De Chernatony et al 2006) and to this end has suggested that attention be paid to the values likely to be held by customers as well as to those held and exhibited by individual employees (ibid.). Ideally, these two sets of values should match and it is suggested that this can be achieved through internal communication and quality control of the Human Resources (HR) function which acts as gatekeepers to those working on the brand.

This recent research crucially shows the inter-dependency of marketing and HR on effective branding and this is to be welcomed. However, while this research is focused on how brand values can be conveyed to customers, it does not focus on how these brand values are created and selected and does not look beyond brand values to design values. If these factors are taken into consideration, how easy is it to achieve a match between the design and brand values created by an organization and those held by the customer?

According to Sunil Shibad, a copywriter and brand strategist at the Flea, a non-traditional marketing communication agency 'there is almost no discussion about the consumer and how best he or she can be satisfied or motivated'. Shibad deplores this state of affairs and its negative impact on marketing:

> 'To advertise to your customer, online or offline, you must start by mentally discarding your own identity. You have to become the people you are communicating with … you must learn to speak the language of your prospect. Often it means emotionally becoming someone you would never in a hundred years be like yourself. In many ways, creating advertising is the same discipline as acting'
>
> (ibid.)

Shibad's thoughts have been quoted verbatim here since he has provided a vivid description of the process that needs to be followed if, in order to satisfy to the customer. This is a complex process which places enormous demands on organizations since they need to be able to deliver solutions that will satisfy the customer, rather than just senior management. One of the major obstacles to doing this lies with the potential mismatch that exists between the preferences of senior management and those of customers (Moss 2007a; Moss et al, 2008) and this obstacle is perpetuated by systems of recruitment and promotion that favour the perspective of senior management rather than that of the customer. This is the problem of achieving 'external fit' which would allow an organization's Human Resources strategy to be brought into line with the firm's chosen path in its product market (Purcell, 2003, 51–2).

Barbara Rogoff in her book '*The Cultural Nature of Human Development*' (2003) argues for the difficulty of achieving consensus when there are disparate points of view but insists, inspite of this, on the importance of reaching agreement on the 'truth'. As she writes:

> 'To include the perspective of other communities, communication between community "insiders" and "outsiders" is essential. It is not a matter of which perspective is correct – both have an angle on the phenomenon that helps to build understanding'.

The question which has not adequately been addressed before is how an organization allows the view of outsiders to be reflected inside an organization. This if part of a bigger question as to how to satisfy customer preferences.

Moving Ahead

There are a number of possible ways forward for organizations. As we have suggested earlier, the first step is perhaps to examine the target demographics, the first phase of our three-step approach to achieving congruence, and the next step is to initiate a discussion on possible differences between the perspective of those inside and those outside the organization. This discussion may lead the organization to discuss both the *lifestyle* characteristics of the target market and its *visual* and *linguistic* preferences. A large research base is now available to fuel this discussion and if the discussion prospers, products and advertising should be fashioned around what we now know about men and women's preferences. This knowledge, if applied well, could lead organizations to modify existing designs and advertisements so as to create products that are more closely matched to the preferences of the target market. The modifications that are necessary may be evolutionary or even revolutionary in character, particularly if comparison with the research shows that large-scale change is needed. Whoever said that websites had to be formulaic in character or that household products, which often sit in a domestic environment, need to emphasize functionality and brand name above aesthetic appearance?

Of course, these discussions may not prosper if there is an initial lack of awareness of the role gender can play in influencing perceptions and preferences and we should not be surprised by if this is the case given the conventional neglect of gender as a segmentation variable in marketing (Hirschman 1993) and the continued domination of the sociological perspective.

Evidence of the weight still ascribed to the sociological perspective comes from Andrew Nelkin, Vice- President of the optical group at Panasonic, who has commented that 'If you try to influence design by gender, you end up missing good design'. He recounts how, not long ago, electronics makers concluded that women wanted their devices to be smaller, lighter and easier to use. 'But in reality those are things women want, but men want, too'. In his view, 'The traditional boundary of what we deemed male- and female-oriented is no longer there' (Consumer Electronics Association 2003). A similar sentiment comes from Christine Cryne, former CEO of the Chartered Institute of Marketing from 2005 to 2006 and Senior Director of Consumer Direct at the UK's Office of Fair Trading. In an email to the author on 6 July 2008 she commented on the importance of situational factors:

> 'The forty something woman in a successful career who does not have children has little in common with the twenty year old mother of toddlers who stays at home. It is more meaningful to group these people according to their lifestyle. Consumers, both men and women, all now play varied roles at different times of their lives. For example, the business traveller who flies first class during the week may choose to use a budget airline when travelling with the family on holiday. It is important for the direct marketing industry to understand that the motivation for such buying behaviour are more complex than gender.'
>
> (http://www.broadsystem.com/articles/articles_gender.htm)

Others have, in a similar way, played down the importance of gender as a segmentation variable. By way of example, Catherine Cave, Senior Business analyst at NVH Marketing Services, stated that:

> '...gender is only the first cut – the database then needs to be overlaid and segmented again, possibly using lifestyle and debt information, if you are to achieve accurate targeting.'
>
> (ibid.)

So, we can see that a wide variety of views are held on the importance of gender as a segmentation variable. In point of the evidence for cognitive sex differences in visuo-spatial abilities is extremely robust and this is likely to be a major factor in the powerful evidence we have found for a male and female design aesthetic continuum. Extreme masculine and female production aesthetics may lie at either end with weaker versions of the same in between and we could debate, *ad nauseam*, the importance of social and biological factors. Whatever the underlying factors, the differences are too important and robust to ignore.

Inside-outside Perspective

From an organizational perspective, the first step in achieving a match between the product offering and customer preferences is to acknowledge the role gender plays in people's perceptions. Once this is accepted, the next step is to compare the internal and external demographics and compare the likely perceptions of those inside and outside the organization. This is to offer what Baden-Fuller (1995) calls the 'inside-out' and the 'outside-in' perspectives on strategy.

If a difference in demographics and perceptions emerges between those inside and those outside the organization, then a paradigm shift is required on the part of an organization's thinking, necessitating 'transformational' change. This type of change offers a bigger step change than its alternative of 'realignment' which offers non-paradigmatic change implemented through stages initiatives (Balogun and Hope Hailey 2008). Transformational change, by contrast, is more fundamental change and an organization can choose to do this in a more or less gradual way, with the slow type of change known as 'evolution' and the faster one known as 'revolution' (ibid.). The two options are shown in Figure 9.3 below with the shorter-term option represented as the 'radical' one and the longer-term option as the 'evolutionary' one at the other end of the continuum (see Figure 9.3).

In essence, the radical options involve recruiting and promoting staff whose perceptions and aesthetic preferences match those of the target market. A less radical and more evolutionary strategy would encourage greater diversity in the people's thinking through a process of training and development. This would focus on the diverse nature of people's aesthetic preferences and likely differences between the thinking of customers on the one hand, and those in the design and marketing functions on the other. This second option may produce longer-term change than the first but both would facilitate movement through the three-step change model shown in Figure 9.1.

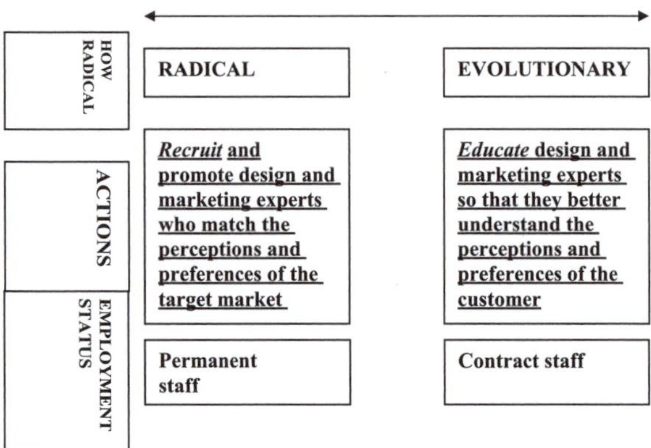

Figure 9.3 The continuum of options available to organizations for effecting change

Without taking one of the courses of action shown in the radical-evolutionary model shown in Figure 9.3 it will be difficult for organizations to achieve the congruence with customer preferences we have discussed in the course of this book. It will also be difficult to fulfil the vision Shibad proposes of internal actors who can take on the thinking of the external customer-base.

If we combine the three-step model with the radical/evolutionary approach, then we have the model shown in Figure 9.4.

Unfortunately, the factors that impact on an organization's ability to successfully achieve congruence do not stop here but include also issues relating to the employment status of those employed, and the availability of appropriate design and marketing experts (that is, experts who can produce the full range of masculine and female design aesthetic responses). We will look at these two points in the next two sections and then examine the way that the homogeneity principle can influence staff selection. In a final section, we will consider the practical implications of the homogeneity principle for the design and advertising industries.

Employment Status

We have outlined a continuum of solutions from a radical one of 'buying in' appropriate skills to the more evolutionary one of educating existing actors in the system. Both solutions could be delivered through the *internal* or *external* labour market, in other words by drawing on the skills of a permanent body of design

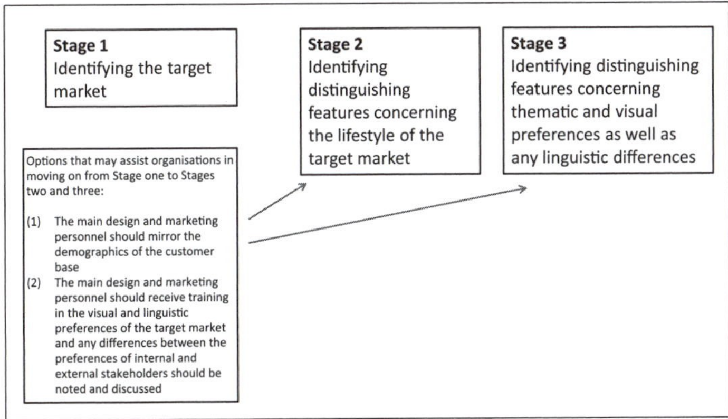

Figure 9.4 Stages that will assist the organization in achieving congruity between the product and customer expectations

and marketing staff (*internal labour market*) or by drawing instead on the skills of non-permanent self-contract or employed staff (*external labour market*). The first implies drawing on the skills of non-permanent, peripheral workers in the external market, while the second implies drawing on the skills of the internal labour market. It needs to be borne in mind that achieving either radical or evolutionary change in the context of the internal labour market presents certain challenges. Lepak and Snell's model (1999) describes the internal labour market as often demarcated internally on hierarchical and gender lines, while Boxall and Purcell characterize them as frequently conservative, sticky systems in which change can be difficult (Boxall and Purcell 2003, 119). These points are reinforced by Wajcman (2000; quoted in Boxall and Purcell 119) who describes organizations as 'profoundly gendered' and the skewed gender demographics of organizations may mean that the dominant male model prevalent in organizations makes it difficult to hire staff whose perceptions and preferences are at odds with those of the male model. In the face of these difficulties, longer-term education of staff may be one way of bringing about change but it may be very ong-term in nature.

Where the option of obtaining skills in the external market is concerned, this offers the possibility of meeting end-user requirements through access to unique skills and knowledge with Lepak and Snell (1999) citing design and ICT specialists as the kind of personnel whose skills might be brought into the company on a non-permanent basis. Hiring staff from the external market still requires that a decision is made within the company to take on this staff and if the internal market of the organization is conservative, then the same obstacles which may prevent an organization from hiring staff whose preferences are at odds with the organizational paradigm would apply to the hiring of external staff. Where the education option is concerned, moreover, one has to wonder whether an organization would commit resources to training non-permanent staff.

Of course, the extent to which it is feasible to think of turning to the 'radical' option of hiring in staff that can reflect the perception and preferences of the external market will depend on the demographics of the design and marketing industries and the extent to which skilled staff of a particular gender are available in the market. Information on the demographics of design and advertising staff is therefore of paramount importance.

Before looking at this data, it is necessary to consider for a moment the underlying assumption which is that people can most easily reflect the perception / preferences of the external market where they share the demographic characteristics of that market. The focus of this book is gender and it needs to be said that not all men, or women, share the same design production and preference aesthetics. However, in the research I have conducted, I have found that the majority of people of one gender (say 75–80 per cent) produce work that conforms to the norms summarized in Table 9.1. The strength of preference tests suggests that similarly high proportions conform to preference norms as well, although it needs to be acknowledged that there will not be 100 per cent conformance. This last fact leaves an important role for recruitment to ensure that those appointed into design and advertising roles really do reflect the preferences of the target market.

The radical option of employing staff whose demographics match those of the target market is possible where these staff are available. If, by contrast, the demographic data shows a skewed gender distribution (as we find in web design, for example) then more evolutionary strategies would be needed, for example training staff in customers perception. This training option is one we explore in more detail later.

The Demographics of the Design and Marketing Sectors

It is important to know something about the demographics of the design and marketing sectors in order to gain an appreciation of how our new understanding of gender aesthetics can be implemented in organizations. In this section, we present the information that is currently available from primary and secondary sources, mainly related to the UK it has to be said. This overview covers is fairly extensive so readers who are not interested in this aspect should fast-forward to the section which follows concerned with the psychology of performance.

We will begin by looking at the demographics of the web design industry, followed by those of the advertising and design industries.

(A) Demographics of the web design industry

Given the importance of web design, it may come as a surprise to learn that there is a relative dearth of information on the demographics of this new industry. Until recently, there were only two studies of relevance, one of which was concerned with small businesses (Thelwall 2000) and the other with the extent to which web design was a male-dominated discipline (Simon and Peppas 2005). This finding was confirmed in a survey conducted by E-consultancy on UK affiliates (organizations creating websites for other companies – see E-consultancy 2007) showing that 83 per cent of the staff employed by affiliates were male. Relevant extracts from the survey are shown at Table 9.4 and corroboration of the low involvement of women in web development emerges from a report highlighting the consistently low proportion of women speakers at web conferences (Kottke 2007).

With the exception of these studies, there was no published data on the demographics and *modus operandi* of this relatively young industry so new research was called for. I conducted this research through telephone interviews and in the first phase, questioned web design managers about the gender distribution of web designers and in the second, questioned Project and Human Resource managers about the skills base of web designers.

In the first phase, interviews were conducted with a sample of web design managers in the three industries discussed earlier (Higher Education, the beauty and the angling sectors) and the results are set out in Table 9.5. These show that the majority of web designers working in these three industries are male and as such are consistent with the male domination of the IT sector (Baroudi and Igbaria 1994/5; Igbaria and Parasuraman 1997; Equal Opportunities Commission 2002).

The interviews also shed light on the way tasks were shared between web designers and business personnel showing that in the angling firms exclusive reliance was placed on the design and creative input of the male web designers. In the Beauty salons, by contrast, 50 per cent of salons provided a range of creative inputs to the website designs even where a web designer had been employed.

Table 9.4 The gender of those who consider themselves to be active affiliates and whether affiliate marketing is the day job or done in spare time (E-Consultancy 2007)

↓ 10. Do you consider yourself to be an active affiliate?
→ 2. Are you male or female?

	Male	Female	Total
Active	83.69% (631)	16.31% (123)	754
Inactive	75% (108)	75% (36)	144
Occasionally active when I get the time	85.1% (497)	85.1% (87)	584
Total	1236	1236	1482

↓ 11. Is affiliate marketing your day job?
→ 2. Are you male or female?

	Male	Female	Total
I do affiliate marketing as my day job	82.91% (325)	17.09% (67)	392
I do affiliate marketing in my spare time	84.01% (909)	16.99% (173)	1082
Total	1234	240	1474

Table 9.5 The design history of the higher education, angling and beauty salon websites with data deriving from telephone interviews (Moss et al. 2008)

Gender of person(s) who undertook the design of the company's website	Angling websites % (No)	Beauty salon websites % (No)	HE websites % (No)
One or more men	77 (34)	78 (37)	74 (38)
One or more women	8 (3)	18 (9)	7 (5)
A man and a woman	7 (3)	4 (2)	19 (11)
Interview responses	73 (44)	73 (44)	84 (54)

The interviews shed light on the nature of this additional input and showed that in only 25 per cent of salons were staff proactively involved in web design. In another 25 per cent of cases, the input of the beauty salon was limited to suggesting that the website contained material from the salon sales materials, whilst in a further 50 per cent of cases, salon personnel made either a negligible or no contribution to the design of the website.

In a second phase of the research, I conducted in-depth telephone interviews with Project or Human Resources managers in six of New Media Age's top ten interactive agencies (NMA 2007). All six interviewees described the skills base of those working in web design as being from one of three backgrounds: computing or IT, graphic design or some unrelated area. The respondents considered that the bulk of web designers came from the first two of these sectors (that is, graphic design and computing) so investigating the gender distribution in these industries would strengthen our understanding of the web design industry.

Unfortunately, there is a similar dearth of information for the graphics industry as for that of web design. Makela and Lupton (1994), suggest that the paradigms taught in graphic gesign derive from Modernism and have a patriarchal origin but this does not make us any the wiser where demographics are concerned. The only other source of information on the graphics profession comes from membership statistics from the Chartered Society of Designers (CSD), the professional body representing designers in the UK. This body operates a professional code of conduct that its members follow and in 2007 it counted a total of 3200 members, all working to professional standards. In the view of Christina Martinez-Tsyrklevich, Development Manager there, 'all the indicators are that CSD's membership figures are representative of the design industry as a whole' (personal communication). This makes them very significant in terms of the light they shed on the demographics of the industry.

Where graphics is concerned, women in 2006 constituted 56 per cent of Graduate Members, 21 per cent of Members and 12 per cent of Fellows. Unfortunately, statistics on the professional status of CSD members are not available but we assume that seniority of membership grade correlates with professional or organizational seniority, then it would appear that the majority of those of middle and senior rank are male, while those on entry-level grades, and in relatively junior positions consist of roughly equal proportions of men and women. A tentative conclusion might therefore be that men and women are equally numerous at entry levels but vertically segregated in the years that follow.

What of the distribution of men and women in the Information Technology (IT) and computing fields? This is a question on which there is sizeable literature. Average participation rates for women in IT and computing fluctuated during the 1990s between 19 per cent and 22 per cent (Robertson *et al* 2001) but there was an overall dominance of men at all levels and across the three fields of information systems, information technology and computer science (ibid.). The situation varied only in different parts of the world and different IT specialisms. For example, in the US, the proportion of women among computer professionals fell in the 1990s from 35.4 per cent to 29.1 per cent. While in the UK in 1994, women made up 30 per cent of computer scientists, 32 per cent of systems analysts, 35 per cent of computer programmers, 10 per cent of ISS directors, 18 per cent of project leaders and 14 per cent of applications development managers (Baroudi and Igbaria 1994/5).

If we are looking for trends, then clearly the proportion of women in IT is on the decline. So, while the 1980s saw an influx of women into IT, with a fourfold increase between 1980 and 1986 in the number of women awarded bachelor's degrees in computer science and a three fold increase in the number of women with master's degrees (Igbaria and Parasuraman 1997), recent years have seen a sharp decline in the number of women pursuing undergraduate and postgraduate degrees in computer-related fields (ibid.). Figures for the IT profession for 2002 (see Table 9.6) show the consequences of this, namely a male-dominated industry (Robertson et al. 2001).

The skewed distribution of men and women in IT has produced a 'masculine computer culture' with a 'masculine discourse' and a prioritization of technical issues (Robertson et al. 2001), all of which are thought to deter women from entering or remaining in the field (ibid.). The authors suggest that it is only by

Table 9.6 Percentage of men and women in the IT profession (Equal Opportunities Commission 2002)

Occupation	% Males	% Females
Software professionals	84	16
ICT Managers	83	17
IT operations, technicians	71	29

including a 'broader set of skills and discursive practices' that a more diverse group of people can be attracted into the profession, and that the masculine nature of the culture can be altered.

What we have seen of the demographics of the web design industry, and the feeder industries of IT and graphic design, indicate an industry that is heavily male-dominated. What of the related areas of advertising and design more generally? These are the focus of the next section.

(B) Demographics of the advertising and design industries

The worldwide market for the conception and development of advertising campaigns is in the area of $45 billion with three main advertising centres in the world, namely New York, Tokyo and London. The US market dominates and the UK is the fourth largest advertising market in the world in terms of revenues after the US, Japan and Germany. The UK advertising industry employs around 92,000 people (Andriopoulos and Dawson 2009).

Where gender demographics are concerned, a survey by the Institute of Practitioners in Advertising survey of the media buying, advertising and marketing communications sectors (Brooke 2006) showed that women make up approximately half of the workforce but only 15.1 per cent of managing directors or chief executives. According to this survey, the percentage of women at the top of the advertising industry has more than doubled from a low of 7 per cent in 1998, but increased by only one percentage point since 2004. Meanwhile, at lower management levels, the survey shows female representation in the industry to be less than 30 per cent (ibid.).

The results of this survey are not surprising since the picture it paints of low female representation in the higher ranks and in creative functions has been shown before. In 2000, for example, research by the UK's Institute of Practitioners in Advertising showed that while women's presence as account handlers had increased from 27 per cent in 1986 to 54 per cent in 1999 (with women accounting for half of those in planning and research), just 14 per cent of art directors and 17 per cent of copywriters were women (*The Independent* 2001). A more recent article shows the figures largely unchanged with figures quoted of 83 per cent of 'creatives' being men, a figure said to be worse than 30 years ago (Cadwalladr 2005)

It is not surprising, given the male domination of the creative side of advertising, that women's representation in creative roles should be referred to as 'a closed shop when it comes to bridging the gender divide' (Doward 2000). It is not surprising, either, that the creative arm of the advertising industry should be described as one that 'does not seem to be too keen on thinking out of the box on gender issues' (Doward 2000). A contributory factor may, according to a report on women in the advertisement industry by Debbie Klein, Chief Executive of WCRS, be the 'stereotypical laddish atmosphere' which is said to be still very much in existence' (Doward 2000).

So much for the UK. In the US, as we have seen, a 2002 survey of advertising staff by AdAge found that on average 35 per cent of creative staff were female. This is a low figure, but almost twice that of the proportion of women in creative roles in the UK (Barletta 2006). So, the staunchly masculine aspect of the creative arm of advertising seems to be particularly pronounced in the UK.

What of the design industry? Figures from *The Business of Design: Design Industry Research,* a UK Design Council Report in 2005, puts the proportion of male designers at 61 per cent, and female at 39 per cent. A more detailed picture of the gender demographics of the industry emerges from membership statistics of the Chartered Society of Designers (CSD), the professional body as we have seen for designers in the UK. The proportion of male and female members for 2006, by design discipline, is shown in Table 9.7.

Table 9.7 The proportion of male and female members of the UK's Chartered Society of Designers by membership level (MCSD = Members of the CSD; FCSD = Fellows of the CSD) in 2006

Discipline	Males (%)	Females (%)
Design Management		
MCSD	86	14
FCSD	84	16
Design Education		
MCSD	86	14
FCSD	70	30
Product Design		
MCSD	92	8
FCSD	92	8
Graduate	66	34
Fashion and Textile		
MCSD	30	70
FCSD	53	47
Graduate	25	75
Interiors		
MCSD	75	25
FCSD	88	12
Graduate	30	70

A quick look at the table shows that men outnumber women in all the design disciplines with the exception of fashion and textiles. Christina Martinez-Tsyrklevich was quick to express concern about these figures. 'If you remove the Fashion and Textile figures from the totals, then you have a situation in which females represent ever decreasing numbers as you advance up the profession. Overall, 9 per cent of Fellows are women, 18 per cent of Members and 40 per cent of Graduates. The absence of women is particularly acute in product design (a discipline classed as covering furniture, ceramics, jewellery, automotive, glass and industrial products) where women constitute a meagre 8 per cent of members at all levels.'

As we saw earlier when looking at the proportion of men and women in graphic design, the CSD does not keep data on the relationship of membership grade to job seniority but one might reasonably expect membership seniority to correlate with professional status. So, following this logic, one might assume from CSD's figures that the vast majority of middle and senior ranks of design managers, design educators and product designers in the UK are male. It is only in the case of fashion and textile design (and then only at Member and Graduate level) that female members outnumber males. At the highest level of Fellow, even in this otherwise female-dominated field, men outnumber women. A tentative conclusion, might be that the design profession is one in which small proportions of women move up the ranks.

Christina Martinez-Tsyrklevich agreed: 'Some of the factors leading to women's low representation in the design industry have been identified by the Women in Work Commission's 2006 report *Shaping a Fairer Future*. This described the difficulties faced by women returning to part-time or full-time work as designers after a break, say for child rearing'. What precisely are these difficulties? 'After a break, if they are able to get work, women frequently return at a lower level of job than before. The reason for this is that after a woman has children, part-time work can be an useful option allowing women to combine childcare with work responsibilities but the shortage of part-time opportunities obliges women to take up freelance work. Unfortunately, the opportunities for freelance work are limited and this could be a major factor in the small proportion of female designers progressing up the ranks'.

Regrettably, statistics on the proportion of men and women who have employed as against self-employed status are not currently available in the UK although the Design Council Report *The Business of Design: Design Industry Research* (2005) puts the number of self-employed in the profession at 47,400 (working either freelance or in a non-employing capacity) and the number employed at 77,000 (working in-house in 5,900 businesses employing at least 100 people). These figures show that 40 per cent of designers are self-employed and since, according to Christina Martinez-Tsyrklevich, the lack of full-time or part-time opportunities are the main reasons women take up freelance work, one might expect the proportion of women in the self-employed category to be high. The availability of statistics stratified by gender would therefore be a useful.

We should note that the declining position of female designers in institutional life contrasts with the position of boys and girls at school leaving stage. In 1996, an analysis I conducted of Art and Design examinations showed not only that the majority of candidates at both GCSE and particularly 'A' level were girls (Moss 1996a), but also showed that the majority of those achieving 'A' grades were girls. Ten years on, the situation at this stage remains largely unchanged since the 2006 report by the Women and Work Commission refers to 'A' level Art and Design as a subject favoured by female candidates. Not surprisingly, the majority of design students at tertiary level are then female (60 per cent) but the big question remains whether women will stay the course in design or fall away from the profession as the statistics suggest they do.

We have now completed our review of the demographics and have seen that the advertising, web and design industries to be male-dominated industries. In the discussion that follows, we will discuss how best the mirroring principle can best be achieved so that customers are presented with products that are maximally appealing. We presented two options earlier, the first involving the parachuting of people into the system who could mirror the demographics of the customers, and the second being an injection of education so that employees who did not match customers demographically could nevertheless gain an understanding of the preferences and perceptions of the target market. We will now explore the feasibility of these two options in the light of the psychological factors underlying the principle of congruence.

The Principle of Congruence: Psychological Factors

In the course of this book, we have seen many reminders of the importance of the congruity principle both from a theoretical and practical perspective. Marketing experts have been pressing the theoretical case for congruence and my own research has put this theory to the test. On repeated occasions, working singly and jointly with psychologists, marketing and statistical experts, I have found that each gender tends to prefer designs produced by people of the same gender as themselves. This shows that the principle of congruence is tried and tested and that empirical work supports and underpins marketing theory.

In this final section, we will lay bare the psychological factors that impact on an organization's ability to achieve the principle of congruence. Understanding these factors rests on appreciating the elements that can influence the *production* as well as *preference* aesthetics and although some of this ground has been covered earlier, we will focus here on the elements that have a bearing on an organization's ability to achieve the congruity principle.

Before going any further, we should note that it is not altogether surprising if the *production* aesthetic links with someone's gender and personality. Popular culture is frequently concerned to explore the links binding a person to their art-work and well-known creatives are frequently the object of media attention with attempts at linking the celebrity's life with the work they produce. This habit of analysing celebrities in order to gain a better understanding of their work, a phenomenon euphemistically referred to as 'celebrity culture', is now so well-established that there is an entry on it in Wikipedia (Wikipedia: Celebrity) and a blibliography on the phenomenon (*Culture of Celebrity*).

In point of fact, a close look at the impact of gender and personality on production and preference aesthetics shows these two variables having a parallel influence on what might be dubbed 'performance' and 'preference' elements (Moss 2007). So, they can influence both what is created and how it is managed (twin elements that I have dubbed 'performance' elements) and can also influence people's responses to what is created (what elsewhere I term the 'preference' element).

Where *performance* elements are concerned (Page et al.2006), these can relate to a range of activities including new product development, innovation and the organizational context within which products and designs are created (Bass 199; Alimo-Metcalf and Alban-Metcalf 2003). Given the extent to which brand managers permeate the brand with their own values (Schneider 2001), and the extent to which senior management is involved either in spearheading new brand values (Driscoll and Hoffman 2000; Moss et al.2006a), the potential for managers to influence design and marketing values is great. *Preference* issues, on the other hand, relate to the responses of those inside and outside the organization to the product or service offered.

In terms of the specific influence of gender, research has highlighted its impact on both 'performance' and 'preference' elements. Where the first is concerned, we have seen earlier, the extensive impact that gender can have on performance elements such as paintings, drawings and designs. In terms of preference elements, we have also discussed the impact the gender can have on people's reactions to designs, whether product, graphic or web design. Preference elements also extend to reactions to people's professional competence and there is an extensive literature demonstration the natural bias and preferences individuals have for interactions with others who are similar. This is the 'similarity-attraction' paradigm (Byrne 1971; Byrne and Newman 1992) and studies have shown the extent to which it influences the recruitment selection and attrition cycle (Schneider 1987; Stockdale and Crosby 2004). Schneider's model shows organizations becoming increasingly homogenous, not only because individuals are attracted to organizations where they believe they will 'fit in' but because organizational members are likely to feel comfortable with applicants who are similar. Perceived similarity will also impact retention as employees are more likely to be satisfied and remain with an organization where they feel that they 'fit in'.

Since there is a direct link between staff recruitment and the type of design and marketing staff employed, the 'similarity-attraction' paradigm will also influence the kind of products and advertising produced. As a consequence, if an organization has a senior management that consists predominantly of men, they will tend to appoint other men and these men, if they are designers or brand managers, will tend to produce designs and brands that are at the masculine end of the production aesthetic continuum. In this situation, achieving congruity with a largely female customer base may be difficult and this would deprive organizations of the many assumed benefits of congruity (Brock 1965; Crozier and Greenhalgh 1992; Hammer 1995; Karande et al 1997; De Chernatoney et al 2004) including enhanced customer pleasure and purchasing (Groppel 1993; Donovan et al 1994; Yahomoto and Lambert 1994). These benefits are too important for organizations to ignore.

Underpinning the congruity principle is the interactionist perspective which, as we saw earlier, views aesthetic perceptions as a function of individual rather than universal values (Porteous 1996). This perspective inspires the search for segemented values and links, in turn, with the 'empathy principle' according to which aesthetic value does not inhere in objects but is the product of empathy between object, perceiver and artist (Dipboye and Macan 1988). This empathy can be expressed as a link between 'performance' and 'preference' elements as indicated in Figure 9.5.

Achieving the match between 'performance' and 'preference' elements shown in Figure 9.5 is vital since it ensures that design and marketing values match those

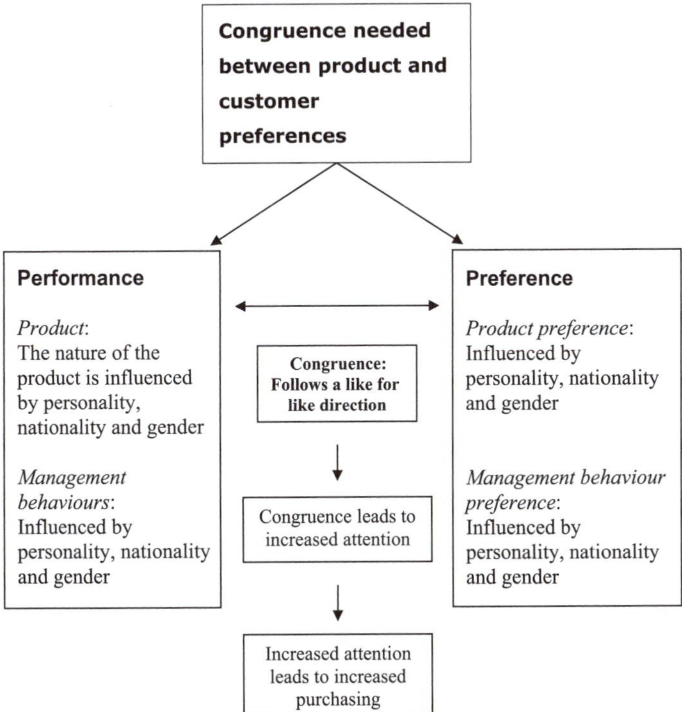

Figure 9.5 The performance – preference link to product/customer congruity

of the target market. Conversely, a failure to achieve this match will mean that design and marketing activities are sub-optimized. By way of example, Vibrandt, a UK-based design consultancy, conducted research on the Kotex brand, discovering that women across Europe perceived brands in the sector to be 'designed and marketed by men' (Lorenz 2005). In a case such as this in which a product with a clearly female market is branded in largely male terms, the model would alert one to the possibility that the brand would be sub-optimal in impact.

It is worth noting that the use of the female aesthetic to target a largely female market is not necessarily synonymous with the use of the female aesthetic as a device to brand products with a feminine aura, the subject of an article by Trish Lorenz in *Design Week* in 2005. She speaks here of the tendency for brands to embrace 'feminine values as part of their core positioning' and cites Stephen Bell, Creative Director of Coley Porter Bell, as taking the view that the trend towards the feminization of brands 'has its origin in major world events'. One might ask, of course, whether this explanation tells the full story or whether in fact the incorporation of feminine features into products serves an additional function in acting as an aid to congruity.

As we have seen, the principle of homogeneity lies at the heart of the principle of congruity insofar it turns on offering customers products that match their preferences. While this is a positive application of the congruity principle, a potentially negative application occurs when an organization selects staff whose preferences are attuned to those of *internal* stakeholders such as senior management but at odds with those of external stakeholders such as customers. The negative effect of poor recruitment has been linked by Boxall and Purcell with organizational 'failure or, at the very least … stunted growth' (2003, 140) and Windolf's recommended move from *status quo* to *innovative* recruitment (1986), can help creative firms mitigate these problems (see Figure 9.6).

Boxall and Purcell (2003, 141) underline the importance of innovative recruitment when they describe the tendency for *status quo* recruitment 'to be conservative, often recruiting from the same social strata and age groups'. By contrast, 'innovative firms attempt to recruit talented people who can help them develop a stream of new products and processes. They therefore use all possible channels to generate a heterogenous group of applicants'.

Whether design and marketing organizations are recruiting a more or less heterogenous group will be explored after we have looked at the organizational obstacles to achieving gender heterogeneity in recruitment.

Performance Elements: Obstacles to Heterogeneity in Management Selection

We have referred earlier to the powerful effect of the homogeneity principle and the fact that it is very much a two-edged sword. As far as satisfying customers is concerned, providing a product that mirrors the preferences of the customer

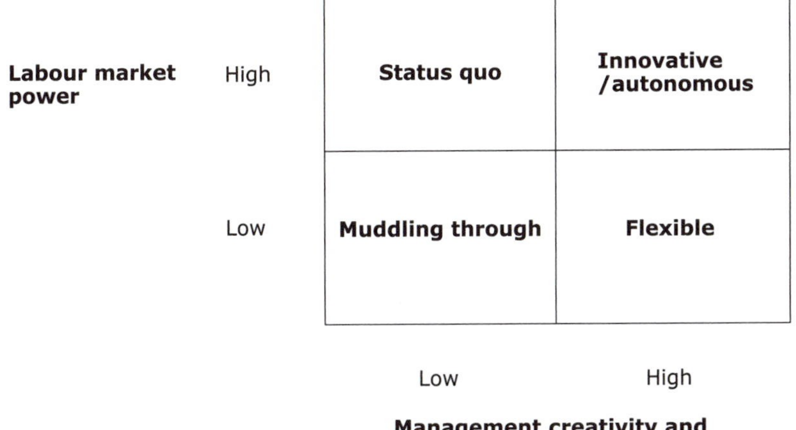

Figure 9.6 Status quo and innovative recruitment

is a positive application of the homogeneity principle. On the other hand, we know about the negative impact this principle can have on management selection. As authors of a text on the psychology and management of workplace diversity have said 'most organizational leaders continue to be white males [and] there is a natural bias for such leaders to attract and select other white males' (Stockdale and Crosby, 2004, 105).

How deep are the obstacles to achieving a greater gender heterogeneity and would be it be possible to overcome the effects of the 'similarity-attraction' paradigm if the job specification referred to characteristics that were not typical of a largely male senior management? In order to understand how deeply entrenched the homogeneity principle could be, and how and whether a dominant way of seeing could be overturned, I conducted research with Lyn Daunton into management selection (Moss and Daunton 2006). This research exposed the extent to which senior management may unwittingly impose its own values during the recruitment process, substituting values that are congruent with their own preferences for the official criteria laid down in the job specification (Moss and Daunton 2006). In some cases, these values may in be at odds with those of the customer constituency (Moss et al. 2006a).

The organization we were investigating was a large public sector organization and we selected it on the basis that the management selection criteria in the job specification were 'transformational' in nature, emphasising those skilled normally defined as 'transformational' in character. There is a large literature on this and the key elements highlighted include charisma (defined as influence based on the perception and behaviour of the leader as charismatic), inspirational motivation, intellectual stimulation and individual consideration (defined as attention to followers' individual needs and individual communication followers). In this particular organization, the female Head of Human Resources had identified these as being the key management skills needed and Lyn Daunton and I interviewed her and the other interviewers (the majority of whom were male) about the management skills they valued.

It was striking to find that all but the two women on the interview panel prioritized the skills of information command and control as well as management by exception (a technique focusing on highlighting failures in performance rather than positive features of performance), features normally categorized as 'transactional' rather than 'transformational' leadership. Interestingly, research has highlighted men's preference for the former and women's for the latter (Moss and Daunton 2006) so the fact that the men prioritized transactional leadership, substituting transactional criteria for the transformational ones in the Job Specification, shows the homogeneity or congruity principle in action. What this shows is people selecting management criteria that match their own style rather than those laid down in the job specification.

It was only in a second organization that the effects of the congruity principle were avoided (Moss et al. 2006a, 2006b) and the research team, joined this time by Ros Gasper, found a contributory factor to be the existence of a complex set of leadership competences informing everything from selection interviewing, to appraisal, to training (Moss et al 2006a, 2006b). Such a strong and concerted emphasis on transformational leadership had helped embed it in the organization and the presence of a high proportion of women in senior management (47 per cent of the total) may also have helped. The first organization had a much smaller female senior management (only 17 per cent of the total) and it is good to be reminded by Judi Marshall, Professor in Leadership and Learning at Lancaster University, of the fact that 'organizational contexts, especially if "highly masculinised" are often hostile to transformational approaches' (Marshall 2008).

We have alluded here and earlier to the extent to which men and women are connected with Transactional and Transformational Leadership respectively and some brief background on this will help interpret these results. The earliest research by Rosabeth Moss Kanter of Harvard back in the 1970s, found no evidence of differences in men's and women's leadership styles (1977) while later research from Europe and America concluded that men and women 'manage differently' (White 1995; Vinnicombe and Singh 2002; Bird and Brush 2002; Eagly et al.2003). The last of these studies compared several studies (a so-called 'meta-analysis') and concluded that 'female leaders were both more transformational than male leaders in their leadership style' and also more likely to use the contingent reward aspect of the transactional style (offering rewards in response to performance). Two points are of note. Firstly, Transformational Leadership coupled with the contingent reward element is credited with producing elevated productivity and High Performance Working (Judge and Piccolo 2004). Secondly, the discrepancy between Kanter's early study and the later ones may relate to a concern by some women to adopt leadership styles that reduces role incongruity (Eagly et al. 2003; Eagly 2004) and decreases visibility and stereotyping by men (Kanter, 1977; Davidson and Burke 2004). This tendency to want to decrease visibility is particularly likely in male-dominated industries (Gardiner and Tiggerman 1999) and may lead women to display a more stereotypically masculine style than males (Rosener 1990; Eagly and Johnson, 1990; Ferrario and Davidson, 1991; Miller 1996; Schneider 2001; Alimo-Metcalfe and Alban-Metcalfe 2003). This impulse may be reduced, however, where the proportion of women has reached near-parity, the case of women managers in Latvia for example. Here women were found to freely exercise transformational leadership (Moss et al 2008; Moss et al in press) in a context where this style was widely accepted.

There is a further factor to consider. The gender differences appear to relate not just to the way that men and women enact leadership (that is, their management *performance* styles) but to their evaluations of leadership styles too (that is, their management *preferences*). One study for example (Luthar 1996), asked men and women to evaluate the leadership skills of other men and women, and the results showed a tendency for men to ascribe higher values to men's skills than women's, and vice versa for women. Given that much of the recent literature on leadership associates men and women with the exercise of contrasting styles of leadership, the tendency for men and women to ascribe higher values to the leadership style typically exercised by people of their own gender, may be a further example of the tendency for *productions* or *performance* elements (in this case the exercise of a particular management style) to mirror *preferences* (the evaluations men and women make of particular management styles). It may also, of course, lead men to select women managers who display male-typical styles of leadership.

What consequences can we infer from this? The evidence on leadership selection shows a tendency for the congruity principle to influence decisions regarding the 'best' leaders and although statistics show a dramatic increase in the number of women pursuing managerial and professional careers, they still appear to be experiencing vertical segregation and encountering a 'glass ceiling' in private and public sector organizations in all developed countries (Burke 2002; Burke and Nelson 2002). According to Vinnicombe and Singh of Cranfield University (2002), women hold only 32 per cent of managerial positions and 6 per cent of top directorships in the UK and the pervasiveness of the congruity principle may be a factor in the continued domination of management by men in western countries.

It is quite conceivable, in fact, that the congruity principle will act in a similar way in decisions concerning the 'best' creatives, whether in design or marketing and we will turn now to up-to-date thinking on this topic in the next section.

Performance Elements: Management in the Marketing Sector

We saw earlier the extent to which design and the creative aspects of advertising are dominated by men and this produces a situation in which, according to Peter Souter, executive creative director of AMV and a former president of the British

Design and Art Direction Association (D & AD), the demographics of the marketing world are predominantly male (Moss 2007a). Importantly, his explanation for the male domination of these industries is that 'people are slightly guilty of hiring themselves' (Moss 2007a) and this is tantamount to acknowledging the all-pervasive impact of the homogeneity principle in the marketing sector, with men appointing other men into management positions.

Souter's own reaction is to impute negative consequences to this, describing this as 'a lamentable state of affairs'. He points to statistics showing that '75 per cent of all purchase decisions are made by women' and concludes from this that the demographics do not make sense 'if you believe that the person *writing* the ad should know as much as possible about the person receiving it'. He is not alone in perceiving the negative consequences of the skewed demographics since Rita Clifton, chairwoman of Interbrand, describes the shortage of female creatives as 'absolutely bizarre and extraordinary' (Cadwalladr 2005). A similar sentiment comes from Debbie Klein, Chief Executive of WCRS and author of the Institute of Practitioners in Advertising report on women in advertising (2000), who writes that 'the balance between people who write the ads and those whom they should be aimed at is completely out of whack' since 'more than 70 per cent of expenditure is made by women' (Doward 2000).

The problems identified by Peter Souter, Rita Clifton and Debbie Klein get to the heart of what we have been discussing in this book, and show how the forces of congruity *within* an organization may impede the achievement of congruity with customers *outside* it. Clearly, the process by which managers are selected is of enormous importance and a way of overcoming the effect of the homogeneity principle *inside* and organization needs to be found.

In the remaining sections, we will discuss practitioners' thoughts on how best to do this.

Practical Steps to Congruence

In the course of this book, we have recommended two strategies for achieving congruence with external customers the first of which is selecting personnel with demographics similar to match those of the target market and the second of which is to educate those who may not reflect the demographics of the target market in the ways of seeing characteristic of that group. Just how feasible are these strategies?

The first option appears, on the face of it, to be an attractive one. In 1995, with the growing awareness that 80 per cent of television advertisements are targeted at women, the group managing director of brand consultancy at Leo Burnett (a leading London advertising agency) commented that 'agencies began to realize that it was a great advantage to appoint people to the team who intimately understood their target audience' (Horsman 1995). More recently, Debbie Klein, Chief Executive of WCRS and author of the 2000 Institute of Practitioners in Advertising report on women in advertising, supported the notion of employing more women in the creative industries on the basis that "it would bring different ways of looking at things' (Doward 2000).

However, while there are attractions to involving people in organizations who offer a different perspective, academics have long been aware, at a theoretical level, of the extent to which design paradigms are concentrated around the male production and preference aesthetic, and the way this can create barriers for those whose thinking may be different. Buckley (1987), for example, speaks of the fact that male designers promote a particular approach to design and that the dominance of the profession by men makes it difficult for a female approach to gain acceptance. We can see this in the fact that design is defined in terms of mass production design, the design favoured by the male sex, and craft design, the design traditionally favoured by women, is accorded secondary status. In this way, the interests of the dominant group are presented as 'universal' rather than just a reflection of the interests of the dominant group and this leads Attfield and Kirkham (1989) to a hierarchy of design values in which industrial design and the 'machine aesthetic', areas which she describes as 'more obviously masculine', are accorded pride of place. Meanwhile, areas which are more obviously 'feminine' are ascribed lesser importance. This notion that there is a specifically male set of values has been further developed by Professor Penny Sparke, Pro Vice-Chancellor for the Arts at Kingston University and a prolific writer on design. As we saw earlier, she writes in *As Long As It's Pink* (1995), her book on gender and design, that 'women's tastes stand outside the "true" canon of aesthetic values of the dominant culture', noting that:

> 'Architectural and design modernism imposed on goods and their design a stereotypically masculine aesthetic, not only because it was undertaken by men but because it was now embedded within masculine culture.'
>
> (ibid. 10)

So, while injecting staff with a new way of thinking into an organization may appear on the face of it to be a useful strategy, in practice it can be problematic. Aside from the demographic difficulties in finding the necessary staff (as a result, for example, of the shortages in female product and web designers), actually succeeding in hiring a new style of recruit whose demographics and values may differ from that of the majority in the organization may be difficult. There are two main factors, the first of which relates to the fact that people are unwittingly subject to the congruity principle and, unless a concerted attempt is made to counter this such as was the case with the organization that initiated a new leadership framework (Moss et al. 2006a), the congruity principle will lead people to recruit people like themselves (Lewis 2006).

The second factor relates to the problems that surface when recruiting people with norms at odds with those of the majority. As Amanda Walsh, founder of the agency Walsh Trott Chick Smith, has said 'You do feel slightly lonely and there are situations when you feel alien and wish you weren't in the room.'

(*The Independent* 2001). In a similar vein, the chairman of the PHD media agency, Tess Alps, says that men 'just don't value the kinds of ads that women write and that women like' (Cadwalladr 2005). This can lead men in the agencies to freely offer negative feedback to the female employees as Christine Walker, founder of Walker Media, writes, 'If they [the men] don't like it', [the women] are 'often told they've got no sense of humour. If I've heard that once, I've heard it 50 times. It can be hurtful, but what's more worrying is the guys don't know that they're doing it' (*The Independent* 2001).

The problem of different values has led Rita Clifton, chairman of Interbrand, to suggest that a strategy of employing people who match the values of the customer base but not those of the organization (for example, employing a female creative team in a male-dominated environment) is not necessarily the solution: 'What I've found is that female creatives are working within this culture, and they are being judged by these standards so they're creating stuff that's framed by that.'

The problems can extend to working cultures too. Christine Walker, founder of Walker Media, writes of the laddish culture in place in advertising agencies: 'I can see why women may not want to work in media agencies,' says Walker. 'Media owners are dominated by men. There is a very laddish culture where people are expected to work hard and play hard. In order to be successful you have to network. You have to be out every night and for most women, the priorities lie elsewhere' (*The Independent* 2001). Changing these cultures can be difficult as Kathy Gornik, former chairwoman of the American Consumer Electronics Association has said: 'There's a lot of intertia when things are done in a particular way. You are talking about having to change the entire orientation and culture of a company' (Palmer 2003).

Clearly, for as long as organizations are unbalanced demographically (for example, employing a higher proportion of men than women) it will be difficult for new people with a different way of seeing not to feel tempted to model their performance on that of the majority. The impulse to do this has been demonstrated in the case of leadership (Gardiner and Tiggerman 1999) and the same may apply where aesthetic responses are concerned. It may in fact only be possible to subvert this natural tendency to conformity through a radical and innovative recruitment strategy that seeks a match between *performance* and *preference* elements (see Figures 9.3 and 9.6) and that offers continued support to demographic minorities in the organization. This approach may focus on the key stages of recruitment, appraisal and promotion until the demographic has become more balanced at which point the minority will be mainstream and better able to maintain its separate identity.

Until that point, it may be helpful to educate the mainstream in the values of the customer, an 'evolutionary' option (see Figure 9.3) which may is longer-term in its timespan and focus. Although evolutionary change is often presented as an easier to achieve than transformational change, we should not be deluded into thinking that this is an easy option. According to Rita Clifton, chairwoman of Interbrand, 'while a good creative should be able to think themselves into any role or profile, and men can do this as well as women, the difference is they don't feel it'. She spells out what she sees as the consequence when she says that 'this comes across in the ads. In lingerie ads the women are very observed figures. These are women who are set up to be watched. The same with some of the supermarket ads' (Cadwalladr 2005).

The recognition of people's limited ability to think beyond their own way of seeing into that of another person, suggests that effecting change in the context of existing organizational and skills demographics is challenging. It may yet be possible to train a man to think more like a women, and vice versa, but targeted and repeated training is likely to be necessary. I can recall the time, for example, when I trained a company in how to optimize its website for its female market and how quick the male web designers were to introduce the recommended female features. However, within a short time, the website had reverted to type its old forms and was displaying the same masculine aesthetic it displayed before the training. This suggests that the effectiveness of any interventions relies on regular inputs over time, and not just one-off inputs. Moreover, the message conveyed in the first session may meet with resistance, and so repeated sessions will be necessary to get past this stage.

Conclusions and Practical Lessons

Ensuring that congruence is achieved between product and customer preferences may not be a simple process. It faces a number of obstacles, not least of which are the presence of values in the workforce (design values and management or teamwork values) that fail to achieve congruence with those of the target market. Careful discussion of these issues and well-organized training may assist in achieving the congruence between staff and customer segmentation variables needed to achieve product/customer congruence but any such initiatives will need to be prepared with great care and accompanied by regular interventions and evaluation.

Bibliography

Aaker, D. (1991), *Managing Brand Equity: Capitalising on the Value of a Brand Name* (New York: Free Press).

Adweek (2000), 27 May, 2.

Alcoff, L. (1988), 'Cultural feminism versus post-structuralism: The identity Crisis in feminism', *Signs* 13:3, 402–36.

Alexander, G. (2003), 'An evolutionary perspective of sex-typed toy preferences: Pink, blue and the brain', *Archives of Sexual Behaviour* 32, 7–14.

Alimo-Metcalfe, B. and Alban-Metcalfe, J. (2003), 'Leadership: A masculine past, but a feminine future?', paper presented at the BPS Occupational Psychology Conference, Bournemouth, 8–10 January.

Allen, D. (2004), 'How do I become … a car designer?', *Times Online*, 21 October. http://business.timesonline.co.uk/tol/business/career_and_jobs/graduate_management/article496826.ece>.

Allport, G.W. and Vernon, P.E. (1933), *Studies in Expressive Movement* (New York: Macmillan).

Alschuler, R.H. and Hattwick, L.W. (1947), *Painting and Personality* (Chicago: University of Chicago Press).

Alvesson, M. and Billing, Y. (1997), *Understanding Gender and Organisations* (London: Sage).

Anderson, P.M. and Rubin, L.G. (1986), *Marketing Communication* (Englewood Cliffs, NJ: Prentice-Hall Inc.).

Andriopoulos, C. and Dawson, P. (2009), *Managing Change, Creativity and Innovation* (Los Angeles: Sage).

Archer, J. (2004), 'Sex differences in aggression in real-world settings: A meta-analytic review', *Review of General Psychology* 8, 291–322.

Archer, J. and Lloyd, B. (2002), *Sex and Gender*. 2nd edition (Cambridge: Cambridge University Press).

Aries, Elizabeth (1976), 'Interaction patterns and themes of male, female, and mixed groups', *Small Group Behavior* 7:1, 7–18.

Aries, E. (1987), 'Gender and communication', in Shaver, P. and Hendrick, C. (eds) , *Sex and Gender*, pp. 27–36 (Newbury Park, CA: Sage).

Aronof, N. and McCormick, N. (1990), 'Psychodiagnostic processes: Projective techniques, sex, sex role identification and college students' projective drawings', *Journal of Clinical Psychology* 46:4, 460–66.

Assael, Henry (1998), *Consumer Behavior and Marketing Action*, 6th edition (Cincinnati: South-Western).

Attfield, J. and Kirkham, P. (1989), *A View from the Interior: Feminism, Women and Design* (London: Woman's Press).

Auto-Observer (2007), 'Why did top GM designer leave?', 2 July. <http://www.autoobserver.com/2007/07/why-did-top-gm-designer-leave.html>.

Baden-Fuller, C. (1995), 'Strategic innovation, corporate entrepreneurship and matching outside-in to inside-out approaches to strategy research', *British Journal of Management*, 6 (Special issues), 3–16.

Bakan, D. (1966), *The Duality of Human Existence: Isolation and Communion in Western Man* (Chicago: Rand McNally).

Ballard, P.B. (1912), 'What London children like to draw', *Journal of Experimental Pedagogy*. 1:3, 185–97.

Balogun J. and Hope Hailey, V, (2008), *Exploring Strategic Change* (London: Prentice Hall).

Barclays (2006), 'More women go it alone to set up their dream business'. <http://www.newsroom.barclays.co.uk/Content/Detail.asp?ReleaseID=821&NewsAreaID=2>. Accessed 5 June 2008.

Barletta, M. (2006), *Marketing to Women: How to Understand, Reach, and Increase Your Share of the Largest Market Segment*, 2nd rev. edition (New York: Kaplan Publishing).

Barmes, L. and Ashtiany, S. (2003), 'The diversity approach to achieving equality: Potential and pitfalls', *Industrial Law Journal* 32:4, 274–96.

Baron-Cohen, S. (2003), 'They just can't help it', *The Guardian,* 17 April. <http://www.guardian.co.uk/life/feature/story/0,13026,937913,00>.

Baron-Cohen, S. (2006), *The Essential Difference: Men, Women and the Extreme Male Brain* (London: Allen Lane).

Baroudi, J.J. and Igbaria, M. (1994/5), 'An examination of gender effects on career success of information system employees', *Journal of Management Information Systems* 11, 3.

Barron, F. (1963), *Creativity and Psychological Health* (Princeton, NJ: Van Nostrand Press).

Bass, B. (1998), 'Current developments in transformational leadership: Research and applications; invited address to the American Psychological Association', San Francisco, CA, August.

Batstone, M. (1994), 'Men on the supermarket shelf', *The Financial Times,* 27 October, 15.

BBC Radio 4's Money Box, Saturday, 31 December 2005. <http://216.239.59.104/search?q=cache:0ppHmkvNEh4J:www.rochdalewomensenterprisenetwork.co.uk/womensnews/womensnews_interface/Results/moneybox%25202%255B1%255D.doc+women+%2Bwealth&hl=en&ct=clnk&cd=24&gl=uk>. Accessed 29 April 2008.

Beetles, A. and Harris, L. (2005), 'Marketing, gender and feminism: A synthesis and research agenda', *The Marketing Review* 5:3, 205–31.

Belch, M.A. and Willis, L.A. (2002), 'Family decision at the turn of the century: Has the changing structure of households impacted the family decision-making process?', *Journal of Consumer Behaviour*, 2:2, 111–24.

Bergson, H. (1999), *Laughter: An Essay on the Meaning of the Comic*, trs Brereton, C. and Rothwell, F. (Los Angeles: Green Integer).

Bernays, E. (1955), *The Engineering of Consent* (Oklahoma: University of Oklahoma Press).

Berscied, E. and Walster, E. (1978), *Interpersonal Attraction* (Cambridge: MA).

Bevan, J. (2007), *The Rise and Fall of Marks and Spencer* (Croydon: Profile Books).

Bieliauskas, V.J. (1960), 'Sexual identification in children's drawings of human figure', *Journal of Clinical Psychology* 16:1, 42–4.

Bimber, B. (2000), 'Measuring the gender gap on the Internet', *Social Science Quarterly*, 81, 868–76.

Binet, A.L. (1904), 'La graphologie et ses revelations sur le sexe, l'âge et l'intelligence', *L'Année Psychologique* 10, 179–210.

Bird, B. and Brush, C. (2002), 'A gendered perspective on organization creation', *Entrepreneurship Theory and Practice* 26, 41–65.

Birren, F. (1961), *Color Psychology and Color Therapy* (New Hyde Park, New York: University Books Inc.).

Birren, F. (1973), 'Colour preference as a clue to personality', *Art Psychotherapy* 1, 13–16.

Bitner, M.J. and Booms, B. (1981), 'Marketing strategies and organizational structures for service firms', in Donnelly, J. and George, W. (eds), *Marketing of Services* (Chicago: American Marketing Association).

Bloch, P.H. (1995), 'Seeking the ideal form: Product design and consumer response', *Journal of Marketing* 59, 16–29.

Bloch, P.H. et al. (2003), 'Individual differences in the centrality of visual product asesthetics: Concept and measurement', *Journal of Personality and Social Psychology* 71, 665–79.

Boeree, George, <http://webspace.ship.edu/cgboer/kelly.html>.

Bonnardel, V. and Herrero, J. (2006), 'Memory for colours: A reaction time experiment, publication', *Proceedings of the Third European Conference on Colour in Graphics, Imaging, and Vision,* Leeds, UK.

Boxall, P. and Purcell, J. (2003), *Strategy and Human Resource Management* (Hampshire, Palgrave Macmillan).

Boyette, N. and Reeves, J. (1983), 'What does children's art tells us about gender?', *Qualitative Sociology* 6:4, 322–33.

Brand, S. (2004), *The Girls' Guide to DIY* (London: Mitchell Beazley).

Brantenberg, Gerd (1977; transl. 1985), *Egalia's Daughters: A Satire of the Sexes* (Seattle: The Seal Press).

Bretl, D., and Cantor, J. (1988), 'The portrayal of men and women in US television commercials: A recent content analysis and trends over 15 years', *Sex Roles* 18, 595–609.

Briffault, R. (1927), *The Mothers: A Study of the Origins of Sentiments and Institutions* (New York: Macmillan).

Bristor, J.M. and Fischer, E. (1993), 'Feminist thought: Implications for consumer research', *Journal of Consumer Research* 19, 518–36.

Brizendine, L. (2006), *The Female Brain* (New York: Morgan Road Books).

Brock, T.C. (1965), 'Communicator-recipient similarity and decision change', *Journal of Personality and Social Psychology*, 1, 650–54.

Brody, L. (1999), *Gender, Emotion and the Family* (Cambridge, MA: Harvard University Press).

Brooke, S. (2006), 'Women miss out on top advertising jobs', *The Guardian,* 25 January. <http://www.guardian.co.uk/media/2006/jan/25/marketingandpr.advertising>.

Broom, M.E. et al. (1929), 'Sex differences in handwriting', *Journal of Applied Psychology* 13, 159–66.

Brown, D.G. and Tolor, A. (1957), 'Human figure drawings as indicators of sexual identification and inversion', *Perceptual Motor Skills* 7, 199–211.

Buchanan, R. (1995), 'Rhetoric, humanism and design', in Buchanan, R. and Margolin, V. (eds), *Discovering Design* (Chicago, University of Chicago Press), 23–68.

Buck, N. et al. (1995), *Changing Households: The BHPS 1950 to 1992* (Essex: ESRC Research Centre on Micro-Social Change).

Buckley, C. (1987), 'Made in patriarchy: Towards a feminist analysis of women and design', *Design Issues* 3:2, 3–14.

Burke, R. (2002), 'Career development of managerial women', in Burke, R. and Nelson, D. (eds), *Advancing Women's Careers* (Oxford: Blackwell).

Burke, R. and Nelson, D. (2002), 'Advancing women in management: Progress and prospects', in Burke, R. and Nelson, D. (eds), *Advancing Women's Careers* (Oxford: Blackwell).

Burt, R.B. (1968), *An Exploratory Study of Personality Manifestations in Paintings*. Doctoral dissertation, Duke University (Dissertation Abstracts International 29, 1493–B Order number 68–14, 298).

Butler, J. (1990), *Gender Trouble: Feminism and the Subversion of Identity* (New York and London: Routledge).

Butler, J. (1991), 'Gender trouble, feminist theory and psychoanalytic disconnect', in Nicholson, Linda J. (ed.), *Feminism/Postmodernism* (New York: Routledge).

Byrne, D. (1971), *The Attraction Paradigm* (New York: Academic Press).

Byrne, D. and Nelson, D. (1965), 'Attraction as a linear function of positive reinforcement', *Journal of Personality and Social Psychology* 1, 659–63.

Byrne, D. and Neuman, J. (1992), 'The implications of attraction research for organizational issues', in Kelley, K. (ed.), *Issues, Theory and Research in Industrial and Organizational Psychology* (New York: Elsevier).

Cadwalladr, C. (2005), 'This advertising boss thinks women make "crap" executives. It seems he's not alone', *The Observer*, 23 October. <http://observer.guardian.co.uk/focus/story/0,6903,1598649,00.html>.

Calas, M. and Smircich, L. (1991), 'Voicing seduction to silence leadership', *Organization Studies* 12:4, 567–601.

Cameron, D. (1985), *Feminism and Linguistic Theory* (London: Macmillan).

Cameron, D. (1992), *Feminism and Linguistic Theory* (London: Macmillan).

Cameron, D. (2007a), *The Myth of Mars and Venus* (Oxford: Oxford University Press).

Cameron, D. (2007b), 'What language barrier', *The Guardian,* 1 October. <http://lifeandhealth.guardian.co.uk/relationships/story/0,,2180812,00.html>.

Cameron, D. et al. (1992), *Researching Language: Issues of Power and Method* (New York: Routledge).

Carpenter, S. (2000), 'Biology and social environments jointly influence gender development', *Monitor in Psychology* 31:9. <http://www.apa.org/monitor/oct00/maccoby.html>.

Carrabis, J. (2006), 'Gender marketing web design differences', *iMedia Connection.* <www.imediaconnection.com/content/11359.asp>. (accessed 7 May 2008).

Caterall, M. and Maclaran, P. (2002), 'Gender perspectives in consumer behaviour: An overview of future directions', *The Marketing Review* 2:4, 405–25.

'CE designers: The brains behind the designs' (2005), *CE@Home* 2:10, 73–5. <http://www.firstglimpsemag.com/Editorial/article.asp?article=articles/2005/y0210/27y10/27y10.asp&guid>.

Chamblee, R. et al. (1993), 'When copy complexity can help ad readership', *Journal of Advertising Research* 33:4, 23–8.

Chandler, J. (1981), 'A long drive for recognition', *Advertising Age* 52:26, 2.

Changini, M. et al. (2006), 'Bare skin, blood and the evolution of primate colour vision', *Biological Letters* 2, 217–21.

Chau, P.K. et al. (2000), 'Impact of information presentation modes on online shopping: An empirical evaluation of a broadband interactive shopping service', *Journal of Organizational Computing Electronic Commerce* 10:1, 1–22.

Cheshire, J. (1982), 'Dialect features and linguistic conflict in schools', *Educational Review* 34:1, 53–67.

Chicago, J. (1982), *Through the Flower, My Struggle as a Woman Artist* (London: Women's Press).

Cianni, M. and Romberger, B. (1997), 'Life in the corporation: A multi-method study of the experiences of male and female Asian, Black Hispanic and white employees', *Gender, Work and Organization* 4:2,116–27.

Clarke, M. (2005), 'Women's wealth soars', *This is Money*, 6 June. <http://www.thisismoney.co.uk/saving-and-banking/article.html?in_article_id=401113&in_page_id=7>. Accessed 29 April 2008.

Clickz Stats (2007), *Stats – Web Worldwide!,* 22 July. <http://www.clickz.com/stats/web_worldwide>.

CNN.com (2004), 'Study: Women buy more tech than men' (published online 16 January 2004) <http://www.cnn.com/2004/TECH/ptech/01/16/women.gadgets.ap/>. Accessed 29 April 2008.

Coates, J. (1993), *Women, Men and Language*. (London: Longman).

Coates, J. (ed.) (1998), *Language and Gender: A Reader* (Oxford: Blackwell).

Cohen, B. (1993), 'Signature kettles', *Design* April, 40–41.

Cohen, D. (1989), 'Laugh: You must be joking – the serious business of research into humans', *New Scientist Tech*, 8 July. <http://technology.newscientist.com/article/mg12316725.800>.

Coldsborough, R. (2000), 'Stickier sites: A primer', *Restaurant Hospitality* 87:7, 86–8.

Colman, A. et al. (1986), 'Familiarity and liking: Direct tests of the preference-feedback hypothesis', *Psychological Reports* 58, 931–8.

Commuri, Suraj and Gentry, James W. (2005), 'Resource allocation in households with women as chief wage earners', *Journal of Consumer Research* 32:2 (September), 185–95.

Conde Nast Motoring Survey (1996), directed by Julia Dunn, February.

Connellan, J. et al. (2001), 'Sex differences in human neonatal social perception', *Infant Behavior and Development* 23, 113–18.

Consumer Electronics Association (2003), 'What women really want in CE', *Vision* Jan/Feb. <http://www.ce.org/print/1520_1864.asp>.

Consumer Electronics Association (2004), *Five Consumers to Watch: An In-depth Look at Emerging Consumer Groups in the CE Marketplace*, Publication ID: CEA960235.

Coolican, H. (2004), *Research Methods and Statistics in Psychology*. 4th rev. edition. (London: Hodder Arnold).

Cooper, G. (1994), 'Women in the driving seat', *The Independent* 5 July 1994, 4.

Costa, J.A. (ed.) (1991), *Gender and Consumer Behaviour* (Salt Lake City: University of Utah Printing Service).

Council of Europe (2006), *Family 2006 in 46 Council of Europe Member States*. <http://66.102.9.104/search?q=cache:zYJfnhmP2wkJ:www.coe.int/t/E/Com/Press/Source/figures_family2006.doc+single+parents%2Bfrance%2Bstatistics&hl=en&ct=clnk&cd=4&gl=uk>. Accessed 29 April 2008.

Cowan, R.L. et al. (2000), 'Sex differences in response to red and blue light in human primary visual cortex: A bold fMRI study', *Psychiatry Research Neuroimaging* 100:3, 129–38.

Cox, M.V. (1993), *Children's Drawings of the Human Figure* (Hove: Lawrence Erlbaum).

Craig, S. (1992), 'Men's men and women's women: How TV commercials portray gender to different audiences', in Kemper, R. (ed.), *Issues and Effects of Mass Communication: Other Voices* (San Diego, CA: Capstone Publishers). <http://www.rtvf.unt.edu/html/craig/pdfs/menmen.pdf>. Accessed 5 June 2008.

Croft, R. et al. (2007), 'Say what you mean, mean what you say: An ethnographic approach to male and female conversations', *International Journal of Market Research*, 49:6, 715–34.

Cronin, H. (2005), 'The vital statistics', *The Guardian* 12 March. <http://www.guardian.co.uk/world/2005/mar/12/gender.comment>. Accessed 4 August 2008.

Cross, S.E. and Madson, L. (1997), 'Models of self: Self-construals and gender', *Psychological Bulletin* 122, 5–37.

Crozier, W. and Greenhalgh, P. (1992), 'The empathy principle: Towards a model for the psychology of art', *Journal for the Theory of Social Behaviour* 22, 63–79.

Culture of Celebrity: A Bibliography of Critical Writings. <http://blake.intrasun.tcnj.edu/celebrityculture/Celebrity%20Bibliography.htm>. Accessed 7 August 2008.

Daily Mail (2007), 'Why Womenomics is the force of the future' 18 October. <http://www.dailymail.co.uk/femail/article-488270/Why-womenomics-force-future.html>. Accessed 5 June 2008.

Daly, M. (1991a), *Gyn/ecology: The Metaethics of Radical Feminism* (London: The Women's Press).

Daly, M. (1991b), 'I thank Thee Lord, that Thou has not created me a woman', in Ashton-Jones, E. and Olson, G.A. (eds), *The Gender Reader* (Boston, MA: Allyn and Bacon).

Daly, M. and Wilson, M. (1988), *Homicide* (Hawthorne, NY: Aldine De Gruyter).

Danger, E.P. (1987), *The Colour Handbook* (Vermont: Gower Technical Press).

Davis, Harry L. and Rigaux, Benny P. (1974), 'Perception of marital roles in decision processes', *Journal of Consumer Research*, 1 (June), 51–62.

Dealix (2006), *Women Internet Sales Professionals – Why Dealerships Need Them.* <http://www.dealix.com/corporate/shownews.aspx?pressID=412>. Accessed 29 April 2008.

De Chernatony, L. (1995), 'The managerial challenge of brand diversity', *Open University Working Paper Series*, also presented as Prof de Chernatony's inaugural lecture on January 18.

De Chernatony, L, Cottram, S. and Segal-Horn (2006), 'Communicating services brands' values internally and externally', *Services Industries Journal* 28:8, 819–836.

De Chernatony, L. and McDonald, M. (1992), *Creating Powerful Brands: The Strategic Route to Success in Consumer Industrial and Service Markets* (Oxford: Butterworth-Heinemann).

De Chernatony, L. et al. (2004), 'Identifying and sustaining services brands values', *Journal of Marketing Communications* 10, 73–94.

Design Council (2005), *The Business of Design: Design Industry Research* (London: Design Council).

Dipboye, R. and Macan, T. (1988), 'A process view of the selection/recruitment interview', in Schuler, R. et al. (eds), *Readings in Personnel and Human Resource Management* (St Paul, MN: West).

Dix, A. et al. (2004), *Human Computer Interaction* (Englewood Cliffs, NJ: Prentice Hall).

Donovan, R.J. et al. (1994), 'Store atmosphere and purchasing behaviour', *Journal of Retailing* 70:3, 283–94.

Doward, J. (2000), 'Why adland is still lad land', *The Observer*, 19 November. <http://www.guardian.co.uk/business/2000/nov/19/pressandpublishing.media1> or <http://www.guardian.co.uk/Archive/Article/0,4273,4093039,00.html>.

Downey, J.E. (1910), 'Judgements on the sex of handwriting', *Psychologial Review* 17, 205–6.

Driscoll, Dawn-Marie and Hoffman, W. Michael (2000), *Ethics Matters: How to Implement Values-Driven Management* (Waltham MA; Bently College Center for Business Ethics).

Duncan, C. (1975), *The Pursuit of Pleasure: The Rococo Revival in French Romantic Art* (New York: Garland).

Duncan, C. (1993), *The Aesthetics of Power: Essays in the Critical History of Art* (Cambridge: Cambridge University Press).

Eagly, A. (2004), 'Few women at the top: How role incongruity produces prejudice and the glass ceiling', in Van Knippenberg, D. and Hogg, M.A. (eds), *Identity, Leadership, and Power* (London: Sage Publications).

Eagly, A. et al. (2003), 'Transformational, transactional, and laissez-faire leadership styles: A meta-analysis comparing women and men', *Psychological Bulletin* 129:4, 569–92.

Eagly, A. and Johnson, M. (1990), 'The leadership styles of women and men', *Journal of Social Issues* 57:4, 781–797.

Eakins, B. and Eakins, R. (1978), *Sex Differences in Human Communication* (Boston: Houghton Mifflin).

Economist (2006), 'A guide to Womenomics'. <http://neweconomist.blogs.com/new_economist/2006/04/the_economist_a.html>. Accessed 5 June 2008.

E-Consultancy (2007), *UK Affiliate Census Report*. <http://www.e-consultancy.com/publications/affiliate-census/>.

Eden, C. (1989), 'Using cognitive mapping for strategic options development and analysis', in Rosenhead, J. (ed.), *Rational Analysis for a Problematic World* (Chichester: John Wiley).

Environment Agency (2001), *Public Attitudes to Angling: A Survey of Attitudes and Participation in England and Wales* (Bristol: Environment Agency).

Equal Opportunities Commission (2002), *Facts About Women and Men in Great Britain* (Manchester: Equal Opportunities Commission).

Erikson, E.H. (1970), *Childhood and Society* (Harmondsworth: Penguin).

Eubanks, S.B. (1975), 'Sex-based language differences: A cultural reflection', in Ordoubadian, R. and Von Raffler Engel, W. (eds), *Views on Language* (Murfreesboro, TN: Inter-University Publishers).

Evans, J. (1939), *Taste and Temperament* (London: Jonathan Cape).

Evereklioglu, C. et al. (2002), 'Craniofacial anthropometry in a Turkish population', *The Cleft Palate-Craniofacial Journal* 39:2, 208–18.

Eysenck, H.J. (1941), 'A critical and experimental study of color preferences', *American Journal of Psychology* 54, 385–94.

Eysenck, H.J. (1981), 'Aesthetic preferences and individual differences', in O'Hare, D. (ed.), *Psychology and the Arts* (Brighton: Harvester Press).

Fancher, R.E. (1979), *Pioneers of Psychology* (New York: W.W. Norton).

Fausto-Sterling, A. (1992), *Myths of Gender: Biological Theories about Women and Men*. 2nd edition (New York: Basic Books).

Fausto-Sterling, A. (1993), 'The five sexes; why male and female are not enough', *The Sciences*, March/April, 20–24.

Feinberg, S. (1977), 'Conceptual content and spatial characteristics in boys' and girls' drawings of fighting and helping', *Studies in Art Education* 18:2, 63–72.

Feingold, A. (1994), 'Gender differences in personality: A meta rnough', *Psychological Bulletin* 116:3, 429–56.

Ferrario, M. and Davidson, M. (1991), 'Gender and management style: A comparative study', paper presented at the British Academy of Management Conference, University of Bath, Bath, September.

Fischer, E. and Arnold, S. (1990), 'More than a labor of love: Gender roles and Christmas gift shopping', *Journal of Consumer Research* 17:3, 333–45.

Fisher, J. (1961), 'Art styles as cognitive maps', *American Anthroplogist* 63:1, 79–93.

Fisher, E. (1979), *Woman's Creation* (New York: McGraw–Hill).

Fishman, P.M. (1978), 'What do couples talk about when they're alone?', in Burtturff, D and Epstein, E.L. (eds), *Women's Language and Style* (Akron: L and S Books).

Fishman, P.M. (1983), 'Interaction: the work women do', in Thorne, B. et al. *Language, Gender and Society* (Rowley, MA: Newbury House).

Fitzgerald, G. et al. (2005), 'Organizational perceptions of e-commerce: Re-assessing the benefits', *Electronic Markets* September, 15:3, 225–34.

Flanagin, A. and Metzger, M. (2003), 'The perceived credibility of personal web page information as influenced by the sex of the source', *Computers in Human Behaviour* 19, 683–701.

Foster, I.R. and Olshavsky, R.W. (1989), 'An exploratory study of family decision-making using a new taxonomy of family role structure', in Srull, T.S. (ed.), *Advances in Consumer Research*, 16:1, 665–70.

Franck, K. and Rosen E. (1949), 'A projective test of masculinity–femininity', *Journal of Consulting Psychology* 13:2, 247–56.

Frow, P. and Payne, A. (2007), 'Towards the "perfect" customer experience', *Journal of Brand Management* 15:2, 89–101.

Gagnon, S. and Cornelius, N. (2000), 'Re-examining workplace equality: The capabilities approach', *Human Resource Management Journal* 10:4, 6887.

Galbraith, J. (1973), *Designing Complex Organizations* (Reading, MA: Addison-Wesley).

Gardiner, M. and Tiggerman, M. (1999), 'Gender differences in leadership styles, job stress, and mental health in male- and female-dominated industries', *Journal of Occupational and Organizational Psychology* 72, 301–315.

Geary, D. (1992), 'Evolution of sex differences in spatial ability', *Yearbook of Physical Anthropology* 35, 125–51.

Geary, D. (1998), *Male, Female: The Evolution of Human Sex Differences* (Washington, DC: American Psychological Association).

Gentry, J. et al. (2003), 'Review of literature on gender in the family', *Academy of Marketing Science Review,* Vol 1. <http://www.amsreview.org/articles/gentry01-2003.pdf>. Accessed 29 April 2008.

Gesell, A. (1940), *The First Five Years of Life* (New York: Harper).

Gilligan, C. (1982), *In a Different Voice* (Cambridge, MA: Harvard University Press).

Gilly, M. (1988), 'Sex roles in advertising', *Journal of Marketing* 52, 75–85.

Goos, L.M., and Silverman, I. (2002), 'Sex related factors in the perception of threatening facial expressions', *Journal of Nonverbal Behaviour* 26:1, 27–41.

Graves, K.N. (2007), 'Not always sugar and spice: Expanding theoretical and functional explanations for why females aggress', *Aggression and Violent Behaviour* 12:2, 131–40.

Groppel, A. (1993), 'Store design and experience orientated consumers in retailing: comparison between the United States and Germany,' in Van Raaij, W.F. and Bassomy, G.J. (eds), *European Advances in Consumer Research* (Amsterdam: Association for Consumer Research).

Gross, R.D. (1991), *The Science of Mind and Behaviour* (London: Hodder and Stoughton).

Grover, V. and Saeed, K.A. (2004), 'Strategic orientation and performance of Internet-based businesses', *Information Systems Journal* 4, 23–42.

Gunn, R. et al. (2007), *The Advertising Effectiveness of Maltese Banks* (Kingston: Academy of Marketing).

Gupta, S. (1995), 'HERMES: A research project on the commercial uses of the World Wide Web', < http://www.umich.edu/~sgupta/hermes>.

Hackley, C. (2002), 'The panoptic role of advertising agencies in the production of consumer culture', *Consumption, Markets and Culture* 5:3, 211–29.

Halpern, D. (2000), *Sex Differences in Cognitive Abilities* (Hillsdale, NJ: Lawrence Erlbaum Associates).

Hammer, E.F. (1980), *The Clinical Application of Projective Drawings* (Springfield: Charles C. Thomas).

Hammer, M. (1995), *Reengineering the Corporation* (London: Nicholas Brearley Corporation).

Hammitt, W.E. et al. (2004), 'Experience use history, place bonding and resource substitution of trout anglers during recreation engagements', *Journal of Leisure Research* 36:3, 256–378.

Hampson, E. (2000), 'Sexual differentiation of spatial functions in humans', in Akira Matsumoto (ed.), *Sexual Differentiation of the Brain* (Florida: CRC Press).

Harding, S. (1987), 'The instability of the analytical categories of feminist thought', in Harding, S. and O'Barr, Jean F. (eds), *Sex and Scientific Inquiry* (Chicago: University of Chicago Press).

Hargreaves, D.J. (1977), 'Sex roles in divergent thinking', *British Journal of Educational Psychology* 47, 25–32.

Harris, A. and Nochlin, L. (1976), *Women Artists* (California: Los Angeles County Museum of Art).

Harshman, R.A. and Pavio, A. (1987), 'Paradoxical sex differences in self-reported imagery', *Canadian Journal of Pscyhology* 41:3, 287–302.

Hassenzahl, M. (2007), 'Aesthetics in interactive products: Correlates and consequences of beauty', in Schifferstein, H.N.J. and Hekkert, P. (eds), *Product Experience* (Amsterdam: Elsevier).

Haste, H (1994), *The Sexual Metaphor* (Cambridge, MA: Harvard University Press).

Haste, H. (n.d.), personal website at <http://people.bath.ac.uk/hssheh/resint.htm>.

Heide, G.A. (1991), *Dancing Goddess, Principles of a Matriarchal Aesthetic* (Boston: Beacon Press).

Heilman, C. et al. (2006), *Luxury Good Expenditures of Husband and Wife Dyads Incorporating User Attitudes*, 11 December. <http://216.239.59.104/search?q=cache:xD_IUXyN67IJ:www.commerce.virginia.edu/faculty_research/Research/Papers/Luxury_Purchase_Behavior_Heilman_Kaefer_Ramenofsky.pdf+joanne+stilley&hl=en&ct=clnk&cd=15&gl=uk>. Accessed 29 April 2008.

Heinrich, P. and Triebe, J.K. (1972), 'Sex preferences in children's human figure drawings', *Journal of Personality Assessment* 36, 263–7.

Herring, S.C. (1993), 'Gender and democracy in computer-mediated communication', *Electronic Journal of Communication/La Revue Electronique de Communication* On-line serial, 3:2.

HESA website, <http://www.hesa.ac.uk/index.php?option=com_datatables&Itemid=121>.

Hewett, T.T. et al. (1996), 'ACM SIGCHI curricula for human–computer interaction', <http://sigchi.org/cdg/cdg2.html#2_1>. Accessed 17 June 2006.

Hines, M. (2004), *Brain Gender* (New York: Oxford University Press).

Hirschman, E.C. (1993), 'Ideology in consumer research, 1980 and 1990: A marxist and feminist critique', *Journal of Consumer Research* 19 (March), 537–55.

Hoffman, D. et al. (1995), 'Commercial scenarios for the web: Opportunities and challenges', *Journal of Computer-Mediated Communication* 5:1 (Special Issue on Electronic Commerce), 1–20.

Hofstede, G.H. (1980), *Culture's Consequences: International Differences in Work-related Values* (Beverly Hills, CA: Sage Publications).

Holbrook, M. (1990), 'The role of lyricism in research on consumer emotions', in *Advances in Consumer Research* 17 (Provo, UT: Association for Consumer Research), 1–18.

Holding, C.S. and Holding, D.H. (1989), 'Acquisition of route network knowledge by males and females', *Journal of Genetic Psychology* 116, 29–41.

Holland, C. (2008), 'Preface to the focus theme section: Internet marketing', *Electronic Markets* 18:2, 104–5.

Holmes, J. (1988), '"Of course": A pragmatic particle in New Zealand women's and men's speech', *Australian Journal of Linguistics* 8:1, 49–74.

Honkavaara, S. (1958), 'The relationship of interpersonal preference and emotional attitudes of the subjects', *Journal of Psychology* 46, 25–31.

Horsman, M. (1995), 'What a week it was for ... ad women', *The Independent* 17 March.

Horvath, G. et al. (2007), 'Gender and web design software', CITSA, Florida, 13–15 July

Hume, D. (1987), 'Of the standard of taste', Part I, Essay XXIII, in Miller, Eugene F. (ed.), Essays Moral, Political, and Literary. Revised edition (Indianapolis: Liberty Fund, Inc).

Hurlbert, A. and Ling, Y. (2007), 'Biological components of sex differences in color preference', *Current Biology* 17:16, 623–25.

Hurlock, E.B. (1943), 'The spontaneous drawings of adolescents', *The Journal of Genetic Psychology* 63, 141–56.

Hutt, C. (1972), *Males and Females* (Harmondsworth: Penguin).

Hyde, J.S. (2005), 'The gender similarities hypothesis', *American Psychologist* 60:6, 581–92.

Ibeh, K. et al. (2005), 'E-branding strategies of internet companies: Some preliminary insights from the UK', *Journal of Brand Management* 12:5, 355–73.

Igbaria, M. and Parasuraman, S. (1997), 'Status report on women and men in the IT workplace', *Information Systems Management* 14:3, 44–54.

Iijima, M. et al. (2001), 'Sex differences in children's free drawings: A study on girls with congenital adrenal hypoplasia', *Hormones and Behaviour* 40, 99–104.

IITA (1994), *Electronic commerce and the NII*, Information Infrastructure Technology and Applications Task Group, National Coordination Office for High Performance Computing and Communications, February, 13–14.

Ing, E. et al. (2006), 'Ocular adnexal asymmetry in models: A magazine photograph analysis', *Canadian Journal of Opthalmology* 41, 175–82.

Institut national d'études démographiques (INED), 'How many children in France live in a single parent family?', <http://www.ined.fr/en/everything_about_population/faq/marriage_famille/bdd/q_text/how_many_children_in_france_live_in_a_single_parent_family_/question/217/>. Accessed 14 June 2008.

Irwin, T. and Flass, R. (2003), 'Diversity moves to the forefront', *Adweek* Western Edition, 1, 13.

Ivanoff, E. (1908), 'Le dessin des écoliers de la Suisse Romande', *Archives de Psychologie* VIII, 97–157.

Jacoby, J. (1969), 'Personality and consumer behaviour, how not to find relationships', *Purdue Papers in Consumer Psychology* 102.

Jaffe, L.J. and Berger, P.D. (1994), 'The effect of modern female sex role portrayals on advertising effectiveness', *Journal of Advertising* 34 (July/Aug), 32–42.

Jaffe, J. Michael et al. (n.d.), 'Gender, pseudonyms and CMC: Masking identities and baring souls', <http://research.haifa.ac.il/~jmjaffe/genderpseudocmc/gender.html >.

Jagger, A. (1983), *Feminist Politics and Human Nature* (Totowa, NJ: Rowman and Allenheld).

Jameson, K. et al. (2001), 'Richer color experience in observers with multiple photopiment opsin genes', *Psychonomic Bulletin and Review* 8, 244–61.

Janz, B.D. and Prasarnphanich, P. (2003), 'Understanding the antecedents of effective knowledge management: The importance of a knowledge-centred culture', *Decision Sciences* 34:2, 351–84.

Joergensen, J. and Blythe, J. (2003), 'A guide to a more effective World Wide Web', *Journal of Marketing Communications* 9, 45–58.

Johnson, L. and Learned, A. (2004), *Don't Think Pink* (New York: American Management Association).

Jolles, I. (1952), 'A study of the validity of some hypotheses for the qualitative intrpretation of the H-T-P for children of elementary school age – Sexual identification', *Journal of Clinical Psychology* 8, 113–18.

Jones, D. (1980), 'Gossip: Notes on women's oral culture', in Kramarae, C. (ed.), *The Voices and Words of Women and Men* (Oxford: Pergamon).

Jones, M. (2007), 'Dorks, dweebs and dummies', *Times Online,* 31 July, http://www.timesonline.co.uk/tol/life_and_style/men/article2167748.ece.

Jordan, P. (1998), 'Human Factors for Pleasure in Product Use', *Applied Ergonomics* 29:1 (February), 25–33.

Judge, T. and Piccolo, R. (2004), 'Transformational and transactional leadership: A meta-analytic test of their relative reliability', *Journal of Applied Psychology* 89:5, 755–68.

Jupiter Communications (2004), Market Forecast Report, *Portrait of the Online Population Through 2009.* <http://www.jupiterresearch.com/bin/item.pl/home/>.

Kacen, J. and Nelson, M. (2002), 'We've come a long way baby – or have we? Sexism in advertising revisited', in Maclaran, P. and Tissier-Desbordes, E. (eds), *Proceedings of the 6th Conference on Gender, Marketing and Consumer Behaviour*, 291–308 (Paris: ESCP-EAP Printing Services).

Kanner, B. (2004), *Pocketbook Power: How to Reach the Hearts and Minds of Today's Most Coveted Consumers – Women* (New York: McGraw Hill).

Kant, E. (1978), *Critique of Judgement* (Translated by J.C. Meredith). (Oxford: Clarendon Press).

Kanter, R. (1977), *Men and Women of the Corporation* (New York: Basic Books).

Kapferer, J. (1992), *Strategic Brand Management* (New York, Free Press).

Kaplan, N. and Farrell, E. (1994), 'Weavers of webs: A portrait of young women on the net', *The Arachnet Journal on Virtual Culture* 2, 3.

Karande, K. et al. (1997), 'Brand personality and self concept: A replication and extension', *American Marketing Association, Summer Conference* 165–71.

Kashani, J.H. et al. (1999), 'Youth violence: Psychosocial risk factors, treatment, prevention, and recommendations', *Journal of Emotional and Behavioral Disorders* 7, 200–210.

Kashima, Y. et al. (1995), 'Culture, gender and self: A perspective from individualism–collectivism research', *Journal of Personality and Social Psychology* 69, 925–37.

Katz, J.E. et al. (2001), 'The Internet 1995–2000', *American Behavioural Scientist* 45, 405–19.

Katzaroff, D. (1910), 'Qu'est-ce que les enfants dessinent?' *Archives de Psychologie* 9, 125–32.

Kelly, G. (1955), *The Psychology of Personal Constructs* (New York: W.W. Norton).

Kerns, K. and Berenbaum, S. (1991), 'Sex differences in spatial ability in children', *Behaviour Genetics* 21, 383–91.

Kerschensteiner, G. (1905), *Die Entwicklung der zeichnerischen Begabung* (Munich: Gerber).

Khouw, Natalia, *The Meaning of Color for Gender*, Published online on J.L. Morton Graphics and Text Color Matters website. <http://www.colormatters.com>, accessed 15 March 2003.

Kimura, D. (1992), 'Sex differences in the brain', *Scientific American* 267, 119–225.

Kinder, J.S. (1926), 'A new investigation of judgements on the sex of handwriting', *Journal of Educational Psychology* 17, 341–44.

Kirton, G. and Greene, A. (2000), *The Dynamics of Managing Diversity* (Oxford: Butterworth-Heinemann).

Kirton, M.J. and McCarthy, R.M. (1988), 'Cognitive climate and organisations', *Journal of Occupational Psychology* 61, 175–84.

Klassen, M. et al. (1993), 'Men and women: Images of their relationships in magazine advertisements', *Journal of Advertising Research* 33, 30–39.

Knapp, R.H. (1964), 'An experimental study of a triadic hypothesis concerning the sources of aesthetic imagery', *Journal of Projective Techniques and Personality Assessment* 28, 49–54.

Knapp, R.H. and Green, S.M. (1960), 'Preferences for styles of abstract art and their personality correlates', *Journal of Projective Techniques and Personality Assessment* 24, 396–402.

Knapp, R.H. and Wolff, A. (1963), 'Preferences for abstract and representational art', *Journal of Social Psychology* 60, 255–62.

Knopf, I. and Richards, T.W. (1952), 'The children's differentiation of sex as reflected in drawings of the human figure', *Journal of Genetic Psychology* 81, 99–112.

Koch, S. and Leary, D. (eds) (1992), *A Century of Psychology as Science* (Washington DC: American Psychological Association).

Kotler, P. (1973–74), 'Atmospherics as a marketing tool', *Journal of Retailing* 49 (Winter), 48–63.

Kotler, P. (1999), *Kotler on Marketing: How to Create, Win and Dominate Markets* (New York: Free Press).

Kottke, Jason (2007), 'Gender diversity at web conferences', <http://www.kottke.org/07/02/gender-diversity-at-web-conferences>.

Kubacki, K. et al. (2007), 'Purchases in provider mode: The case of children's music education', *The Marketing Review*, 7:1, 2–22.

Kuhn, M.H. and McPartland, T. (1954), 'An empirical investigation of self-attitudes', *American Sociological Review* 19, 68–76.

Kyle, G. et al. (2004), 'An examination of recreationists' relationships with activities and settings', *Leisure Sciences* 126, 123–42.

Lakoff, R. (1975), *Language and Woman's Place* (New York: Harper and Row).

Lamb, P. (2005), *Mrs Fixit Everyday DIY: The Real Woman's Guide to DIY* (London: Collins).

Lark-Horovitz, B. et al. (1967), *Understanding Children's Art for Better Teaching* (Columbus, Ohio: Charles E. Merrill Books). (Later edition in 1973).

Laufert, J. and Fouquet, A. (1997), *Effet de plafonnement de carrière des femmes cadres ar accès des femmes à la décision dans la sphère économique*, Groupe HEC-Centre d'étude pour l'emploi et le service du droit des femmes – HEC Group, November. Quoted in Thévenon, Emmanuel, 'Travail des femmes, une irrésistable ascension. Published online at < http://www.diplomatie.gouv.fr/fr/article-imprim.php3?id_article=24361 >. Accessed 14 June 2008.

Lavie, T. and Tractinsky, N. (2004), 'Assessing dimensions of perceived visual aesthetics of web sites', *Journal of Human-Computer Studies* 60, 269–98.

Leet-Pellegrini, H.M. (1980), 'Conversational dominance as a function of gender and expertise', in Giles et al. (eds), *Language, Social Psychological Perspectives* (Oxford: Pergamon).

Leigh, T.W. et al. (1987), 'Role portrayals of women in advertising: Cognitive responses and advertising effectiveness', *Journal of Advertising Research* 27:5, 54–63.

Leong, K. (1997), 'Women gaining clout online', *Internet Week* 686, 107.

Lepak, D. and Snell, S (1999), 'The strategic management of human capital: Determinants and implications of different relationships', *Academy of Management Review* 24:1, 1–18

Levine, K.J. et al. (1999a), 'Anglers' attitudes, beliefs, and behaviours as impacted by the Michigan Fish Consumption Advisory', *Journal of Public Health Management Practice* 5:6, 18–28.

Levine, S. (1999b) 'Early sex differences in spatial skill', *Developmental Psychology*, 35, 940–49.

Lewis, C. (2006), 'Is the test relevant?', *The Times* Career section, 30 November, 8.

Liff, S. (1996), 'Two routes to managing diversity: Individual differences or social group characteristics', *Employee Relations* 19:1, 11–26.

Lindgaard, G. et al. (2006), 'Attention web designers: You have 50 milliseconds to make a good impression', *Behaviour and Information Technology* 25, 115–26.

Ling, Y. et al. (2004), 'Colour preference: Sex and culture', *Perception* 33, 15–45.

Linn, M. and Petersen, A. (1985), 'Emergence and characterization of sex differences in spatial ability: A meta-analysis', *Child Development* 56, 1479–98.

Lippard, L. (1976), *From the Centre* (New York: E. P. Dutton).

Lorenz, T. (2003), 'Design must try harder at bringing women on board', *Design Week* 18:47 (20 November), 7.

Lorenz, T. (2005), 'Soft Sell', *Design Week* 20:29, (7 November), 18–19.

Lovdal, L. (1989), 'Sex role messages in television commercials: An update', *Sex Roles* 21, 715–24.

Lundstrom, W. J. and Sciglimpaglia, D. (1977), 'Sex role portrayals in Advertising', *Journal of Marketing* 14 (July), 72–9.

Lupotow, L. et al. (1995), 'The persistence of gender stereotypes in the face of changing sex roles: Evidence contrary to the sociocultural model', *Ethology and Sociobiology* 16, 509–30.

Luthar, H. (1996), 'Gender differences in evaluation of performance and leadership ability: Autocratic vs. democratic mangers', *Sex Roles* 35:5–6, 337–61.

Maccoby, E (1998), *The Two Sexes: Growing Up Apart, Coming Together* (Cambridge, MA: Harvard University Press). Discussion of her acceptance speech is published online at <http://www.apa.org/monitor/oct00/maccoby.html>.

Maccoby. E. E. Jacklin, C .N. (1974), *The Psychology of Sex Difference* (Stanford: Stanford University Press).

Macrae, F (2007), 'Scientists uncover truth behind "pink for a girl, blue for a boy"', *Daily Mail*, 21 August. <http://www.dailymail.co.uk/sciencetech/article-476578/Scientists-uncover-truth-pink-girl-blue-boy.html>. Accessed 4 August 2008.

Madson, L. and Trafimow, D. (2001), 'Gender comparisons in the private, collective, and allocentric selves', *Journal of Social Psychology* 141:4, 551–9.

Maeda, J. (2006), *The Laws of Simplicity* (Cambridge MA: The MIT Press).

Mainardy, Pat (2001), 'A feminine sensibility?' in Robinson, Hilary (ed.), *Feminism-Art-Theory, 1968–2000* (Oxford: Blackwell), 295–6.

Mainord, F.B. (1953), 'A note on the use of figure drawings in the diagnosis of sexual inversion', *Journal of Clinical Psychology* 9, 188–9.

Majewski, M. (1978), *The Relationship Between the Drawing Characteristics of Children and their Sex*. Unpublished doctoral dissertation, Illinois State University.

Makela, L. and Lupton, E. (1994), 'Underground matriarchy in graphic design', *Eye* 4:14, 46. <http://www.elupton.com/index.php?id=51>.

Marriott, M. (2007), 'To appeal to women, too, gadgets go beyond "cute" and "pink"', *New York Times* 7 June. <http://edition.cnn.com/2004/TECH/ptech/01/16/women.gadgets.ap/>. Accessed 14 June 2008.

Marsh, S. (2004), 'Sisters are DIY-ing it for themselves… and stores adore it', *The Times* 11 December.

Marshall, J. (1995), *Women Managers Moving On: Exploring Careers and Life Choices* (London: Routledge).

Marshall, J. (2008), 'Women and leadership: Transforming visions and diverse voices', *Times Higher Education*, 12 June 2008. <http://www.timeshighereducation.co.uk/story.asp?storyCode=402345§ioncode=26>. Accessed 23 December 2008.

Maughan, L. et al. (2007), 'Like more, look more: Look more, like more: The evidence from eye-tracking', *Journal of Brand Management* 14:4, 336–43.

McCarty, S.A. (1924), *Children's Drawings: A Study of Interests and Abilities* (Baltimore: Williams and Wilkins Company).

McCollough, M.L. (1987), 'Blind marking and gender identity', *Bulletin of the British Psychological Society* 40, 103.

McCormack, H. (2004), 'Shopping turns into child's play for men, thanks to adult creches', *The Independent*, 10 December, published online at <http://findarticles.com/p/articles/mi_qn4158/is_20041210/ai_n12824318>.

McElroy, W.A. (1954), 'A sex difference in preference for shapes', *British Journal of Psychology* 45, 209–16.

McGowan, P. (1996), 'What women want from a car', *Evening Standard*, 9 February.

McGuiness, D. (1976), 'Sex differences in the organisation of perception and cognition', in Lloyd, B. and Archer, J. (eds), *Exploring Sex Differences* (London: Academic Press).

McManus, I.C. et al. (1981), 'The aesthetics of colour', *Perception* 10, 651–666.

McNiff, K. (1982), 'Sex differences in children's art', *Journal of Education* 164, 271–89.

Melton, L. (2006), 'Sex differences: Mars and Venus in the lab', *WellcomeScience*, September. <http://www.wellcome.ac.uk/stellent/groups/corporatesite/@msh_publishing_group/documents/web_document/wtx033546.pdf>.

Mercer, D. (1992), *Marketing* (Oxford: Blackwell Business Press).

Meunier, L. (n.d.), 'The psychological impact of the socialization process: Further understanding gender issues', *Perspectives* 1:3, 1–3. <http://www.mentalhelp.net/poc/view_doc.php?type=doc&id=286>. Accessed 4 August 2008.

Meyers-Levy, J. (1989), 'Gender differences in information processing: A selectivity interpretation', in *Cognitive and Affective Responses to Advertising,* Cafferata P., and Tybout A., (eds), (Lexington, MA: Lexington Books).

Midgley, C. (2006), *Lobal Warfare,* 9 August. <http://www.timesonline.co.uk/article/0,,7-2303878.html>.

Miller, D. (1996), 'Equality management: Towards a materialist approach', *Gender Work and Organisation* 3:4, 202–14.

Miller, H. and Arnold, J. (2000), 'Gender and home pages,' *Computers and Education* 34:3–4, 335–9.

Miller, M. (2007), <http://michelemiller.blogs.com/marketing_to_women/2007/04/index.html>.

Miller, M and Buchanan, H (2008), *The Soccer Mom Myth: Today's Female Consumer – Who She Really Is, Why She Really Buys* (Austin, Texas: Wizard Academy Press).

Milroy, L. (1980), *Language and Social Networks* (Oxford: Basil Blackwell).

Minimato, F. (1985), *Male–female Differences in Pictures* (Tokyo: Shoseki).

Mintel (1994), *Report on Small Kitchen Appliances* (London: Mintel International Group Ltd).

Mintel (2005), *Health and Beauty Treatments – UK* <www.mintel.co.uk>.

Mintel (2006), *Nightclubs, UK,* December.

Mobiz (2007), 'Trends and opportunities: Nokia No. 1, Samsung No. 2, Motorola dropped to No. 3'. 30 November. <http://mobchina.blogspot.com/2007/11/nokia-no1-samsung-no2-motorola-dropped.html>. Accessed 11 August 2008.

Mohan, M. (1995), 'The influence of marital roles in consumer decision-making', *Irish Marketing Review* 8, 97–107.

Mohanty, R.P. (1999), 'Value innovation perspective in Indian organizations', *Participation and Empowerment: An International Journal* 7:4, 88–103.

Moir, A. and Jessel, David (1989), *Brainsex* (Great Britain: Mandarin).

Mollon, J. (1986), 'Understanding colour vision', *Nature* 321, 12–13.

Morrison, M. and Shaffer, D. (2003), 'Gender-role congruence and self-referencing as determinants of advertising effectiveness', *Sex Roles* 49:5–6, 265–75.

Moss, G. (1995), 'Differences in the designs and design aesthetic of men and women: Implications for product branding', *Journal of Brand Management* 3:1, 51–61.

Moss, G. (1996a), 'Assessment: Do males and females make judgements in a self-selecting fashion?', *Journal of Art and Design* 15:2, 161–9.

Moss, G. (1996b), 'Gender and consumer behaviour: Further explorations', *Journal of Brand Management* 7:2, 88–100.

Moss, G. (1996c), 'Sex: The misunderstood variable', *Journal of Brand Management* 3:5, 296–305.

Moss, G. (2007a), 'The impact of personality and gender on branding decisions', *Journal of Brand Management* 14:4, 277–83.

Moss, G. (2007b), 'Psychology of performance and preference: Advantages, disadvantages, drivers and obstacles to the achievement of congruence', *Journal of Brand Management* 14:4, 343–58.

Moss, G. and Colman, A. (2001), 'Choices and preferences: Experiments on gender differences', *Journal of Brand Management* 9:2, 89–98.

Moss, G. and Daunton, L. (2006), 'The discriminatory impact of deviations from selection criteria in Higher Education selection', *Career Development International* 11:6, 504–21.

Moss, G., Daunton, L. and Gasper, R. (2006b), 'The positive impact of selection criteria on leadership diversity: A comparison of two organizations', *European Academy of Management*, 16–19 May, Oslo.

Moss, G., Farnham, D. and Cook, C. (in press), 'Women managers in Latvia: A universal footprint for the future?', in G. Moss (ed), *Profiting from Diversity*, Palgrave Macmillan.

Moss, G., Farnham, D. and Cook, C. (2008), 'Lessons on gender and management from Latvia, International Conference new socio-economic challenges of development in Europe 2008', *Labour Market Issues*, October 2–4, 2008.

Moss, G. and Gunn, R. (2005), 'Websites and services branding: Implications of Universities' websites for internal and external communications', *4th Critical Management Studies Conference*, July, Cambridge.

Moss, G. and Gunn, R. (2007), 'Gender differences in website design: Implications for teaching, learning and assessment', CITSA, Florida, 13–15 July.

Moss, G. and Gunn, R. (2009), 'Gender differences in website production and preference aesthetics: Preliminary implications for ICT in education and beyond', *Behaviour and Information Technology*, DOI: 10.1080/0144929080.

Moss, G. and Vinten, G. (2001), 'Choices and preferences: The effects of nationality', *Journal of Consumer Behaviour* 1:2, 198–207.

Moss, G. et al. (2006a), 'Angling for beauty: Commercial implications of an interactive aesthetic for web design', *International Journal of Consumer Studies* 31, 248–57.

Moss, G. et al. (2006b), 'The impact of leadership selection on high performance working', *CIPD Professional Standards Conference*, 26–28 June, Keele University.

Moss, G. et al. (2006c), 'Some men like it black, some women like it pink: Consumer implications of differences in male and female website design', *Journal of Consumer Behaviour* 5, 328–41.

Moss, G. et al. (2007a), 'Evolutionary factors in design preferences', *Journal of Brand Management* 14:4, 313–23.

Moss, G. et al. (2007b), 'Refining our understanding of men and women's design preferences', 3 September, Towards a UX Manifesto, University of Lancaster.

Moss, G. et al. (2007c), 'Successes and failures of the mirroring principle: The case of angling and beauty websites', *International Journal of Consumer Studies* 31:3, 248–57.

Moss, G. et al. (2008), 'Gender and web design: The implications of the mirroring principle for the services branding model', *Journal of Marketing Communications* 14:1, 37–57.

Moss, G. et al. (in press), 'Men and women: Do they value the same things in mainstream nightclubs and bars?', *Tourism and Hospitality*.

Muller, W.H. and Enskat, A. (1961), *Graphologische Diagnostik* (Bern: Verlag Hans Huber).

Myers-Levy, J and Sternthal, Brian (1991), 'Gender differences in the use of message clues', *Journal of Marketing Research* 28:2, 84–96.

NAEA (1996), *The Estate Agent.*

Neave, N. et al. (2005), 'Some evidence of a female advantage in object location memory using ecologically valid stimuli', *Human Nature* 16, 146–63.

Neitz, M. et al. (1998), Expression of L-cone pigment gene subtypes in females', *Vision Research* 38, 3221–5.

Neubauer, P.B. (1932), *The Process of Child Development* (New York: New American Library).

Newhall, S.M. (1926), 'Sex differences in handwriting', *Journal of Applied Psychology* 10, 151–61.

Newland, M. (2006), 'Why women prefer talking to sex', *Daily Mail* 13 September.

Nielson, A.C. (1997), *Beauty Care Service, Homescan* (Henley: NTC Publications).

Nkomo, S. (1992), 'The emperor has no clothes: Rewriting race in organizations', *Academy of Management Review* 17:3, 487–513.

NMA (2007), 'Top 100 Interactive Agencies', <http://www.nmatop100.co.uk/Top100/default.aspx>.

Norwood, Graham (2005), 'It's a woman's world', *Independent* 9 February. <http://money.independent.co.uk/property/homes/article10105.ece>. Accessed 29 April 2008.

Oeser, O.A. (1931–32a), 'Some experiments in the abstraction of form and colour', *The British Journal of Psychology* 32, 200–214.

Oeser, O.A. (1931–32b), 'Some experiments on the abstraction of form and colour: Rorschach tests', *The British Journal of Psychology* 32, 287–323.

O'Gorman, R. (1999), 'Sex differences in spatial abilities: An evolutionary explanation', *Irish Journal of Psychology* 20:2–4, 95–106.

Ono, H. and Zavodny, M. (2003), 'Gender and the internet', *Social Science Quarterly* 84, 111–21.

Orth, U. and Holancova, D. (2004), 'Men's and women's responses to sex role portrayals in advertisements', *International Journal of Research in Marketing* 21:1, 77–88.

Oser, K. (2003), 'Marketing well to women pays off', *Direct,* December.

Packard, V. (1957), *The Hidden Persuaders* (Montreal: Pocket Books of Canada Ltd).

Page, R. et al. (2006), 'The measurement of organisational performance, institute of employment studies. <http://www.employment-studies.co.uk/pubs/summary.php?id=ssda0513>. Accessed on 3 December 2006.

Pahl, J. (2000), 'The gendering of spending within households', *Radical Statistics* 75 (Autumn).

Palmer, J. (2002), 'Web site usability, design and performance metrics', *Information Systems Research* 13:2, 151–67.

Palmer, K. (2003), 'Tech companies try wooing women with girlie marketing', *The Wall Street Journal*, August, 26.

Papadakis-Michaelides, E.A. (1989), *Development if Children's Drawings in Relation to Gender and Culture*. Unpublished doctoral thesis, University of Birmingham, UK.

PBS, 'Women and philanthropy: Sharing the wealth', <http://www.pbs.org/ttc/headlines_economics_philanthropy.html>. Accessed 5 June 2008.

Peugeot Citroen Magazine (2008), 'Women at the wheel ... style on the move', 26 June. <http://www.psa-peugeot-citroen.com/en/magazine/magazine_doss_c1.php?id=309>.

Pérez-Carpinell, J. et al. (1998), 'Color memory matching: Time effect and other factors', *Colour Research and Application* 23, 234.

Petersen, A.C. and Crockett, L. (1985), 'Factors influencing sex differences in spatial ability during adolescence', in Willis, C.L. (Chair) (ed.), *Sex Differences in Spatial Ability Across the Lifespan Symposium Conducted at the Ninety-Third Convention of the American Psychological Association* (Los Angeles, CA: American Psychological Association).

Philips.com, <http://www.philips.com/about/brand/whysimplicity/index.page>.

Phillips, L. (2008), 'B&Q aims to put women in positions of power', *People Management*, 20 March, 14.

Phipps, S.A. and Burton, Peter S. (1998), 'What's mine is yours? The influence of male and female incomes on patterns of household expenditure', *Economica* 65:260, 599–613.

Piron, Francis (2002), 'Singaporean husbands and grocery shopping: An investigation into claims of changing spousal influence', *Singapore Management Review* 24:1, 51–65.

Popcorn, F. and Marigold, L. (2001), *EVE-olution: The Eight Truths of Marketing to Women* (London: HarperCollins Business).

Porteous, J.D. (1996), *Environmental Aesthetics: Ideas, Politics and Planning* (London: Routledge).

Potter, E. (1994), 'WELL topic: Commercialisation of the World Wide Web', *The Internet Conference on the WELL,* 16 November.

Prakash, V. (1992), 'Sex roles and advertising preferences', *Journal of Advertising Research* 32:3, 43–53.

Preece, J. (2002), *Interaction Design: Beyond HCI* (New York: John Wiley).

Price, L.L, et al. (2000), 'Older consumers' disposition of special possessions', *Journal of Consumer Research* 27:2, 179–201.

Putnam, M. and Davidson, W.R. (1987), *Family Purchasing Behavior: II Family Roles by Product Category* (Columbus, OH: Management Horizons, Inc.).

Putrevu, S. (2004), 'Communicating with the sexes. Male and female responses to print advertisements', *Journal of Advertising* 33:3, 51–62.

Qualls, W.J. (1982), 'Changing sex roles: Its impact upon family decision-making', *Advances in Consumer Research* 9, 267–70.

Rach, Lalia (2003), *Coming of Age: The Continuing Evolution of Female Business Travelers: A Study to Determine Changes and Trends*, NYU Robert Tisch Center for Hospitality. <http://www.scps.nyu.edu/docs/general/FBT_II_Report_10–21–03.pdf> (web page no longer available).

Read, H. (1953), *Art and Industry* (London: Faber and Faber).

Read, H. (1958), *Education Through Art* (London: Faber and Faber).

Reed, E. (1954), 'The matriarchal-brotherhood: Sex and labor in primitive society', *Fourth International* 7/54, 15:3, 84–90.

Regan, B. et al. (2001), 'Fruits, foliage, and the evolution of primate colour vision', *Philosophical Transactions of the Royal Society of London: Biological Sciences* 356, 229–83.

RethinkPink (2008), <http://www.rethinkpink.com>. Accessed 16 June.

Robertson, M. et al. (2001), 'The issue of gender within computing: Reflections from the UK and Scandinavia', *Information Systems Journal* 11, 111–26.

Rogoff, B. (2003), *The Cultural Nature of Human Development* (Oxford: Oxford University Press).

Rogoff, I. (1998), 'Studying visual culture', in Mirzoeff, N. (ed.), *The Visual Culture Reader* (London: Routledge).

Rosener, J. (1990), 'Ways women lead', *Harvard Business Review* November/December, 119–25.

Roth, M. (2006), 'Some women may see 100 million colours, thanks to their genes', *Pittsburgh Post Gazette* 13 September. <http://www.post-gazette.com/pg/06256/721190-114.stm>. Accessed 4 August 2008.

Rowe, R. et al. (2004), 'Testosterone, antisocial behaviour, and social dominance in boys: Pubertal development and biosocial interaction', *Biological Psychiatry* 55:5, 546–52.

Rowlands, I.H. et al. (2002), 'Consumer perceptions of green power', *Journal of Consumer Marketing* 19:2, 112–29.

Roy, R. and Wield, D. (1989), *Product Design and Technological Innovation* (Philadelphia: Open University/Taylor and Francis).

Rubin, Z. and McNeil, E. (1987), *Psychology of Being Human*. 4th edition. (London: HarperCollins).

Russell, H. (1981), 'Benefit segmentation, a decision-oriented research tool', *Journal of Marketing* 32 (July), 30–5.

Sabbagh, D. and Blakely, R. (2007), 'Move over geeks, women are top web users', *The Times*, 23 August, 31. <http://technology.timesonline.co.uk/tol/news/tech_and_web/article2310548.ece>.

Sanchez-Martin, J.R. et al. (2000), 'Relating testosterone levels and free play social behaviour in male and female preschool children', *Psychoneuroendocrinology* 25:8, 773–83.

Schenkman, N. and Jonsson, F. (2000), 'Aesthetics and preferences of web pages', *Behaviour and Information Technology* 19, 367–77.

Schiffman, L.G. and Kanuk, L.L. (1994), *Consumer Behaviour*, 5th edition (New Jersey: Pearson Education).

Schiffman, L.G. and Kanuk, L.L. (2004), *Consumer Behaviour*, 8th edition (New Jersey: Prentice Hall).

Schneider, B. (1987), 'The people make the place', *Personnel Psychology* 40, 437–53.

Schneider, R. (2001), 'Variety performance', *People Management* 7:9, 27–31.

Schroeder, J. (2003), 'Consumption, gender and identity', *Consumption, Markets and Culture* 6:1, 1–4.

Schroeder, J.E. and Borgerson, J.L. (1998), 'Marketing images of gender: A visual analysis', *Consumption, Markets, and Culture* 2:2, 161–201.

Schultheiss, O.C. and Brunstein, J.C. (2001), 'Assessment of implicit motives with a research vision of the TAT: Picture profiles, gender differences and relations to other personality measures', *Journal of Personality Assessment* 77, 71–86.

Scott, W.R. (1981), *Organizations: Rational, Natural, and Open Systems* (Upper Saddle River, New Jersey: Pearson Education Inc.).

Shibad, S. <http://www.e-consultancy.com/forum/106530-the-consumer-is-not-a-moron-she-is-a-keyword.html>.

Shneiderman, B. (2003), *Leonardo's Laptop: Human Needs and the New Computing Technologies* (Cambridge, MA: MIT Press).

Silverman, I. and Eals, M. (1992), 'Sex differences in spatial abilities: Evolutionary theory and data', in Barkow, J. et al. (eds), *Evolutionary Psychology and the Generation of Culture*. (New York: Oxford University Press).

Silverman, I. et al. (2000), 'Evolved mechanisms underlying wayfinding: Further studies on the hunter-gatherer theory of spatial sex differences', *Evolution and Human Behaviour* 21, 201–13.

Silverstein, M. and Fiske, N. (2003), *Trading Up: The New American Luxury* (New York: Boston Consulting Group).

Simms, A. (2005), 'The gaudy sameness of Clone Town', *New Statesman* 24 January. <http://www.newstatesman.com/200501240020>. Accessed 14 June 2008.

Simms, A. (2007), *Tescopoly* (London: Constable).

Simon, J. and Peppas, S. (2005), 'Attitudes towards product website design: A study of the effects of gender', *Journal of Marketing Communications* 11:2, 129–44.

Sjoberg, S.A. et al. (1998), 'L-cone pigment genes expressed in normal colour vision', *Vision Research* 38, 3213–19.

Smith, N. and McPhee, K. (1987), 'Perfomance on a coincidence timing task correlates with intelligence', *Intelligence* 11, 161–7.

Smith, P.R. and Taylor J. (2004), *Marketing Communications: An Integrated Approach*, 4th edition (London and New York: Kogan Page).

Soskin, W.F. and John, V.P. (1963), 'The study of spontaneous talk', in Barker, R. (ed.), *The Stream of Behavior* (New York: Irvington Publishers, Inc.).

Sparke, P. (1995), *As Long As It's Pink* (London: Pandora Press).

Speckman, R. and Stern, L. (1977), 'Environmental uncertainty and buying group structure: An empirical investigation', *Journal of Marketing* 43 (Spring), 54–64.

Spender, D. (1980a), *Man Made Language* (London: Routledge & Kegan Paul).

Spender, D. (1980b), 'Talking in class', in Spender, D. and Sarah, E. (eds), *Learning to Lose: Sexism and Education* (London: The Women's Press).

Stanton, W. et al. (1991), *Fundamentals of Marketing*, 9th edition (New York: McGraw–Hill).

Steinem, G. (1991), 'Men and women talking', in Ashton-Jones, E. and Olson, G.A. (eds), *The Gender Reader* (Boston: Allyn and Bacon).

Stern, D.N. (1994), 'The Sense of verbal self', in Roman, C. et al. (eds), *The Women Language Debate* (New Brunswick: Rutgers University Press).

Stewart, J. and Logan, C. (1998), *Together: Communication Interpersonally*, 5th edition (New York: McGraw-Hill).

Stockdale, M. and Crosby, F. (2004), *The Psychology and Managements of Workplace Diversity* (Oxford: Blackwell).

Strodtbeck, F. and Mann, R. (1956), 'Sex role differentiation in jury deliberations', *Sociometry* 19, 3–11.

Sutherland, Ryan (2001), 'Aliens among us: Preliminary evidence of superhuman tetrachromats', <http://www.ryansutherland.com/media/tetrachromats.pdf>.

Sutton, C. (2008), 'Women get in gear for buying process', *Real Business* 23 April. <http://www.realbusiness.co.uk/columnists/clive-sutton/5242086/women_get_in_gear_for_the_buying_process.thtml>. Accessed 14 June 2008.

Swacker, M. (1975), 'The sex of the speaker as a sociolinguistic variable', in Thorne, B. and Henley, N. (eds), *Language and Sex:Difference and Dominance* (Rowley, MA: Newbury House).

Szybillo, George J. and Sosanie, Arlene K. (1979), 'Family member influence in household decision-making', *Journal of Consumer Research* 6:3, 312–16.

Tannen, D. (1990), *You Just Don't Understand. Women and Men in Conversation* (New York: Morrow).

Tannen, D. (2006), 'A brain of one's own', *Washington Post*, 20 August. <http://www.washingtonpost.com/wp-dyn/content/article/2006/08/18/AR2006081800429_pf.html>.

Tarr, M.J. et al. (2001), 'It's Pat! Sexing faces using only red and green', *Journal of Vision* 1, 337.

The Independent (2001), 'How to get ahead in advertising', 2 January. <http://www.independent.co.uk/news/media/how-to-get-ahead-in-advertising-692900.html>. Accessed on 23 December 2008.

Thelwall, M. (2000), 'Effective websites for small and medium-sized enterprises', *Journal of Small Business and Enterprise Development* 7, 150–59.

Thévenon, E, (1999), 'Women in France today', <http://www.diplomatie.gouv.fr/en/france_159/label-france_2554/label-france-issues_2555/label-france-no.-37_4205/feature-women-in-france-today_4298/women-at-work-an-inexorable-rise_6616.html>.

Till, B. and Priluck, R. (2001), 'Conditioning of meaning in advertising: Brand gender perception effects', *Journal of Current Issues and Research in Advertising* 23:2, 1–8.

Tingley, J. and Robert, L. (1999), *Gender Sell* (New York: Simon and Schuster).

Tolor, A, and Tolor, B. (1955), 'The judgement of children's popularity from their human figure drawings', *Journal of Projective Techniques* 19, 170–76.

Tolor, A. and Tolor, B. (1974), 'Children's figure drawings and changing attitudes towards sex roles', *Psychological Reports* 34, 343–49.

Trafimow, D. et al. (1991), 'Some tests of the distinction between the private self and the collective self', *Journal of Personality and Social Psychology* 60, 649–65.

Triandis, H.C. (1995), *Individualism and Collectivism* (Boulder, CO: Westview).

Tribble Advertising Agency (2008), 'Wikipedia Separates "Advertising" and "Internet Advertising"', < http://www.tribbleagency.com/?p=929>. Accessed 7 August 2008.

Tyre, P. and Scelfo, J. (2006), 'Why girls will be girls', *Newsweek*, 31 July. <http://www.newsweek.com/id/46204?tid=relatedcl>. Accessed 4 August 2008.

Underhill, P. (1999), *Why We Buy* (New York: Simon and Schuster).

US Census Bureau (2000), <http://www.census.gov/main/www/cen2000.html>. Accessed 5 June 2008.

Van der Heijden, H. (2003), 'Factors influencing the usage of websites: The case of a generic portal in the Netherlands', *Information Management* 40, 6.

Van der Pool, L. (2002), *Adweek Western Edition* 27 May, 52:22, 27.

Van Iwaarden, J. et al. (2004), 'Perceptions about the quality of web sites: A survey amongst students at North-Eastern University and Erasmus University', *Information and Management* 41, 947–59.

Verkuyten, M. and Masson, K. (1996), 'Culture and gender differences in the perception of friendship by adolescents', *International Journal of Psychology* 31, 207–17.

Vinnicombe, S. and Singh, V. (2002), 'Developing tomorrow's women business leaders', in Burke, R. and Nelson, D. (eds), *Advancing Women's Careers,* Wikipedia entry on Internet Marketing. <http://en.wikipedia.org/wiki/Internet_marketing>.

Vogler, C. and Pahl, J. (1993), 'Social and economic Change and the organisation of money within marriage', *Work, Employment and Society* 7:1, 71–95.

Voyer, D. et al. (1995),'Magnitude of sex differences in spatial abilities: A meta-analysis and consideration of critical variables', *Psychological Bulletin* 117, 250–70.

Wajcman, J. (2000), 'Feminism freeing industrial relations in Britain', *British Industrial Relations* 38:2, 183–202.

Waehner, T.S. (1946), 'Interpretations of spontaneous drawings and paintings', *Genetic Psychology Monograph* 33, 3–70.

Wager, T.D. et al. (2003), 'Valence, gender, and lateralization of functional brain anatomy in emotion: A meta-analysis of findings from neuroimaging', *NeuroImage* 19, 513–31.

Ward, L. (2007), 'Office loses its appeal as more work at home', *The Guardian*, 25 September. <http://www.guardian.co.uk/uk_news/story/0,,2176434,00.html#article_continue>.

Warner, F. (2002), 'Nike's women's movement', *Fast Company* 61, 70. <http://www.fastcompany.com/magazine/61/nike.html>. Accessed 29 April 2008.

Warner, F. (2005), *The Power of the Purse* (New York: Pearson Prentice Hall).

Water-Based Sport and Recreation: The Facts (2001), University of Brighton, School of the Environment, Report Prepared for Department of Environment, Food and Rural Affairs. <http://www.defra.gov.uk/wildlife-countryside/resprog/findings/2001dec.htm>.

Watson, N.V. and Kimura, D. (1991), 'Nontrivial sex differences in throwing and intercepting: Relation to psychometrically-defined spatial functions', *Personality and Individual Differences* 12, 375–85.

Webb, J. (1997), 'The politics of equal opportunity', *Gender, Work and Organization* 4:3, 159–67.

Wedande, G. et al. (2001), 'Consumer interaction in the Virtual Era: Some solutions from qualitative research', *Qualitative Market Research: An International Journal* 4, 150–59.

Weider, A. and Noller, P.A. (1950), 'Objective studies of chidren's drawings human figures. I. Sex awareness and socio-economic level', *Journal of Clinical Psychology* 6, 319–25.

Weider, A. and Noller, P.A. (1953), 'Objective studies of children's drawings human figures. II. Sex, age, intelligence', *Journal of Clinical Psychology* 9, 20–23.

Welsh, G.S. (1949), *A Projective Test for Diagnosis of Psychopathology*. Unpublished PhD thesis, University of Minnesota.

West, C. (1984), 'When the doctor is a lady', *Symbolic Interaction* 7:1, 87–106.

West, C. and Fenstermaker, S. (1993), 'Power, inequality and the accomplishment of gender: An ethnomethodological view', in England, P. (ed.), *Theory on Gender. Feminism on Theory* (Hawthorne, NY: Aldine de Gruyer).

Westcott, M. (1979), 'Feminist criticism of the social sciences', *Harvard Educational Review* 49 (November), 422–30.

Whissell, C. and McCall, L. (1997), 'Pleasantness, activation, and gender differences in advertising', *Psychological Reports* 81, 355–67.

White, J. (1995), 'Leading in their own ways: Women chief executives in local government', in Itzin, C. and Newman, J. (eds), *Gender, Culture and Organizational Change* (London: Routledge).

Wilkie, W.L. (1994), *Consumer Behaviour* (New York: Wiley).

Wikipedia, 'Celebrity', < http://en.wikipedia.org/wiki/Celebrity>.

Wikipedia, 'David Ogilvy', < http://en.wikiquote.org/wiki/David_Ogilvy>.

Wikipedia, 'The family', <http://en.wikipedia.org/wiki/Family>. Accessed 29 April 2008.

Wikipedia, 'Sex diffferences in cognitive abilities', <http://en.wikipedia.org/wiki/Sex_Differences_in_Cognitive_Abilities>.

Wind, Yoram (1976), 'Preference of relevant others and individual choice models', *Journal of Consumer Research* 3:1, 50–57.

Wind, Yoram (1978), 'Introduction to special section on market segmentation research', *Journal of Marketing Research* 15:3 (August), 15–16.

Windolf, P. (1986), 'Recruitment, selection and internal labour markets in Britain and Germany', *Organisational Studies* 7:3, 235–254.

Witelson, S. (2005), 'Male, female and Einstein's brains', <http://infoproc.blogspot.com/2005/07/male-female-and-einsteins-brains.html>.

Wittig, M. (1992), *The Straight Mind* (Boston: Beacon Press).

Wolff, W. (1948), *Diagrams of the Unconscious* (New York: Grune and Stratton).

Wolin, L.D. (2003), 'Gender issues in advertising – An oversight synthesis of research: 1970–2002', *Journal of Advertising Research* 43:1, 111–29.

'Women and the automobile world: Facts and figures on women and the auto industry', *Road and Travel*. <http://www.roadandtravel.com/newsworthy/newsandviews04/womenautostats.htm>. Accessed 14 June 2008.

Women and Work Commission (2006), *Shaping a Fairer Future: Report Presented to the Prime Minister* (London: Department of Trade and Industry).

Wong, M. (2004), 'Consumer electronics companies woo women: Women spent more on technology than men in 2003', 16 January. <http://www.msnbc.msn.com/id/3966261/>.

Yahomoto, M. and Lambert, D.R. (1994), 'The impact of product aesthetics on the evaluation of industrial products', *Journal of Product Innovation Management* 11, 309–24.

Zahedi, F. et al. (2006), 'Web documents' cultural masculinity and femininity', *Journal of Management and Information Systems* 23:1, 87–128.

Zajonc, R.B. (1968), 'Attitudinal effects of mere exposure', *Journal of Personality and Social Psychology Monograph Supplement* 9, 1–27.

Zeithaml V. (1985), 'The new demographics and market fragmentation', *Journal of Marketing* 48:3, 64–75.

Zimmerman, D. and West, C. (1975), 'Sex roles, interruptions and silences in conversation', in Thorne, B. and Henley, N. (eds), *Language and Sex: Difference and Dominance* (Rowley, MA: Newbury House).

Zinn, L. (1992), 'Real men buy paper towels, too', *Business Week*, 9 November, 75–7.

Index

Figures are indicated by **bold** page numbers, tables by *italics.*